MUSIC THROUGHOUT THE WORLD

Music

DRAWINGS BY LESTER PETERSON

A COURSE IN UNDERSTANDING
AND APPRECIATION BASED ON
THE MUSIC OF MANY COUNTRIES

throughout the World

BY

MARIAN COTTON

AND

ADELAIDE BRADBURN

OF THE MUSIC FACULTY

NEW TRIER TOWNSHIP HIGH SCHOOL

WINNETKA, ILLINOIS

ADVISORY EDITOR · DON MALIN

C · C · BIRCHARD AND COMPANY · BOSTON

FOREWORD

THIS BOOK has been written with the hope that it may provide a helpful text for classes in Music Appreciation. It is recommended that it be placed in the hands of the individual pupil. When each student has his own book at hand, daily assignments can be made and a greater portion of the recitation time becomes available for helpful discussions and discriminating listening. This does not mean that outside reading should be discouraged, for it is hoped that the student will have his interest sufficiently aroused that he will want to gather information from many sources.

Teachers may adapt the use of this book to their particular needs and the chapters may be studied in any order that is preferred. It may prove profitable to start with the chapters devoted to the "Instruments of the Orchestra." This seems feasible because so many musical illustrations are orchestral in character. Others may wish to begin with the study of American music or with the folk music of various countries.

It will be noted that under "Listening Suggestions" only the titles of compositions are given. These are the representative compositions of the composers or countries under discussion, and all are available in recorded form. Since many new recordings reach the market each month, it is recommended that the teacher consult with record dealers as to the best available recordings.

It is further recommended that students be encouraged to keep a record of their own listening and report on their own listening experiences in connection with radio, television, and concert programs. Printed schedules of significant concert, radio, and television programs may be posted on bulletin boards to remind students of good music that may be heard.

Other listening experience may be provided through records or tape recordings of school groups. Members of the school band or orchestra may also be called upon for demonstrations of their own instruments.

Courses in Music Appreciation should be closely linked to the student's daily life. Participation through singing is provided for by the representative folk songs contained in MUSIC THROUGHOUT THE WORLD. This experience may be extended by means of such song collections as SINGING AMERICA, the TWICE 55 BROWN and GREEN BOOKS, and other inexpensive collections.

Theodore Thomas once said, "Popular music is familiar music." Familiarity with music through judicious selection and repeated listening and singing will help to make friends for music in the appreciation class. It may not be wise to play long compositions, such as symphonies, in their entirety. A class may profit more if the most tuneful and easily understood portions are played at first. A desire to hear the complete work will usually follow.

Music is often called the "Universal Language." How each of us interprets that language is not important, but it is important that we seek to develop a sincere love for good music. The teacher's ingenuity will suggest many approaches to the development of this appreciation.

CONTENTS

LIST OF ILLUSTRATIONS

⇴ 1 ⇴

FOLK MUSIC

TO APPRECIATE fully the folk songs and folk dances of the countries in this world, we must get an idea of their origin and source of inspiration. We should try to picture the peoples of these many lands in their gay and colorful costumes. We need to consult our knowledge of the geography and climate of these countries and to take into consideration their national customs and their racial characteristics.

Folk music, as you know, is the outgrowth of the national expression of the people in song and dance. The songs have often been referred to as the "heart songs" of a nation, or the "wild flowers" of music. They are the spontaneous and sincere bits of expression of unsophisticated people — music that has never come under cultivation any more than has the wild flower. But just as beautiful specimens of new plants have been developed from these "wanderers," so have the great composers used this inspirational material as the basis of some of our greatest composed music.

In this very sophisticated machine age in which we are living, it is difficult for us to experience the emotions or picture the activities and lives of the people who have given us such a wealth of folk music. We must remember that our folk singers made music a part of their very existence. They sang and danced as they played and they sang as they worked. They expressed all of their deepest emotions in song. Love, hate, joy, sadness, patriotism and religious fervor, all found a way into their music. Often their only means of recreation depended upon the inspiration of the moment. These tunes were rarely written down but passed along from one generation to another by word of mouth. This gave to folk music a simplicity of words and music and a certain vigor and sincerity.

Nearly all of this beautiful and inspiring music has come to us from the rural districts and sparsely populated sections of the different countries. City life makes possible certain cultural opportunities. It may make people more sensitive to beauty and refinement, but it can also make them more self-conscious and perhaps less sincere. When we live too close to highly developed civilization, we are likely to refrain from expressing a full measure of emotion and feel that those

1

who do make too much show of their deepest feelings. Here in America, at the present time, many of us, unfortunately, refrain from singing at all.

Until recent years, all mothers sang their babies to sleep; now they no longer even rock the cradle. In the past, candlelight and open fireplaces were more conducive to occasional song than are radiators and electric lights. The old cook stove was more romantic than the gas range and the open sleigh more suggestive of a song than is the closed limousine. Not many years ago our little children sang, with appropriate movements, harvest songs, shoemaker songs and songs about the blacksmith; but the modern garage and filling station do not inspire us.

Naturally, none of us wants to give up his modern comforts just to be romantic, but perhaps it is this "call of the wild" within our souls that beckons many of us to the forest preserve and to summer camps. Certainly we need some spiritual or emotional outlet, or this machine age in which we live will become our master.

Perhaps the pendulum has already begun to swing in another direction. Many housekeepers today treasure the furniture and belongings of their ancestors. Homes are built with open fireplaces and rooms lighted with candles. Religion, art, and music find a more important place in the lives of boys and girls and men and women. Singing societies and community orchestras abound, and in many cities people of different nationalities gather together to help preserve the songs and dances of their countries. Their handwork is prized as it never was before, and a real appreciation of "homemade" arts is at hand.

QUESTIONS

1. How do we sometimes refer to folk songs?
2. What do we mean by "unsophisticated"?
3. Do you know any piece of composed music where a great composer has employed a folk song or folk dance or a national anthem as the principal theme or tune in his composition?
4. Name four emotions that have been expressed in folk songs.
5. From what districts does most folk music spring and why?
6. Why was the civilization of our grandparents more romantic (in a way) than our civilization of today?

2

Chester

WILLIAM BILLINGS

Fervently

Let ty-rants shake their i - ron rod, And slav-'ry clank—her
What grate-ful off-'ring shall—we bring? What shall we ren - der

gall - ing chains. We'll fear them not; we— trust— in
to— this Lord? Loud hal - le - lu - jah— let— us

God, New— Eng-land's God——— for - ev - er reigns.
sing, And—praise His Name— on ev - 'ry chord.

≥ 2 ≤

MUSIC IN AMERICA

To many people of our time, American music means a favorite
dance tune or the latest popular song heard over the radio. An
increasing number of Americans, however, are becoming interested
in serious music, often referred to as "classical," and they know the
important works of the great European masters and those of our own
American composers. Americans in general, however, are not familiar
with the story of musical growth in our country. It is a romantic and
interesting history and one in which we may take pride.

American culture is younger than those of the European countries
and our youthfulness as a nation has given our music an enthusiasm
and a self-confidence that reflects the Yankee spirit which enabled the
American pioneers to overcome many obstacles and build a great
nation.

The United States is unique among nations because it was settled
by people from so many parts of the world. America is often referred
to as the "Melting Pot," and our musical expressions reflect in some
measure the temperamental and racial characteristics of the peoples
of many nations.

Music in the Early Colonial Days

A quick view of the whole picture of our musical history will
reveal some of the interesting sources which have contributed to it.

Picture for a moment our Puritan and Pilgrim ancestors with their
sober countenances and drab attire. Think of the "stern and rock-
bound coast" upon which they landed and the hardships they were
forced to endure. It is not surprising that music and the other arts
had comparatively little place in the lives of these people. They had
homes to build, soil to cultivate, enemies to guard against, and their
days were very full. They were imbued with a religious zeal which
had originally brought them to these shores. And yet they were not
without music, although it was solemn music devoted to their religious services. Longfellow has written of Priscilla:

4

*Open wide on her lap lay the well-worn psalm-book of Ainsworth
Printed in Amsterdam, the words and the music together.*

The Ainsworth Psalter, with its Psalms set to music, was a source of spiritual strength to these early Americans, and after their colony had been established one of the first books they printed was the Bay Psalm Book. Some of the tunes they sang more than three hundred years ago are still familiar to us, especially *Old Hundredth,* often called *Old Hundred* or the *Doxology.*

The stern attitude toward music held by these New England pioneers gradually softened to such a degree that after the American Revolution Boston was considered the musical center of America. From the landing of the Pilgrims until after the Revolution music necessarily developed slowly in the New World, for its people generally led a rather rugged life. At the same time Europe was passing through one of her most colorful, even extravagant, periods, and the arts were flourishing. When the American pioneers were hewing a nation out of the wilderness, their European cousins were enjoying the music of Bach, Handel, Mozart, and Haydn.

The colonial history of music in Philadelphia differs from that of New England. Germans, Swedes, and Moravians settled in and near Philadelphia, and while they, too, were deeply religious, they did not believe in limiting music to the service of the church. Many of these people understood music as well and valued it as highly as the people of eighteenth century Europe.

The Moravians established settlements at Bethlehem, Pennsylvania, and Salem, North Carolina. They brought from Europe many fine musical instruments, and some historians credit these early Pennsylvanians with the first American performances of Haydn's string quartets and oratorios. Certain it is that they established a fine musical tradition which flourishes today. The first music festival in Bethlehem was held as long ago as 1742, and the annual Bethlehem Bach Festival has been a tradition for nearly seventy years.

Although the Quakers, and, some say, the early Presbyterians, took a dim view of music, the art, even in its lighter forms, was generally favored by the Pennsylvania colonists. There is record of a dancing master in Philadelphia as early as 1710, and the first public concert in Philadelphia was given in 1757. The first American-made piano was produced in Philadelphia in 1775, and it was in Philadelphia (in 1730) that Benjamin Franklin published the large hymnbook known as the *Ephrata Collection.* Franklin was a man of many interests, and one of them was music. He is said to have played the guitar well, and to have had some ability with the violin and cello. Some of his letters show him to have been well informed on music.

5

The Cavaliers who came to Virginia, Maryland, and the Carolinas brought with them European ideas and customs in contrast to the Pilgrims who came to America to get way from Europe. The early Virginians and their neighbors in the other Southern Colonies wore the powdered wigs and lace and ruffles common to European dress of the time, and they danced the minuet, gavotte, and other courtly dances.

George Washington, like many an American since his time, was fond of dancing and the theater. He visited America's first playhouse, built in Williamsburg, Virginia, in 1722. Thomas Jefferson interested himself in several of the arts, and attained fame as an architect as well as a statesman. History tells us also that he was fond of music and could play the violin with some degree of skill. When he was president of the United States, he sometimes turned to music for relaxation, playing violin duets with Patrick Henry, author of the famous phrase, "Give me liberty or give me death." In the Virginia-Maryland atmosphere, life, particularly for the upper classes, was gayer and more romantic than in New England, and the music of these colonies was more like that of Europe. It was in these colonies that a love for the old English, Scottish, and Irish ballads was fostered — songs which traveled westward from Virginia to Tennessee and Kentucky and eventually to other parts of an expanding America.

In the French colony at New Orleans there was always music, and opera flourished there before it was well accepted in other American cities. An opera house was built in New Orleans as early as 1808 and for many years the best-known opera house in this country was the French Opera House, built in New Orleans in 1859. Many French and Italian operas had their first American performances in this opera house.

New York was also interested in opera, and the first American opera, *The Archer,* was produced there in 1796. Its composer was Benjamin Carr, who also opened the first music store in Philadelphia. In 1825 opera became well established in New York through the visit of the famous Garcia company, brought to America partly through the efforts of Lorenzo Da Ponte, then living in New York. As court poet to the Vienna Opera, Da Ponte had in earlier life supplied the librettos for Mozart's *Marriage of Figaro* and *Don Giovanni.*

New York has the distinction of sponsoring the first American symphony orchestra, the New York Philharmonic, now more than a century old, having been founded in 1842. The first American-made pipe organ was installed in Trinity Church in New York in 1737.

Each of the colonies brought some musical influence to America.

6

Usually this influence was largely of a folk nature. The Pilgrims with their Psalm tunes, the Germans and Moravians in Pennsylvania, the Dutch in New Amsterdam (New York) and the Cavaliers in the lower colonies all made their contributions. So did the French at New Orleans, in upper New England, and in the Great Lakes area. The Spanish and Mexican influence reached throughout the Great Southwest and especially in Texas, New Mexico, and California. Added to these cultures are the musical contributions of the Negroes and the American Indians. The result is the diverse and highly interesting musical scene which America presents today.

QUESTIONS

1. What kind of music did the Puritans and Pilgrims sing?
2. What familiar hymn-tune was sung by these early settlers?
3. Name the national influences represented among the early settlers of Philadelphia.
4. Discuss the musical activities which center around Bethlehem, Pennsylvania.
5. How did the music of the Southern Colonies differ from that of New England?
6. Relate some interesting facts relative to the French Colony at New Orleans.
7. What was the date of the first opera produced in New York?

≈ 3 ≈

FOLK MUSIC OF AMERICA

A MERICA'S CONTRIBUTION to folk music is both rich and interesting.
The colorful history and geographical extent of the United States,
together with the diverse occupations of its people have contributed to
a great variety of self-expression. We have the songs of the lumber-
jack, the cowboy, the riverboatman, and the miner. There are songs
of the brave pioneers who blazed their trails in covered wagons.
There are bold songs of soldiers and sailors and swaggering tunes
sung by desperadoes. The lives and deeds of our romantic heroes
have been celebrated in song and story.

Prominent in American folk music is the large literature of ballads,
songs and dances originating in our Southern States and known as
Southern Mountain songs or Anglo-American folk songs. The American Indians have their folk music, and there are numerous other distinct types, such as the Latin-American songs of the Southwest and
the Creole songs. The most widespread folk music of our time is
perhaps the popular music of the day, which will be discussed in a
separate chapter.

Much American folk music had its origin in foreign lands and has
been modified and adapted to its present American forms. This is true
of many songs, ballads, and dances brought from Europe, particularly
from the British Isles. It is true of our Latin-American music and to
some degree of our Negro music because of its basic African rhythms.
There exist, nevertheless, many native American folk songs which
are as American as baseball or corn-on-the-cob. Such fiddle tunes as
Arkansaw Traveler, Old Zip Coon, Old Joe Clark, and *Sourwood
Mountain* are definitely American. So also are the cowboy songs,
Old Paint and *The Old Chisholm Trail.* Thoroughly American are
such songs as *The Erie Canal, Red Iron Ore, Casey Jones,* and *John
Henry.* Even in religious folk music we find some songs which are
fully rooted in American soil. Among them are *Poor Wayfaring
Stranger* and *I Wonder as I Wander.*

The Europeans who settled America brought with them their songs
as well as their other possessions. In a day when there was no radio,
phonograph, or television, people made their own music. It was im-

8

portant then to know and to preserve folk songs and ballads. They were a record of legends, of history and customs. Many songs were brought to our eastern coast from the British Isles to be handed down from one generation of Americans to another. These songs were especially preserved among the mountain dwellers of Virginia, the Carolinas, Tennessee, and Kentucky, and some of them may be heard today, little changed from the way in which they were sung in England in the time of "Good Queen Bess." *Barbara Allen* and *The Gypsy Laddie* are excellent examples of these Anglo-American folk ballads. *Billy Boy* and *Frog Went A-Courtin'* are American songs which came originally from England.

Fortunately Americans became aware of the beauty and cultural importance of these folk songs in time to preserve a great many of them through the printed page and the phonograph record. The first to undertake this valuable work was a Harvard professor, Francis James Child. He was followed by the Englishman, Cecil Sharp, who worked with an American woman, Mrs. Olive Campbell, to collect several hundred Anglo-American folk songs. In more recent times such Americans as Mrs. Annabel Morris Buchanan, John Powell, John Jacob Niles, George Pullen Jackson, and Charles F. Bryan have collected and published many of these beautiful songs, with the result that they are now well known in our schools and to our musicians at large. Popular entertainers, such as Susan Reed and Burl Ives, have made extensive reputations by singing these folk songs, and composers have begun to use them in contemporary music. An example is the folk opera, *Down in the Valley*, by Kurt Weill, which employs a number of these Southern Mountain tunes.

The early American was a very busy man, for there were many things to do in building a new country. As a result he often sang as he worked, and many of the truly American folk songs are work songs. The cowboy sang as he tended his cattle and the riverman as he steered his barge. Walt Whitman refers to the work songs of early America in his lines from *I Hear America Singing:*

> *The wood-cutter's song, the ploughboy's on his way in the morning,*
> *   or at noon intermission or at sundown,*
> *The delicious singing of the mother, or of the young wife at work,*
> *   or of the girl sewing or washing,*
> *Each singing what belongs to him or her and to none else.*

Some of these songs were crude and of no great musical value, but many of them have a flavor and an individuality which have given them a permanent place in American musical life. Such songs as

9

Home on the Range, Old Paint, and *The Erie Canal* are not easily forgotten and are sung in home and school and by entertainers.

Our true folk songs are now well known, and having come to the attention of those who make our popular music, many imitations of these true folk songs may be heard on the radio. Often they are of poor quality in both music and words. Many people refer to them as "hillbilly" songs or ballads, and sometimes genuine folk songs and their synthetic imitations (songs written to sound like folk songs) are grouped together in this classification. A few hearings, however, will usually serve to separate the genuine folk song from the "manufactured" variety.

In Southwest America we find, in addition to the songs of the cowboys, folk melodies brought from Spain and Mexico. These in turn inspired songs of American origin, resembling their Spanish ancestors, just as we find today in Texas, New Mexico, and California many people of Spanish and Mexican extraction. Father Junipero (Hoo-nee'pe-ro) Serra, who established the chain of missions which still grace the state of California, was followed by settlers from Mexico and other Latin countries, and in many places in California and in other southwestern areas there grew up a civilization which was predominantly Spanish-influenced. The discovery of gold in California and the entrance of Texas into the Union gradually made these areas more like the rest of our country, but even today the evidences of Latin-American culture are very plain in San Antonio, Santa Fe, Tucson, and other southwestern centers. And from this part of the country has come beautiful folk music reminiscent of the customs of Spanish America. Such songs as *The Hammock* and *At the Gate of Heaven* recall the Southwest before it was brought into the United States.

The French influence in Louisiana and the Great Lakes area can be found in our folk music. *Alouette* is as well known to many Americans as it is to French-Canadians. The songs of the French Voyageurs recall the explorations of La Salle, Marquette, Cadillac, and other Frenchmen who helped to open up our great Midwest, while the French development of Louisiana has enriched our American music with French and Creole folk songs.

INDIAN MUSIC

Some authorities state that the music of the American Indian is the only true American folk music that we have, in that it is the only type that was not influenced by foreign music. Others say that genuine folk music is a fairly highly developed type of music and that the songs and dances of the Indians do not properly come under this head. They also remind us that although the Indians are North America's oldest residents, their lives and customs have always been something quite apart from our civilization. We need not be disturbed by this controversy. We know that the Red Man has played a dramatic part in the history of our country, and it should therefore be of great interest to us to know something about his music and dance and about their relationship to his interesting life.

Centuries ago the North American continent was inhabited by tribes of Indians who spoke more than fifty different languages. Some of these tribes were socially and politically highly organized; others lived very simply. Even today the Office of Indian Affairs at Washington is dealing with more than three hundred separate tribes and sub-tribes. It is not possible here to discuss in detail the music of each group. It is, in fact, really more exact to speak of the music of the Blackfeet or Chippewas than of the music of the Indian. There are, however, traits which are common to the music of many tribes.

Fortunately, historians and collectors of folk music began more than fifty years ago to give serious consideration to the dances and ceremonials of the Indians and to preserve them for future generations. The older Indians have helped by reproducing much of this music, as they remember hearing it sung and played by their ancestors.°

It is difficult to separate Indian music from Indian life. These people use music for specific purposes, rather than for its own sake. The Indian wishes to obtain results with his music. He uses it for success in war and in the hunt, and he believes it will heal the sick. Some tribes sing lullabies to their babies. Some of the young braves play a type of flute at sunset, possibly to attract the attention of their favorite maidens. Marriages, however, are usually arranged by the parents so that such romantic moments are perhaps wasted.

The instruments used by these people are quite simple and consist of flutes, pipes, and many types of rattles and drums. The music of the Indians and many Orientals have qualities in common.

The Indian uses scales containing smaller intervals than ours and often uses the pentatonic, or five tone scale, referred to in other chapters on folk music. Often he sings in one rhythm and beats his drum in another, and usually he sings and plays his instruments in the same fashion at each performance, seldom failing to employ the same intervals or to keep his beat going in the same fashion. Many Indians sing with a distinct tremolo or vibrato, and a favorite trick is to start

---

° We are indebted to phonograph recordings and collections of Indian songs and dances made by such collectors as Thurlow Lieurance, Charles Wakefield Cadman, Arthur Farwell, Harvey Worthington Loomis, Alice Fletcher, Natalie Curtis, Francis Densmore, and others.

11

a note sharp and then slide down. The early tribes had voices which sounded more like instruments. Indians like descending melodies, and if the tune starts upward they soon descend again. Their music seems to be written in no particular key, but, like Orientals, they prefer the minor mode.

The chief character of Indian music is largely lost when reduced to a white man's harmonization, but many fine composers have shown that, like the Negro melodies, some of the Indian's songs and dances can be used as inspirational themes for composition.

Edward MacDowell wrote his famous *Indian Suite*, and we are indebted to other American composers, such as Lieurance, Cadman, and Charles Sanford Skilton for compositions based on Indian themes.

NEGRO MUSIC

America justly claims the music of the Negro as part of her rich heritage. Authorities disagree as to whether or not this folk music can be claimed as truly American, but one of these writers seems to have stated the case clearly. Henry E. Krehbiel, in his book entitled *Afro-American Folk Song*, says, "Their music contains idioms which were transplanted from Africa, but as songs they are the products of American institutions, of the social, political, and geographic environment within which their creators were placed in America . . ."

Negro rhythms are well known to all of us. The syncopations of jazz and the "blues" have been made famous by the crooner and the saxophone player. These are direct products of Negro music.

Music seems to be inborn in the Negro. His sense of rhythm is highly developed and traces back to long experience in Africa with the complex rhythms expressed in dancing and drumming — rhythms which have fascinated many a white musician. The Negro more often than not is blessed with a good voice. We have only to think of such celebrated concert singers as Marian Anderson, Dorothy Maynor, Roland Hayes, Paul Robeson — to name but a few. The Negro has an instinctive feeling for harmony, and his folk music, in its natural state, is characterized by phrases sung by a solo voice which is answered by phrases in harmony.

His music helped to sustain the Negro in time of trouble, and if his lot in life improved, he expressed in music his joys as well as his sorrows. To his rich and varied African rhythms he added elements of the songs he heard in America. The spirituals were often suggested by the hymns he overheard at the religious meetings of the white people. His work songs and his dances were usually an outgrowth of his daily work. And his music, whether the serious and often mournful

12

spirituals or the gay and exciting dances, was always a highly personal expression.

Often the Negro used music as a story-telling medium, just as ballad singers did in Europe centuries ago. Many of the spirituals are Bible stories told in the colorful music and speech of the Negro. Examples are *Go Down, Moses, Ezekiel Saw de Wheel, The Old Ark's A-Mov-erin'*, and *Joshua Fit the Battle of Jericho*. Personal feelings the Negro often expressed in the "blues." Sometimes the "blues" lamented a fickle or a departed lover and sometimes it depicted homesickness or a longing for better times.

Thomas Jefferson called attention to the musical abilities of the Negro, and during the first half of the nineteenth century the Negro's ability to entertain was widely recognized, especially in the Southern States. The minstrel show, with its banjo and its comic songs, and the songs of Stephen Foster, became immensely popular. These, however, presented the Negro as the white man saw him, and they touched very lightly, if at all, on the real music of the Negro. The Negro's best music, especially the spirituals, was first brought to notice through the activities of the Fisk Jubilee Singers. This group, established at Fisk University in Nashville, Tennessee, in 1871, toured Europe and America and interested thousands of people in Negro spirituals. Their activities were supplemented many years later by the choirs of other Negro colleges, such as Hampton Institute, Tuskegee Institute, and Howard University.

Despite the favorable attention which the spirituals received, it remained for European musicians to convince Americans of the real importance of Negro music. When Antonin Dvořák visited this country in 1892, he pointed out to Americans that Negro folk music was a rich storehouse of rhythmic and melodic ideas. He praised the spirituals and when he composed his Symphony, *From the New World*, he used themes which, although his own, were strongly suggestive of Negro tunes. One of them has a similarity to *Swing Low, Sweet Chariot*.

A few years later Samuel Coleridge-Taylor, a Negro of British birth, came to this country to conduct his greatest work, a series of three cantatas on the story of Hiawatha. Coleridge-Taylor's enthusiasm for Negro folk music was such that he even introduced the spiritual tune, "Nobody Knows the Trouble I've Seen," in the overture to his *Hiawatha*.

Spurred by the admonitions of these visitors, Americans, white and Negro alike, began to take the spirituals more seriously, and these fine songs began to appear in print. In looking back it now seems very strange that it was only about fifty years ago that people first

13

had an opportunity to know *Deep River,* one of the greatest of all folk songs. This lovely song, with other traditional spirituals, was arranged by the Negro singer and composer, Harry T. Burleigh,* who had sung these songs to Dvořák a few years before. The spirituals found favor with concert singers and with choruses, for choral arrangements soon followed.

The music of the Negro continues to be important in the entertainment field, but on a higher plane than in the minstrel show days. Playwrights, such as Marc Connelly in *Green Pastures,* have made much of the spirituals, and one of George Gershwin's major works is the folk opera, *Porgy and Bess,* a setting of the play by DuBose and Dorothy Heyward. Mary Garden has been quoted as saying that *Porgy and Bess* will go down in history as the first great American opera. Whatever its place, those who have seen the opera are agreed that Gershwin made excellent use of Negro rhythmic and melodic ideas even though, like Dvořák in the *New World Symphony,* Gershwin fashioned his own tunes.

Other composers for the theater have given substantial recognition to the music of the Negro and have even occasionally contributed a composed folk song, as in Jerome Kern's *Old Man River.* For a century — from Stephen Foster to George Gershwin — American composers have frequently turned to Negro folk music as a source of inspiration.

QUESTIONS

Folk Music of America

1. Name some of the types of folk music to be found in America.
2. Name two songs that seem to be purely American and have no foreign flavor or influence.
3. What type of folk songs are found in the southwestern part of our country?
4. Where is the French influence felt in American folk music?

Indian Music

1. Why is it difficult to classify Indian music?
2. The Office of Indian Affairs at Washington is dealing with how many tribes and sub-tribes?
3. In what way does the music of the Indian become part of his daily life?
4. What sort of instruments does the Indian use?

---

* Other Negro musicians followed the lead of Burleigh, and, as the result of the activities of such men as Nathaniel Dett, William L. Dawson, Clarence Cameron White, J. Rosamond Johnson, John W. Work, and William Grant Still, the music of the Negro has become widely known and appreciated.

5. In what way do the intervals of the Indian scales differ from ours?
6. Name a few American composers who used Indian melodies and rhythms as a basis for their compositions.

Negro Music

1. Name some famous Negro singers.
2. How did music help sustain the Negro when he felt sad?
3. Name some types of songs that belong essentially to Negro music.
4. What famous organization helped bring some of the best of the Negro music to the attention of the public?
5. What famous European visited this country and helped to point out to Americans the real importance of Negro music?
6. What Negro singer and composer was the first to arrange the folk song *Deep River* and bring it to the notice of musicians everywhere?
7. Name a famous folk opera written by George Gershwin.

LISTENING SUGGESTIONS

Arkansaw Traveler
At the Gate of Heaven
Buffalo Gals
Deep River
Erie Canal, The
Go Down, Moses

Good-by, Ol' Paint
Home on the Range
Old Zip Coon
Poor Wayfaring Stranger
Steal Away
Swing Low, Sweet Chariot

⪻ 4 ⪼

POPULAR MUSIC IN AMERICA

THE STORY OF MUSIC in America would be far from complete if we were to omit from consideration our "everyday" music, heard (sometimes far too often) on jukebox, piano or radio. It is a common fashion to consider music as divided into two categories — "classical" and "popular," "classical" having reference to music for the musically educated, and "popular" to that which is enjoyed by the rank and file, especially young people. In actual fact, the distinction is not so simple. Our American popular music may include a dozen different types which vary widely in style. There is a vast difference between a Romberg melody and a boogie-woogie piece, and certainly *Begin the Beguine* and *The Tennessee Waltz* are far apart musically. Popular music frequently reaches out and takes material from the "classics," and the high school boys of a few years ago who whistled "Song of Love" from *Blossom Time* or *Moon-Love* may not have realized that they were really whistling Schubert and Tschaikowsky.

Since America became a nation there has been popular music in our country. Even severe old William Billings, in Revolutionary days, wrote popular songs, and his *Chester*, refashioned from a psalm tune, became an everyday favorite. Our early popular music was largely in the nature of simple, easily-learned songs, accompanied by guitar, banjo, piano, or parlor organ. The history of popular music went through a cycle similar to that of serious music. It had first a singing period succeeded by an instrumental phase.

In the early days of our country, travel and communication were difficult, and people had largely to make their own entertainment. Leisure time was often spent in singing the songs of the day. As facilities for entertainment improved, Americans heard songs in the music hall, the minstrel show, and the vaudeville theatre. If he liked what he heard, our nineteenth century American took the song home with him, and he and his friends and family often sang it at home. This was true of the songs of Stephen Foster. Perhaps the fact that these songs were so often sung in the home helped to maintain the place they have always had in the hearts of Americans.

Aside from Stephen Foster the mid-nineteenth century produced a

16

host of popular songs, a few of which we hear today. Sometimes they were in a humorous vein, such as *Clementine*, a favorite with the California gold-seekers. Sometimes they were inspired by the War between the States — *Just Before the Battle, Mother*. More often they were sentimental and concerned a loved one. And the American parlor resounded to the strains of *I'll Take You Home Again, Kathleen*, *When You and I Were Young, Maggie*, or *Silver Threads Among the Gold*.

The last thirty years of the nineteenth century were rather leisurely years when people had more time for singing than they seem to have now. America had not acquired its twentieth century sophistication and its popular music was usually simple and direct and nearly always sentimental. James Bland, a Virginia Negro, wrote such hits as *Carry Me Back to Old Virginny*, and *In the Evening by the Moonlight*. The waltz was the favorite dance of the time, and many of the popular songs were in waltz-time — *After the Ball*, *The Band Played On*, *Sweet Rosie O'Grady*, and a host of others. Often the songs had to do with a lover's quarrel or a sweetheart. Sometimes the popular songs of the "Gay Nineties" were identified with a city (*The Sidewalks of New York*) or a river (*On the Banks of the Wabash*), but whatever the subject matter, the songs were definitely a part of the American life of their day, and they were easy to remember.

The first fifteen years of the new century largely followed the pattern of the old, and we still had sentimental songs about "love, home, and mother." In theatre and home the favorites were of the style of *Meet Me Tonight in Dreamland*, *Mother Machree*, and *Down by the Old Mill Stream*. Some of them are often heard today in the repertoire of barber-shop quartets. Occasionally there was a real ballad, in folk style, which recorded a tragedy, as in *Casey Jones*, which details the last ride of the "brave engineer."

There were forces at work, however, which were destined to change the style of American popular music. Jazz was beginning to sound its strange rhythms in New Orleans and Chicago. Life in general was speeding up. The automobile, the movies, the phonograph, and the radio were to change the habits and the tempo of American life. Americans learned to dance in greater numbers than ever before. Phonographs, and eventually radios, began to displace pianos, and Americans did more listening and less playing. The rise of the popular dance orchestra did much to carry American popular music from its singing phase to its instrumental phase.

Ragtime had been known even before 1900 and had been gradually working its way into popular dance music. Not until 1911, however, did it begin to affect the songs which came out of "Tin Pan Alley," the

17

section of downtown New York where popular music is written, auditioned, and published. The year 1911 saw the publication of Irving Berlin's *Alexander's Ragtime Band*. Although the ragtime was more in the title than in the song itself, the piece centered attention on this exciting type of music from the South. The piece swept the country and started a career of fame and fortune for young Irving Berlin, who had come from Russia to this country as a boy of five.

Ragtime may have taken its name from its irregular rhythms which some people describe as "ragged." Syncopation is a feature of ragtime, and in syncopation a weak beat in a measure often receives a stress or accent ordinarily given to the strong beat. This is usually brought about in two ways: 1. The note which falls on the strong beat is shorter than the note which follows it; 2. The regular accent is distorted by tying an unaccented note in one measure to an accented note in the next.

Syncopation was not new to music. Bach and the other masters often employed syncopation and excellent examples occur in the music which the first Queen Elizabeth of England knew. But syncopation in Negro folk music, which led to ragtime, is a basic characteristic, not an occasional effect. A good ragtime player kept a steady bass going with his left hand and played a syncopated melody with his right hand. A "boogie-woogie" player does the same thing, merely repeating a phrase in steady rhythm over and over with the left hand while the right plays all sorts of highly decorated and syncopated melodies. Most amateur pianists are right-handed, and it is only natural for the right hand to undertake the more difficult part while the left keeps time.

Ragtime was quickly followed by the Blues. This was another Negro folk type of music, usually a melancholy tune in twelve, instead of the conventional sixteen, measure form. The Blues harmonies were quite different from those in common use in popular music, and the melodies made much use of the third and the seventh notes of the scale, sometimes major and sometimes minor. When sung these notes were usually sung at a pitch halfway between major and minor and were known as "blue" notes. This cannot be exactly reproduced on the piano, but you can get some of the effect of the "blue" notes by playing a piece in the key of C Major and ending it with the note pattern, G - A - G - B-Flat.

William C. Handy, an Alabama-born Negro, made the Blues famous. His first song in the Blues manner to be published was the *Memphis Blues*, written to help elect a mayor in Memphis, Tennessee. Then

18

he wrote one of the landmarks of American popular music, *The St. Louis Blues,* which, like some other masterpieces, went begging so that Handy had to publish it himself because the publishers refused it.

The Blues had long been an authentic type of Negro folk music in which the singers expressed their laments and frustrations resulting from poverty, sorrow and social injustice. They were an important part of the Negro's secular folk music in contrast to the spirituals which were his religious music. It remained for Handy to write them down and to compose Blues songs of his own.

It is very common to hear American popular music described as "jazz" music. This is not strictly true, since jazz is not really a type of music so much as it is a method of performing music. Any tune can be played in jazz style. The melody itself may not contain a syncopated note; the syncopation is provided in the accompaniment which the players weave about the melody. Jazz is unique in music because it is primarily a process of improvisation. In an orchestra, band, or chorus the musicians follow the notes on the printed page. The jazz orchestra player also has printed parts but he does not follow them faithfully, and his most interesting contributions come when he deserts the printed part and embarks on flights of musical imagination. Thus the best examples of jazz music are not found in published music but in the recordings of performances of jazz. And the truest expression of jazz is in the "jam session" where musicians dispense with notes and play whatever comes into their minds. Oddly enough the jazz experts in improvisation have their counterpart in serious music in the dignified organists, who do not, of course, play the "breaks" on their sedate instrument but who often make up their music as they go, just as do the members of a swing band.

There are several musical factors in the jazz style. The Blues influence on harmony and melody and the extensive use of syncopation have been mentioned. Another distinguishing feature is the use of polyrhythms. This rather formidable word simply means that several rhythmic patterns are being played simultaneously.*

Another trademark of jazz is the "break," and here we have an idea which has a very good parallel in serious music. Anyone who has heard a concerto in which a pianist or a violinist as a soloist with orchestral accompaniment will recall that at some point in the music the orchestra stops and the soloist plays an elaborate and brilliant solo part which is called a "cadenza." When a jazz musician "takes a

---

* This can be illustrated by going to the piano and playing a steady four-four rhythm with the left hand and playing with the right hand a three note melody, repeating the latter several times so that the strong beats keep shifting to different notes of the three-note pattern. Try it with G in the bass and G, F-sharp, E repeated in the treble. This superimposing of rhythms is important in the structure of jazz.

break" or puts in some "hot licks," he is really playing a cadenza, for he uses his ingenuity to make it as scintillating as possible. The rest of the dance orchestra allows one or another player at intervals to have the spot-light with a "break." The reputations of such famous popular musicians as Louis Armstrong, Benny Goodman, Harry James, and many another rest to a degree on the brilliance of their "breaks." One of the early jazz musicians who established great traditions for the "breaks" was "Bix" Beiderbecke, who is said to have left school rather than "tone down" his trumpet-playing.

Since jazz is much less influenced by the printed page than other music, and since it is the "everyday" music of the American public, it is subject to whims and fads, changes in style, and to the pull and haul of commercial interests seeking to profit on any new development in popular music. The first jazz bands, like the Original Dixieland which startled New York in 1917, seldom had more than five men. When music is improvised rather than played from written notes, it is obvious that not many musicians can play together effectively. Six or eight men can work together as a team, but forty or fifty trying to play in the free jazz style would have plenty of trouble. The nature of jazz, whether improvised or played from notes, is such that it does not lend itself to large groups. This explains why jazz numbers, played by large school bands and orchestras, never sound as well as when played by a small dance combination.

The entertainment field, always experimenting to find new ways to popular favor, has tried out many jazz styles and many instrumental effects. During the 1920's "sweet jazz" and "symphonic jazz" were high in favor. Sweet jazz used saxophones and the other dance band instruments, but it also retained the violins and other string instruments which had been important in dance music before jazz. With this kind of an orchestra the melody and harmony were more important than in the hot jazz combinations where rhythm was paramount. For the sweet and symphonic styles of jazz it was necessary to have the music specially arranged and this led to the rise of the "arranger," who, in popular music, is often more important than the composer.

Popular dance music thus began to assume the shape which it has now pretty well retained for more than thirty years. There have been various changes of style in jazz — sweet, swing, jive, bebop, etc. One succeeds another, and next year it will be something new. Recently many bands have revived the old Chicago Dixieland style so-called because Chicago was the first large city where it was widely heard.

The expert arrangers agreed quite generally on instrumentation in which drums, string bass, piano, and banjo or guitar kept the steady

20

insistent rhythm going while the melody was handled by clarinet, saxophone, and trumpet with the lower saxophones and the trumpets and trombones providing the harmony. Little did Adolphe Sax, who invented the saxophone a hundred years ago, suspect that the smooth-toned instrument he intended for military bands would become the mainstay of dance orchestras the world over.

The arrangers produced dance music which was smooth, sounded well, and still had some of the freedom of the original jazz, and it was played by expert and well-disciplined groups such as the orchestras of Paul Whiteman, Guy Lombardo, Wayne King, and others. The arrangers became important and well-paid men in the popular field. Ferde Grofé, who was Paul Whiteman's arranger, did much to establish dance orchestra styles. He helped George Gershwin by orchestrating the *Rhapsody in Blue*. Whiteman, Grofé, and Gershwin attempted with some success to establish "symphonic jazz," a more sophisticated style, calling for a larger orchestra and for a musical treatment which often resembled symphonic music. Grofé, Robert Russell Bennett, Andre Kostelanetz, and Morton Gould developed a presentation of popular music which has had a wide vogue in theatre and radio.

Paul Whiteman's concert in New York in 1924 brought jazz to the attention of the "long-hairs," as jazz musicians sometimes describe the devotees of serious music. George Gershwin, whose music is discussed in another chapter, was foremost in the movement to produce jazz music in larger forms suitable for symphony orchestras. Morton Gould has also produced interesting works in the jazz idiom for large orchestra. Some composers, primarily identified with serious music, have made use of jazz rhythms in some of their compositions, among them Roy Harris, Aaron Copland, and Igor Stravinsky.

While jazz has influenced the more serious music of our own time, the most widespread use of jazz continues to be through the dance orchestras which follow the tradition of freedom to improvise and are not too much hampered by notes. Orchestras like those of Duke Ellington, Benny Goodman, Tommy Dorsey, and a host of others have preserved much of the original jazz tradition of making up music on the spot. The tune is much less important than the treatment of it. Duke Ellington is known as a jazz composer, but it is said that his music is really the result of composite composition to which the members of his band contribute, so that an Ellington tune is really a species of folk music in which several people have had a hand.

The heroes of jazz music are thus the performers and not the composers, since the players are to a considerable extent the composers. The jazz field, offering greater financial rewards than the

21

symphonic, has attracted many fine musicians. Some of them are artists of virtuoso stature in their own field just as Milstein and Horowitz tower above the concert field. A list of such celebrities would certainly include Harry James and Louis Armstrong, trumpeters, Jack Teagarden, trombonist; Benny Goodman, clarinetist; Eddie Condon, guitarist; Gene Krupa and Lionel Hampton, drummers; and such pianists as "Jelly Roll" Morton and Count Basie.

It must not be thought that, with the remarkable instrumental development of popular music, the song, as such, disappeared. Far from it, for Tin Pan Alley has produced many a tune which the American public has sung, hummed, and whistled. Irving Berlin, during a fruitful career of more than forty years, has perhaps given Americans more good popular songs than any other one man. Berlin, as is well known, is a "black key" piano-player, playing everything in the key of F-sharp major. His ideas — lyrics, tunes and harmonies — are dictated to others who write them down. Berlin has long had a gift for a turn of phrase, in words or music or both, which will capture the fickle fancies of the American public, and such songs as *Always, Remember,* and *White Christmas* might be termed "classics" in popular song literature, while his *God Bless America* has become an unofficial national anthem.

Our country has received cultural influences from many countries and races, and it is not surprising to find a great variety in the songs which Americans have cherished. Sometimes it is a straightforward, easy-to-sing tune like *God Bless America,* and again it may be a tune of instrumental character like Hoagy Carmichael's *Star Dust,* which originally written as a ragtime piano piece, was made over into a highly popular song, although it is not easy to sing. Sometimes the popular tune has a folk quality, like *Old Man River,* or it may have the sophisticated Park Avenue touch of *Night and Day.*

The promoters and publishers of popular music are shrewd businessmen, ever on the alert for salable material. Frequently they have borrowed extensively from folk songs and the serious composers. There have been years, in fact, when Peter Tschaikowsky and Frederic Chopin could have been called the leading composers on the Hit Parade, since it contained songs derived from their tunes to a larger degree than those of any present-day song writer.

In any country the popular music is inevitably closely identified with the theatre of that country, and the musicians who have written for the American theatre have provided many of our song hits. The American musical comedy developed along somewhat the same lines as the Gilbert and Sullivan operettas in England and the Viennese operettas on the continent. From our American musical shows, on the stage and in lesser degree on the screen, have come many of America's best popular tunes.

The man who did the most to establish the pattern of American musical comedy or light opera was Victor Herbert. This genial Irishman, who came to America at an early age, dominated the American musical stage for thirty years, producing a long line of musical comedies that were vastly popular with the theatre-going public. *Babes in Toyland, Naughty Marietta, The Red Mill, The Fortune Teller, Sweethearts,* and *Eileen* are a few of the stage productions which added luster to the Herbert name. Many of the songs from these works, such as "Ah, Sweet Mystery of Life," "The Gypsy Love Song," and "The Italian Street Song" continue to enjoy great popularity.

Herbert came to this country to play the cello in the Pittsburgh Symphony Orchestra, and he had ambitions to become a composer of serious music. The American public took to his light operas, but his grand operas, *Natoma* and *Madeleine,* are largely forgotten.

It was Victor Herbert who led the battle for recognition of the rights of the composer under the copyright law which resulted in a Supreme Court decision that a composer's works could not be performed for profit without his permission. His leadership to establish this principle led to the establishment of ASCAP (the American Society of Composers, Authors and Publishers) which guards the rights of its membership which includes a great many creative musicians.

The Herbert tradition has been continued by a number of operetta composers. Rudolph Friml, of Czech birth and a student of Antonin Dvořák, has scored with such hits as *The Firefly, Rose Marie,* and *The Vagabond King,* while Sigmund Romberg, born in Hungary, long enjoyed a position of eminence in stage and screen music circles with such successes as *The Student Prince, Blossom Time, The New Moon* and *The Desert Song.* Jerome Kern, like George Gershwin, grew up in New York City and served an apprenticeship as a "song plugger" for Tin Pan Alley publishers to go on to fame and fortune as the composer of the scores of *Sunny, The Cat and the Fiddle,* and one of the most famous of all musical productions, *Show Boat.*

Some of George Gershwin's best tunes were written for his stage productions: *Lady, Be Good, Strike Up the Band,* and *Of Thee I Sing.* The last-named work satirized American politics just as Gilbert and Sullivan did with British affairs, and it was awarded the Pulitzer Prize.

Irving Berlin wrote music for the *Ziegfeld Follies, The Music Box Revue, This Is the Army, Annie, Get Your Gun,* and many other stage and screen productions. Cole Porter whose *Night and Day* and

23

Begin the Beguine could be called "classics" in the popular field, has contributed to many stage successes, while the contemporary team of Richard Rodgers and Oscar Hammerstein has enriched popular music with the tunes of *Oklahoma, Carousel,* and *South Pacific.* Also to be remembered is Vincent Youmans, composer of musical shows distinguished by such song hits as *Tea for Two, I Want to be Happy, Great Day,* and *Hallelujah.*

The singers of popular songs have usually had a special technique quite apart from that of the concert singer. Often this technique is contrary to the best principles of voice culture, and popular singers often depend upon a sort of song-speech. Sometimes the popular singer has an intense, highly dramatic delivery, as in the case of Al Jolson or Sophie Tucker, or the popular song may be done in the suavely smooth style of Dinah Shore or Bing Crosby.

Singing has always been important in popular music, both before and since the advent of jazz, but Fred Waring seems to have been the only director in the popular field to give serious attention to choral singing. His "Pennsylvanians," long a popular orchestra, have in late years featured choral presentations.

The history of American popular music is a long and interesting one which can only be briefly sketched here. Like other phases of our American culture, it has received influences from many sources — the folk music of pioneer America, and especially the folk music of the Negro, the English ballad, the Viennese waltz, and the music of Latin America. All these have contributed to that great body of music which, in distinction to the music of the concert hall, we know as "popular music."

QUESTIONS

1. Is it possible to draw a hard and fast line between popular and classical music? If not, explain why.
2. Name a few songs that were popular during the last thirty years of the nineteenth century.
3. What is meant by ragtime?
4. What changes in our civilization led up to this type of music?
5. Tell something about music designated as the "Blues."
6. Name two jazz players who have made themselves famous for their playing of a brilliant type of cadenza known as the "break."
7. Name two well-known musicians who are famous for their dance orchestras.
8. Name a famous arranger who helped Paul Whiteman and George Gershwin.
9. Who first brought jazz to the attention of serious musicians? In what year was this?

24

10. Who are some of the musicians who direct dance bands and who have especially followed the tradition of freedom to improvise and are not too much hampered by notes?
11. Who are the real heroes of jazz music?
12. Tell something of interest concerning Irving Berlin.
13. Who are some of the serious composers whose music has been borrowed by promoters and publishers?
14. Who did the most to establish the pattern of American musical comedy or light opera in this country?
15. Give some interesting facts concerning this composer.
16. Name other composers who have contributed musically to the American theatre.
17. Name some of the sources which have influenced American music.
18. Name two other famous composers of musical comedy.
19. Name two popular light operas written by Rodgers and Hammerstein.
20. Name a well-known and much-beloved singer of popular songs.

LISTENING SUGGESTIONS

After the Ball — Harris
Ah, Sweet Mystery of Life—Herbert
Alexander's Ragtime Band — Berlin
Always — Berlin
Begin the Beguine — Porter
Gypsy Love Song — Herbert
Hallelujah — Youmans
I'll Take You Home Again, Kathleen — Westendorf
Italian Street Song — Herbert
March of the Toys — Herbert
Memphis Blues — Handy
Mother Machree — Ball
Old Man River — Kern
On the Banks of the Wabash — Dresser
St. Louis Blues — Handy
Star Dust — Carmichael

Tea for Two — Youmans
Who — Kern
Recordings from *Oklahoma, South Pacific, The King and I, The Desert Song, Blossom Time, Rose Marie, The Vagabond King*, and other operettas by Herbert, Romberg, Friml, Kern, and Rodgers and Hammerstein.
Recordings by Louis Armstrong, Count Basie, Sidney Bechet, Eddie Condon, Bing Crosby, Dinah Shore, Harry James, Jelly-Roll Morton, and the orchestras of Duke Ellington, Benny Goodman, Stan Kenton, Wayne King, and Guy Lombardo.

⊰ 5 ⊱

AMERICAN COMPOSERS

I T IS a commonly-held belief that Stephen Foster was the first American composer. It is believed by others that Edward MacDowell
was the first creative American musician. Neither belief is correct,
for there have been American composers since the days of the American Revolution. The man who probably best merits the title of "first
American composer" was Francis Hopkinson. Born in Philadelphia,
he was a member of the first class graduated from the University
of Pennsylvania (in 1757), and as a prominent lawyer he became
important in the affairs of the American Colonies. He was, in fact,
one of the signers of the Declaration of Independence and one of
the men who helped to write our Constitution. Music was his hobby,
and he gave time to it until his death in 1791. Among his works was
a collection of Seven Songs, dedicated to George Washington. Hopkinson's best-known song, *My Days Have Been So Wondrous Free,*
was composed when he was a young man of twenty-two.

In Boston about the same time there was a singing-master named
William Billings. Not a well-educated aristocrat like Hopkinson, Billings was a common man of the people who originally made his living
as a tanner. He gave more and more time to music and thus became
the first *professional* composer in America. Between 1770 and 1794
he published six collections of church music, including in them the
psalms and hymns then known in New England, together with his
own compositions. You may still find in many songbooks his hymn,
Chester, which became a marching song of the American soldiers in
the Revolution. Billings organized and conducted singing-classes, one
of which led to the formation of America's oldest choral society, the
Stoughton (Massachusetts) Musical Society, organized in 1786. Long
neglected, Billings' choral compositions have in late years been
revived and are frequently performed by American choral groups.

STEPHEN FOSTER

As our first great popular song-writer, Stephen Foster introduced a
new note into American music. Born in 1826, he became, as a young

26

man, fully aware of many phases of the American life of his time and knew the sentimental songs highly prized by family groups around the parlor organ, the rather crude songs favored by the minstrel shows so popular in his time, and the songs of the Negro workers. As a youth his preoccupation with music and his lack of interest in business were the despair of his parents. His day-dreams, however, produced a series of songs which captured the hearts of his countrymen to a degree which has probably never been equalled by another songwriter. His early efforts were well received, but his first real success was *Oh! Susanna,* published in 1848 when Foster was twenty-two. It was taken up by the entertainers of the day and became a veritable theme song for the California gold-rush in 1849.

Had Foster lived fifty years later he would have become a wealthy man. Thousands of copies of his songs were sold during his own short life (he died at thirty-eight), but the copyright laws of his time were lax, and many publishers were unscrupulous, with the result that he received little of what should have been his due as a composer. Editions of his songs were frequently "pirated," (printed without permission) sometimes even without his name.

For some years Foster enjoyed the kind of fame that Irving Berlin, George Gershwin, and Rodgers and Hammerstein were to meet at a later time, and the American public looked forward eagerly to the next Foster hit-tune. Such beloved melodies as *Old Folks at Home, Camptown Races, My Old Kentucky Home,* and *Jeanie with the Light Brown Hair* (probably inspired by his wife, Jane) were immensely popular soon after publication.

With the War between the States, Foster's popularity suffered a sharp decline. Although he was a Northerner, born in Lawrenceville, Pennsylvania (now part of Pittsburgh), Foster's songs until 1861 were more popular in the South than in the North. With the coming of the War, the South would not sing the songs of a Northerner and the North refused to sing songs associated with the South. A decade or two later their popularity began to rise again, but it was too late to benefit the composer, who had died in 1864. Now his songs are known to every American and are often called composed folk songs, because they are simple and easy to sing. Stephen Foster's memory is perpetuated in the Foster Memorial on the campus of the University of Pittsburgh. The Foster Library housed there was begun by an Indianapolis admirer, Josiah K. Lilly. Also dedicated to Foster's memory is "My Old Kentucky Home" at Bardstown, Kentucky, a fine old mansion and not a cabin as some might imagine.

27

EDWARD MACDOWELL

In sharp contrast to Stephen Foster, who wrote simple songs for the masses, was Edward MacDowell, born in New York City in 1861, three years before Foster's death. His parents, unlike Foster's, encouraged Edward's musical career and even sent him to Europe for study. There he met Debussy, Liszt, and others, including his European teacher, Joachim Raff. Twelve years passed in Europe where the young MacDowell studied, played the piano, and composed. Boston was his home for eight years after his return to America, and from there he was called in 1896 to Columbia University to become the first chairman of its newly-created music department. It proved an unfortunate move, for MacDowell's independent temperament was ill-suited to the academic routine. He remained at Columbia for several years, giving some attention to composing and to concert tours, for he was in demand as a concert pianist. Eventually he left Columbia and the city for the quiet of the New Hampshire hills.

Edward MacDowell is sometimes called an American Romanticist. A Romanticist, in music, is a composer whose music is descriptive of something which has aroused a personal, emotional response. Thus MacDowell wrote many piano pieces descriptive of the things he saw and felt during his New England vacations. Best known are *To a Wild Rose, To a Water Lily,* and the *Sea Pieces.* His travels helped to shape MacDowell's music, just as had Mendelssohn's a half-century earlier. There are many such evidences in MacDowell's compositions: the *Scotch Poem,* the *Norse Sonata,* the *Keltic Sonata,* the *Indian Suite,* the *New England Idyls.*

Some critics refer to MacDowell's music as more European than American. He did not intend it to be typical of America, for music to him was the very personal expression of the composer. He wanted more than anything else to prove to the world that there was a place in America for a serious musician. Even as a youth he is said to have delighted in proving to his associates that he could excel in sports as well as in playing the piano and that music was not a "sissy" activity for a young man. His career proved another point in music — that a little thing, well done will outlast many a grandiose work. MacDowell wrote sonatas and concertos, and good ones, but thousands of music-lovers remember him best for *To a Wild Rose* and other brief piano gems.

MacDowell was a nature-lover and spent his happiest hours in his log cabin near Peterborough, New Hampshire, a "house of dreams untold," as he called it. He had hoped to establish a colony there where creative artists might work. He was not to see his dreams

28

realized, but the colony has now existed for more than forty years as
a result of the untiring efforts of his widow, Marian MacDowell, a
truly remarkable woman, who raised thousands of dollars through
her concerts and lectures to establish the MacDowell Memorial Association. The Colony at Peterborough has become a lasting memorial
to a distinguished American composer and it annually affords a haven
to American composers, writers, and artists, who may there pursue
their creative activities undisturbed.

OTHER AMERICAN COMPOSERS

At times a certain fortunate association of personalities and circum-
stances results in a brilliant period of creative activity within a single
city. London was a center of musical creativity in the seventeenth
century, Paris in the eighteenth, and Vienna in the nineteenth century.
In the early days of the twentieth century, Boston was a center of
musical culture, not perhaps of the worldwide importance of the
Vienna of Schubert, Beethoven, and Brahms, but important in the
musical development of America. There were in these years several
men in Boston who contributed importantly to American music
through their compositions and, in even greater degree, through their
teaching. These men are known as the "New England Group." Among
them was George Whitefield Chadwick (1854-1931), long director
of the New England Conservatory of Music and one of America's
greatest music teachers, as well as an excellent composer. Arthur
Foote (1853-1937) won distinction as composer and teacher. Horatio
Parker (1863-1919), pupil of Chadwick, attained renown in Europe
as well as America through his oratorio, *Hora Novissima*, and eventually became chairman of the music department at Yale University.

Also in the "New England Group" were John Knowles Paine (1839-
1906), earliest of the group, who founded the music department at
Harvard; Mrs. H. H. A. Beach, (1867-1949), America's first prominent
woman composer, and three composers who owed their early training to Chadwick — Henry Hadley (1871-1937), Frederick Converse
(1871-1940), and Arthur Whiting (1861-1936).

Now and then since Stephen Foster's time the American public has
taken to its heart a song in much the same fashion that it adopted
the familiar Foster melodies. One such song is *The Rosary*, written
in 1898 by Ethelbert Nevin (1862-1901), who also composed much
piano music, some of which (*Narcissus* and *A Day in Venice*) once
enjoyed great popularity. The songs of Carrie Jacobs Bond have
enjoyed a great vogue in the American home, especially *A Perfect
Day* and *I Love You Truly*.

Charles Wakefield Cadman (1881-1946) was the composer of songs which became immensely popular (*At Dawning* and *From the Land of the Sky-Blue Water*). Cadman wrote in larger forms also, with some success, and his opera *Shanewis* (*The Robin Woman*) is one of the few American operas ever produced at the Metropolitan in New York. It is based on an American Indian story. Cadman made a study of the music of the Indians, and a considerable number of his compositions were inspired by it. Sometimes he gave attention to other American subjects, as in his opera, *A Witch of Salem*, produced in Chicago.

Daniel Gregory Mason (1873-   ) who has won distinction as composer and author, once said that America had not one music but ten musics. We know that America's folk music includes many and diverse types, and this great variety is found in the work of American composers who are now living and writing. This is perhaps not at all surprising in our country which is of great extent and has musicians of widely varying types of thought. A number of our present-day American composers have been influenced by European training or experience; others have found their material in our American folk music. Some follow rather closely the traditions of the past; others want nothing to do with the past and strive valiantly to be "different." It is difficult to know how much of their music will last, how much will not. Do not expect all American music to sound alike or to follow an "American" pattern. There are, after all, many types of music in any other country — England, Germany, or Italy.

In listening to American music of our own time, the listener does find one thing which is common to nearly all present-day American composers — an over-powering interest in the symphony orchestra. A few recent Americans have written songs, choral works, or piano music; quite a number have shown interest in chamber music (for small groups of instruments), but practically all of them have had ambitions to conquer the symphony orchestra.

In a book of this size it is not possible to discuss in detail the music of contemporary Americans, but it is possible to list a number of Americans who have won recognition for their compositions and to suggest that the listener hear their music when opportunity presents.

John Alden Carpenter (1876-1950), who combined two successful careers — music and business — is remembered for his songs and his orchestral pieces, especially the humorous suite, *Adventures in a Perambulator*, and the ballet *Skyscrapers*. Howard Hanson (1896-   ), director of the Eastman School of Music, is respected here and abroad as the composer of several symphonies and the opera, *Merrÿmount*, produced at the Metropolitan in New York in 1933.

30

Carpenter, born in Illinois; Hanson, a native of Nebraska, and Roy Harris (1898-   ), who came from Oklahoma, have proved that American composers may come from the Middlewest as well as from the older eastern states. Harris is widely known for his symphonies and string quartets.

Other middle-western Americans who have become established American composers are Leo Sowerby (1895-   ), native of Michigan, known especially for his church music and organ compositions, and Gardner Read (1913-   ), born in Illinois, though now living in Boston, and Virgil Thomson (1896-   ), born in Kansas City, but now of New York and known both as composer and critic.

Arthur Shepherd (1880-   ) born in Idaho, educated in Massachusetts, and long a resident of Cleveland, is typical of numerous American musicians whose experience has included various parts of America. Other composers have come from the West. George Frederick McKay (1899-   ) was born and lives in the State of Washington. Much of his music is influenced by American folk characteristics, and his *Music of the Americas* series is well known to American school orchestras. Harl McDonald (1899-   ), born in Colorado, did not forget the West though long a Philadelphia resident. His music often evokes pictures of the West and Southwest. His first symphony is sub-titled *The Santa Fe Trail* and his *Second Symphony* contains a rhumba as its third movement.

Many of these composers have eventually become established in New York, Boston, or Philadelphia because of the importance of these cities as teaching and performing centers. Deems Taylor (1885-   ), widely known in radio and television and as an author and a composer, was born in New York City. His operas, *The King's Henchman* and *Peter Ibbetson*, were well received, and his suite for orchestra, *Through the Looking Glass,* is frequently heard.

William Schuman (1910-   ), head of the noted Juilliard School of Music, is a native New Yorker. His symphonies and chamber music have commanded attention, as well as several choral works. Paul Creston (1906-   ), a native of New York City, has won a name as a composer for orchestra and also for band. Randall Thompson (1899-   ), now on the music staff at Harvard, was born in New York City. He is notable for his symphonies and his choral compositions, one of which, his *Alleluia,* is in the repertoire of many high school and college groups. Samuel Barber (1910-   ), a native of Pennsylvania, has won distinction for his works for voice and for orchestra. Barber's *Adagio for Strings* and *Essay for Orchestra* were the first American works selected by Arturo Toscanini for the N.B.C. Symphony Orchestra program when he assumed its leadership. Barber served in World War II and his Second Symphony is dedicated to the Army Air Force.

From Brooklyn came Aaron Copland (1900-   ) and George Gershwin (1898-1937). Copland has given considerable attention to music for the ballet (*Rodeo, El Salon Mexico, Appalachian Spring,* etc.). He has also been interested in providing music for the movies. Copland is an excellent example of the present-day composer who is thoroughly aware of many phases of American life. Many of his works are based on American scenes and history. One of his compositions, *A Lincoln Portrait,* for orchestra and narrator, honors Abraham Lincoln and for other works, especially his ballets (*Rodeo, Billy The Kid,* and others) he has chosen American subjects. Copland is also an apostle for new ideas in music. He founded the American Festival of Contemporary Music held yearly at Yaddo in Saratoga Springs, New York, and is a member of the faculty at the noted Tanglewood School in Massachusetts, a center each summer for American musical activity. He has lectured extensively and written books on modern music.

To many young Americans the name of George Gershwin is perhaps better known than that of any other American composer. Almost everyone has heard *Summertime* and the *Rhapsody in Blue,* and Gershwin occupies a unique place in American music in bringing together jazz music and serious music. Gershwin grew up in the field of popular entertainment. As a youth of twenty or so he wrote such songs as *Swanee,* made famous by Al Jolson. Gershwin was then a "song-plugger" on Broadway, which means that he was employed by publishers of popular music to popularize their tunes in cafes and theaters. He wrote numerous musical comedies but took greater pride in his folk-opera, *Porgy and Bess,* based on a Negro story. Tunes from this opera, *Summertime* and others, became, and remain "hit-tunes" in America.

Gershwin believed the musical elements of jazz could be employed in symphonic music in a way that would interpret contemporary American life. Recognition of his success in this direction began when he played his *Rhapsody in Blue* with Paul Whiteman's Orchestra in Aeolian Hall in New York City in 1924. Gershwin then knew little about writing for orchestra, and the scoring (arranging for orchestra) of the *Rhapsody* was done by Ferde Grofé, whose composition, *Grand Canyon Suite,* is often heard.

Gershwin then studied orchestration and a little later achieved another success with his *Piano Concerto in F,* written for the New York Symphony, and another orchestral work, *An American in Paris.* Had his career not been cut off by death when he was still under

32

forty, George Gershwin might have succeeded still further in making jazz music an important element in serious concert music. While jazz effects are heard now and then in our newer American music, our present-day composers do not seem to have followed Gershwin's lead.

The opera has occupied the attention of the young Italian-American composer, Gian-Carlo Menotti (1911-   ), who has won fame as the composer of *The Consul, The Medium, The Telephone,* and *Amahl and the Night Visitors.* The last-named opera has the distinction of being the first opera composed especially for presentation on television.

Along with the creative musicians who are producing America's new music are native Americans who can interpret it. The stars of concert and opera now include each year a higher proportion of native-born talent. Audiences which once applauded operatic casts imported entirely from Europe now enjoy the singing of American-born singers. Helen Traubel, Eleanor Steber, Gladys Swarthout, Lawrence Tibbett, Robert Merrill, James Melton, are but a few American singers to win fame, while such Americans as Albert Spalding (1888-1953), Yehudi Menuhin, William Kapell, and others have become celebrated violinists or pianists.

Not many years ago there seemed to be a unanimous feeling among symphony orchestra boards that the qualifications of a conductor included European birth. That attitude has now been modified to the degree that several important American orchestras employ native-born conductors. Among them are Thor Johnson, conductor of the Cincinnati Symphony Orchestra; Alfred Wallenstein, conductor of the Los Angeles Philharmonic Orchestra; Walter Hendl, who conducts the Dallas Symphony Orchestra, and Howard Mitchell, conductor of the National Symphony Orchestra in Washington, D.C.

QUESTIONS

1. Name several important composers in the New England group.
2. What American composer made a study of the American Indians and what was the name of his opera based on an Indian story?
3. Name several other American-born composers and a well-known composition of each.
4. Who was George Gershwin?
5. What compositions illustrate his employment of the musical elements of jazz in symphonic music?
6. Name several prominent American-born performers of music.

7. Do you think that America has a great musical future? If so, give your reasons.
8. How do you feel about opera in English?

LISTENING SUGGESTIONS

Adagio for Strings — Barber
A Day in Venice — Nevin
Adventures in a Perambulator — Carpenter
A Lincoln Portrait — Copland
American Salute — Morton Gould
An American in Paris — Gershwin
Appalachian Spring — Copland
Concerto in F — Gershwin
El Salon Mexico — Copland
From the Land of the Sky-Blue Water — Cadman
Indian Suite — MacDowell
Jeanie with the Light Brown Hair — Foster
Latin-American Symphonette — Morton Gould

My Days Have Been so Wondrous Free — Hopkinson
Nordic Symphony — Hanson
Oh! Susanna! — Foster
Porgy and Bess — Gershwin
Rhapsody in Blue — Gershwin
Rodeo — Copland
Rhumba — Harl McDonald
Shepherd's Carol, The — Billings
Skyscrapers — Carpenter
Symphony No. 4 — Hanson
Symphony No. 3 — Roy Harris
Symphony No. 3 — Schuman
Through the Looking Glass — Taylor
To a Water Lily — MacDowell
To a Wild Rose — MacDowell
White Peacock, The — Griffes

Cielito Lindo

English: David Stevens   Mexican

In gay waltz time

1. De la Sie - rra Mo - re - na, Cie -
1. I'm wait-ing near __ by the foun-tain here, __

li - to Lin-do, vie - nen ba - jan-do __
Come, my love-ly Cie - li - to Lin-do. __

Un par de o - ji - tos ne-gros Cie -
O - ver there __ in the vil - lage square,

li - to Lin-do de __ con-tra-ban-do. __
there is mu-sic, Cie - li - to Lin-do. __

CHORUS

Ay ay ay ay! __ Can - ta y no llo - res __
Ay ay ay ay! __ Come to your win - dow __

por - que can-tan - do se a - le-gran, Cie -
Ere moon-light fails __ and the star-light pales, __

li - to Lin-do los __ co - ra - zo - nes. __
We must has-ten, Cie - li - to Lin-do. __

⨽ 6 ⨼

CENTRAL AND SOUTH AMERICA

FOR MANY YEARS North American people were accustomed to think of Central and South America as foreign lands, remote from us and inhabited by people who spoke other languages and thought differently from us. In a vague way we knew that the Mayas, the Incas, and the Aztecs had once developed important cultures, but our knowledge of the past and present cultures of the countries which make up Latin America was quite limited. If we thought of them as having any music, it was in terms of such songs as *La Paloma* or *La Golondrina.*

Both North and South America, having been settled by Europeans, necessarily retained many European influences, but as the Americas grew independent of Europe, politically and economically, they began to realize that they had many interests in common as inhabitants of the Western Hemisphere. The airplane and the radio brought the Americas closer together, and in recent years there has been a cultural and an economic interchange which has brought us to a much better knowledge of our neighbors to the south.

We now realize that in these countries there is a highly interesting and complex literature of folk music which, for purposes of convenience, is usually called "Latin-American" music. The term "Latin-American," of course, came about because the South and Central American countries were colonized largely by people from Spain, Italy, and France, who spoke languages which were derived in large part from the Latin tongue. Some South and Central Americans resent the term "Latin-American" but it has nevertheless come into very common usage.

To many listeners Latin-American music is a rather standardized product of rumba or tango patterns, punctuated with certain characteristic rhythms. Much of the music exported to us from these countries has, like our own popular music, been subjected to changes brought about by entertainment demands and has thus lost much of its original folk character, just as the commercial jazz we hear day in and day out is quite different from genuine jazz music.

Actually, "Latin-American" music is often more African than Latin,

36

CENTRAL AND SOUTH AMERICA

and some of it is neither Latin nor African but Indian. There is a considerably greater variety of folk melody and rhythm in South and Central America than there is in our own folk music, and this should not surprise us when we remember that there are important differences in the racial populations of these countries. Such countries as Bolivia, Colombia, Ecuador, Guatemala, Mexico, Nicaragua, Paraguay, Peru, and El Salvador are inhabited very largely by Indians and mestizos (people of mixed white and Indian blood). In Argentina, Brazil, Chile, Uruguay, and Venezuela, white people predominate. Except in Brazil, where the majority of people trace back to Portugal, the people of these countries represent Spanish blood more than that of any other country, although in some sections the people may trace back to colonists from France, Germany, Italy, or England. Haiti is populated almost entirely by Negroes, and in Cuba perhaps a fourth of the people are Negroes. The folk music of Latin America is thus a blend of three influences — Indian, African, and Spanish (in Brazil, Portuguese). In Indian countries like Ecuador and Peru one hears slow-moving melodies, solemn or plaintive, and often in the ancient five-tone scales. In Haiti and Cuba the rhythms are more vigorous and drums and other percussion instruments are prominent. In Argentina, Brazil, Chile, and other countries the music tends to show some of the characteristics of each of the three basal sources.

Only a few years after Columbus discovered America the Spanish *conquistadors* (conquerors) subdued the Indian populations of Central and South America. Cortez conquered Mexico City in 1521 and Pizarro founded the city of Lima in Peru in 1535. Spain was then one of the most influential countries in the world and Spanish traders and priests followed the soldiers, so that a Spanish civilization was soon superimposed on the ruins of the Indian culture. Music, especially the music of the church, was cultivated by those early colonists, and as a result Latin America has a musical tradition considerably older than ours in the United States. Nearly a century before the Pilgrims landed at Plymouth a conservatory of music was established in Mexico City. Seven books of music were printed in Mexico before 1600, although the first music printed in the United States did not come until 1698, in an edition of the Bay Psalm Book. The Spanish priests brought with them the mystery plays of a religious nature through which they gave instruction to the Indians. The tradition of these survives to this day in *Las Posadas* and *Los Pastores*, the Christmas plays which may be seen in Mexico and in Southern California. Theatres were established and Spanish plays were frequently performed, especially in Peru, before 1600.

The Spanish were zealous colonists, and they endeavored to stamp

37

out the Indian culture. They did succeed in establishing the Spanish language as the predominant tongue, except in Brazil, but fortunately they did not succeed in obliterating the folk music and legends of the Indians.

The Negro was brought to the islands of the West Indies and to the eastern shore of South America only a few years after the Spaniards and Portuguese discovered the new lands. With him came the drums and that uncanny sense of rhythm which is innate in the Negro, and which has played so large a part in our North American popular music. Most of the rhythms in the Latin-American music of today may be traced to African sources, either directly through the Negro or indirectly through the Spaniard, whose musical heritage derives in no small part from the Moors who came to Spain from Africa more than a thousand years ago.

Practically all of the Latin-American dances with which we are familiar have an African origin. The *tango,* while modified by the Spanish, descended from a Negro dance called the tangano, described by visitors to Central America in the sixteenth century. The Cuban *conga* and *rumba* and the Brazilian *samba* have the energetic rhythms so characteristic of African music. The *beguine,* made famous by Cole Porter's *Begin the Beguine,* is essentially an African dance with a French name.

In Mexico the popular dances, *jarabe* (hah-rah'bay) and *huapango* (whah-pahn'go), have more of a Spanish background, while the dances of the western countries, such as Peru, Chile, and Ecuador, have more of an Indian and less of a Spanish flavor. Such dances are the *yaravi,* the *cueca* (kway'ka), and the *huyano* (whee-ahn'o).

The *habanera* (ah-bah-nay'ra), long popular in Cuba, has been traced back through Spain and France to the country dance of England. It received its name in Cuba, from Havana, and from there it was reintroduced into Spain, where it became immensely popular. The famous "Habanera," used by Bizet in the opera *Carmen,* is said to have been written by Sebastian Yradier (Ee-răhd'yay), a Spaniard who spent some time in Cuba. The *Habanera* and Yradier's famous *La Paloma,* also in the habanera rhythm, doubtless grew out of the composer's Cuban sojourn.

The native instruments of Central and South America are many and varied. The Incas and Aztecs (the Indian groups overcome by the Spanish explorers) had various types of flutes made from bone, clay, or wood. The *quena* (kay'na), a rather primitive flute, is still found in Peru and Ecuador, and the *panpipe,* a combination of two or three flutes, may still be found in Bolivia and other countries.

Many of the drums in Latin America are derived from African

38

instruments, but some of them are native to their countries, for drums were employed in the early music. They also had an important role in communication and were the "jungle telegraph" whereby messages were sent, in the same way that drums have long been used by the natives in Africa. At one time the Cuban government banned the use of conga drums because they were being used by enemies of the government for the transmission of secret information. The drums in Haiti have long been used to carry messages and to perform a role in the Voodoo rites.

The early Indians had instruments which made a noise when shaken. Usually they were dried gourds which resounded to the seeds inside them. The descendants of these instruments are found in the *maracas* (mah-rah'kas), now often seen and heard when dance orchestras are playing a rumba or a tango. The *claves* (clah'ves), a pair of hardwood bars, probably of Cuban origin, are also familiar to us.

With the Spaniards came the *guitar,* and it eventually became as indispensable to popular music in Latin America as it has been for hundreds of years in Spain. Here again is an African influence, for the guitar was brought to Spain by the Moors. The guitar is a convenient instrument for the accompaniment of singing, particularly songs of a romantic character such as the *corridos* (cor-ree'dos) so popular in Mexico.

Some time later the guitar, the violin, harp, and other European instruments were brought to the New World, and today it is very common to encounter, especially in Mexico, a *mariachi* (mah-ree-ah'chee) band, a small group of strolling musicians with guitars, a violin, and occasionally a trumpet, who entertain by playing and singing favorite folk songs.

The folk music of Latin America, being simpler than the composed music of our southern neighbors, found its way to our shores first. Several generations of school children have come to know such songs as *Cielito Lindo, Chiapanecas, Ay, Ay, Ay!,* and *La Cucuracha.* Before them such melodies as *La Paloma, La Golondrina,* and the familiar waltz, *Over the Waves,* became so well known in the United States that, like the songs of Stephen Foster, they came to be regarded as folk music.

There is now a flourishing art-music throughout Latin America, which is gradually becoming known in our country. Composers and conductors like Carlos Chavez (Shah'veth) of Mexico and Heitor Villa-Lobos (Vee-ya-loh'bos) of Brazil have visited the United States and their music is frequently heard. There are numerous fine concert halls, opera houses, and symphony orchestras in the larger cities.

39

The Latin-American composers of today are building their compositions to a large extent on the folk music of their countries, often employing folk themes or writing their own in a folk style. Many North American composers are also resorting to their folk music for inspiration, but Mexican and South American composers in general are probably more independent of European influences than many of our own creative musicians.

In Latin America the native artist is more highly regarded than his counterpart in our country. Every Latin-American republic has a Department of Fine Arts which promotes and supports musical and other artistic activities, and a composer of talent enjoys considerable prestige. In our own country our State Department has given some promotion to American music, but our government has no well organized Fine Arts Department, such as may be found in several South American countries.

The roster of Latin-American composers is long, but the music of most of them is not yet known to us. Manuel Ponce of Mexico is known to us for his song, *Estrellita,* while the compositions of Ernesto Lecuona (Lay-kwo'na) of Cuba have been widely played, especially his *Malagueña* and his song, *Siboney.* He has written symphonic works but is quite at home in popular music, and his rumba band, Lecuona's Cuban-Boys, is so well known throughout Latin America that Lecuona enjoys a reputation comparable to that of Benny Goodman, Guy Lombardo, and other North American dance band leaders.

Heitor Villa-Lobos of Brazil is an enormously prolific composer of music in many styles, nearly all of which retains some mark of Brazilian folk music. He has written choral music as well as instrumental, and one of his favorite activities is to arrange music for school children to sing in vast outdoor festivals in which several thousand children take part. Villa-Lobos has been interested in school musical activities since 1932 when President Vargas appointed him Director of Musical Education for Brazil.

The music of other Brazilians has been heard in the United States. Carlos Gomez, a nineteenth century composer, wrote the opera *Il Guarany,* the overture to which is often played by American bands. Some of the most interesting Brazilian music of today has been written by Oscar Lorenzo Fernandez, whose settings of the Brazilian dance form known as the *batuque* (ba-too'kay) are especially exciting.

Mexico's best known contemporary composer is Carlos Chavez, who is also the founder and conductor of the Orquesta Sinfonia de Mexico, in Mexico City. His compositions often pay tribute to the

40

earlier Indian culture of Mexico, and Chavez frequently uses Indian folk themes and traditional Indian instruments. Half Indian himself, Chavez is an authority on the Indian culture. Much of the music of Chavez has been published in the United States, and performances of it here are frequent.

Latin America has given us some excellent musical interpreters. Two famous women pianists have come from South America. Teresa Carreño (Kah-rayn'yo) of Venezuela became world-famous at the keyboard, and Guiomar Novaes (Ghee-o-mar' Noh-vah'ays), also internationally known as a pianist, is a Brazilian. Frequently heard in this country also is Claudio Arrau (Ah-rah'oo), a native of Chile, and the name of Jesús María Sanromá, Porto Rican pianist, is well known to American music lovers.

There is, therefore, much music in the countries to the south of us. Fortunately, it is becoming better known in our country, for it has much to tell us of the interesting peoples and countries "south of the border." We are now able to hear the folk music and the concert music of our Latin-American friends and when we listen to popular music in the United States we often hear echoes of the music of Latin America. The frequently heard rhythms of the conga and samba and the popularity of such tunes as Cole Porter's *Begin The Beguine* bear testimony to the degree to which Latin-American music has influenced our own popular music. In return, we have exported American jazz to South and Central America and the casual radio listener in Mexico City or Rio de Janeiro is likely to hear a type of popular music which combines Latin-American and jazz characteristics and is often known as "Latin swing."

QUESTIONS

1. Why has our knowledge of the Central and South American culture been limited?
2. How is this changing today?
3. What do we mean by the term "Latin-American" music?
4. The folk music of Latin America is a blend of what three influences?
5. Tell something about the music of Central and South America after their subjugation by the Spanish conquistadors.
6. What did the Negro bring to these countries?
7. Name several popular dances found in Latin-American countries.
8. How did the habanera receive its name and what is its origin?
9. What instruments are used in Latin America?
10. Name several folk songs of these countries.

11. What have several Latin-American countries done to support artistic activities?
12. Name several well-known composers from Mexico and South America.
13. What famous pianists have come from South America?

LISTENING SUGGESTIONS

Ay, Ay, Ay! — folk
Bachianas Brasilieras 1, 2, or 5 — Villa-Lobos
Cielito Lindo — Mexican Folk
Estrellita — Ponce
Flowing River — Chilean Folk
La Cucuracha — Mexican Folk
La Cumparsita — Rodriguez (Tango)

La Golondrina — Serradell
La Paloma — Yradier
Malagueña — Lecuona
Mexican Hat Dance
Siboney — Lecuona
Sinfonia India — Chavez
Tico Tico — Abreu (Samba)
Tutu Maramba — Brazilian Folk
Vidalita — Argentine Folk

The Loreley

Heinrich Heine
English: Stephen Fay

Friedrich Silcher

1. O tell me, what is this sad-ness
2. Up-on a rock sits the maid-en

that fills my heart with woe?
of won-drous form and fair,

A strange old leg-end haunts me, a tale of long a-go.
In all her daz-zling beau-ty, and combs her gold-en hair.

The fad-ing light grows dim-mer,
A comb so bright and shin-ing

a-cross the flow-ing Rhine,
she plies and sings the while,

While red with sun-set glo-ry the loft-y moun-tains shine.
In strains of wierd en-chant-ment that hearts of men be-guile.

≫ 7 ≪

GERMANY AND AUSTRIA

THE MUSIC of the great composers of Germany and Austria is solidly based on folk song. Bach, Haydn, Mozart, Beethoven Schubert, and Brahms found many of their musical ideas in their native folk tunes. Even when they did not use actual folk tunes but invented their own, their musical utterances were shaped by their contacts with folk music. One authority has stated that eighty per cent of Johann Sebastian Bach's great musical output is based on folk sources. The *Seventh Symphony* of Beethoven draws practically all its themes from folk music. Even Richard Wagner, although making less use of actual folk melodies, was greatly inspired by the folk legends and chronicles of early Germany, and his music dramas are thus of the very essence of Germany.

When Europe emerged from the period known as the "Dark Ages," music began to flourish in the numerous small principalities and kingdoms which eventually were to be united under the name of Germany. As in other parts of Europe, the churches and monasteries had kept music alive, but with the development of such groups as the Minnesingers and the Mastersingers, musical knowledge became more general and musical expression became a part of the life of the Germanic peoples.

It was through music that the peasants, soldiers, and townspeople of early Germany received some of their education. They listened to the songs of the Minnesingers and the chorales (ko-rahls′) of the church founded by Martin Luther. Through these experiences they came to know and love their native language and song. Every daily activity and every emotion found expression in German song four and five hundred years ago. The student, the peasant, the artisan, the housemaid, the soldier — all had their own folk songs. Like the folksongs of other countries, they reflect the character of the people who made them. The songs of pleasure-loving Austria are gayer and more lively, rhythmically, than those of the serious-minded Germans, whose songs tend to be direct, vigorous, and square-cut, and often with more than a touch of sentiment.

44

An example of the solid, vigorous type of folk tune is found in *Gaudeamus Igitur*, a melody which Brahms used in his *Academic Festival Overture*. Like numerous other German student songs, this one has a Latin text, for Latin was important in German studies. Other tunes, like *Du, du, liegst mir im Herzen*, and *Ach, du lieber Augustin* are simple and sentimental with strongly accented dance rhythms.

In the twelfth and thirteenth centuries the art of music flourished in what is now Germany through the activities of the Minnesingers. "Minnesinger" means "singer of love songs." The Minnesingers, like the Troubadours of France of the same time, were from the more favored classes of society. Usually they were knights and often of noble birth. They were poets as well as composers, and their songs were nearly always of love and in the courtly style of "The Age of Chivalry." Tannhäuser, Wolfram, and other principal figures in Wagner's music drama, *Tannhäuser* (Tahn'hoy-zer), were Minnesingers, and the action of the drama includes a "tournament of song," such as delighted these musicians of five hundred years ago.

In the time of Minnesingers there was often strife and war, as there has been so often in Europe, and the political upheavals of the time took from the knights and the aristocrats much of their influence. There was a corresponding decline in the importance of the Minnesingers. Their place was largely taken over by the Mastersingers. In the fourteenth and fifteenth centuries in Europe, every group of workers or artisans had its guild or trade organization. There were guilds of bakers, tailors, wood-carvers — practically every occupation — and the Mastersingers constituted the musicians' guild. As may easily be seen, the guilds were really the ancestors of our present day trade or labor unions.

The Mastersingers had elaborate rules governing the composition and performance of their songs, and, as is usual when musicians are too much occupied with rules, the songs of the Mastersingers were sometimes lacking in inspiration. Richard Wagner pokes fun at this preoccupation with rules in his immortal music drama, *Die Meistersinger von Nürnberg* (The Mastersingers of Nuremberg), in which he contrasts the free and imaginative song of Walther von Stoltzing with the dull and stilted utterances of Sixtus Beckmesser, clerk of the Mastersingers. Beckmesser, Hans Sachs, the shoemaker, and various other characters in this Wagner opera were not fictitious, for the records of sixteenth century Nuremberg show these names on the rolls of the Mastersingers. Wagner's Hans Sachs is probably more noble and his Beckmesser less so than were their namesakes in real life, but *Die Meistersinger* stands, not only as a musical masterpiece, but as an unforgettable picture of the people of Germany with their colorful guilds·and their great love and respect for music.

There were also, in sixteenth and seventeenth century Germany, many "Stadt-Pfeifferei" (shtaht-pfi'fer-eye), the town pipers whose duty was to provide music for important civic occasions. These town pipers or town musicians were instrumentalists and were in charge of the town bands or orchestras. Johann Sebastian Bach's father was a town musician, and some idea of the activity of these men may be had today when the brass instrument players assemble to play chorales at a Bach festival in Bethlehem, Pennsylvania, or at a church festival in Winston-Salem, North Carolina.

The church, too, had an important part in determining the shape of German music. When Martin Luther founded his church, he wanted the people in his congregation to have a part in the singing, and he published a German hymnbook even before he translated the Bible into German. To help the people he had to provide simple melodies which could be easily learned. He gathered together folk tunes and wrote tunes himself, such as the majestic *Ein Feste Burg* (A Mighty Fortress). He enlisted other musicians, such as Johann Walther, and their solid, dignified tunes came to be known as chorales. They have been the foundation of the music of the Lutheran Church and were of great inspiration to Bach, Mendelssohn, Brahms, and others.

Some of our most beloved music dates from this period when German composers were beginning to construct their splendid art on a foundation of folk song and chorale. Every Christmas we hear the beautiful *Lo, How a Rose E'er Blooming*. It is not a chorale but is generally considered to be a composition of Michael Praetorius, although it is probably a folk song which he harmonized. Praetorius was in his day the leading writer on musical subjects. Another seventeenth century German, Hans Leo Hassler, a Nüremberg organist, is credited with the chorale, *O Sacred Head*, a melody which Bach esteemed highly and used in numerous works. Hassler had employed it as a love song in madrigal style, but Bach transformed it into the beautiful chorale now so well known. Still other tunes from this period which we often sing are *Wake, Awake, for Night is Flying,* and *The Morning Star,* both of them ascribed to Rev. Philipp Nicolai, a minister who was also a composer.

With the beginning of the eighteenth century came the first of a series of great composers who owe their origins to Germany and Austria and whose music was influenced by the folk song of the Germanic peoples.

46

QUESTIONS

1. Explain how the great composers of Germany used the folk songs of their country.
2. How did the Minnesingers and the Mastersingers affect the music of Germany?
3. What does Wagner's great opera, *Die Meistersinger*, describe?
4. In what way did the church take an important part in determining the shape of German music?

LISTENING SUGGESTIONS

Ach, Du lieber Augustin
All Glory, Laud, and Honor —
  Teschner
Du, Du, liegst mir im Herzen
Gaudeamus Igitur
German Dances — Schubert
Ländler (any recording)
Lo, How a Rose — Praetorius

The Loreley — Silcher
A Mighty Fortress — Luther
Now Thank We All Our God —
  Cruger
O Sacred Head — Hassler-Bach
Silent Night — Gruber
Soiree de Vienne — Schubert
Wake, Awake — Nicolai-Bach

47

GERMAN COMPOSERS — XVIIIth CENTURY

Johann Sebastian Bach (1685-1750)

SOME COMPOSERS achieve fame and riches in their own lifetimes. The reverse was true in the case of Johann Sebastian Bach (Bahk), now almost universally regarded as the greatest of all composers. He lived a quiet, uneventful life, although a very busy one, occupied as he was with the duties of training choir-boys, writing new music for the church services, and meeting the needs of his large family of twenty children. He was respected in his own lifetime, but no one then saw anything remarkable in the masterpieces for chorus and for organ which now have the highest place in the literature of music.

Eighty years passed after Bach's death before he was recognized as a genius. That recognition came about when Felix Mendelssohn unearthed the manuscript of Bach's *St. Matthew Passion* and gave it a performance in Berlin. Now, two hundred years after his death, the tremendous greatness of Bach is fully appreciated by musicians, and schools, churches, organists, choral societies, and symphony orchestras pay tribute to his memory in their frequent performances of his works.

Johann (Yo'hahn) Sebastian Bach was born in Eisenach (I'zenahk), Germany, in 1685. He came from a long line of musicians, and it is not surprising that he showed an early interest in music. Left an orphan at the age of ten, Johann went to live with an older brother who taught him to play the clavichord and the violin. When he was fifteen, the boy had an opportunity to enter the St. Michael's Church Choir School at Lüneburg. There was a fine library at Lüneburg, and Bach studied its musical treasures carefully. This was a stimulation to the future composer, and Lüneburg helped to shape his career in another way, for it was there that he learned to play the organ.

At eighteen the young Bach was engaged as a violinist in the court orchestra at Weimar (Vy'mar). Soon, however, he accepted the post of organist in a church at Arnstadt, for his first love was the organ. He would travel long distances, sometimes on foot, to hear the famous organists of the day. Once the church board gave him a month's vacation to go to Lübeck to hear the celebrated organist Buxtehude (Books-tuh-hoo'deh). Bach was so enchanted by the music he heard at Lübeck that he stayed three months. When he returned, the church board reprimanded him but did not dismiss him.

Bach held several church positions where his responsibilities were to play the organ and to instruct the boys of the choir, not only in music, but in other subjects. His compensation was paid partly in money and partly in food and firewood. With all his duties and responsibilities, he found some time to compose.

When he was thirty-two, Johann Sebastian accepted his second position as a court musician. He was engaged as Kapellmeister for Prince Leopold of Anhalt-Cöthen (Ahn-hahlt-Kuht'en). Kapellmeister means literally "master of the chapel," but actually the music director so designated had charge, not only of the music in the chapel, but at all court functions as well.

These were happy years for the composer. Some of his music which we often hear, such as the six Brandenburg Concertos, came from this period, and Bach also wrote much chamber music — music for two, three, or four instruments, suitable for small rooms.

At the age of thirty-eight, Bach was successful in obtaining the post of Cantor (Director of Music) in St. Thomas Church in Leipzig, a position for which several of Germany's leading musicians competed. Here he passed the remainder of his life — busy years, occupied with the training of the choir, occasional quarrels with the church authorities, and constant composition. In Leipzig he wrote 265 church cantatas and all his great choral works — the *Mass in B Minor,* the *Christmas Oratorio,* and the various settings of the Passion Music, of which the *St. Matthew* is regarded as the greatest.

Throughout all these magnificent works are heard the melodies of the German chorales which had such a profound influence upon Bach. Some of them are tunes which are found in practically all hymnbooks — such tunes as *A Mighty Fortress; Now Thank We All Our God; All Glory, Laud, and Honor* — and the recognition of these melodies helps us to understand Bach's music. He used these chorale tunes in much of his choral work and wrote dozens of organ "chorale-preludes" based on them. His skillful use of these melodies as a basis for composition eventually caused the world to recognize in him the greatest genius in the history of music.

Johann Sebastian was a serious-minded, religious man. Often he signed his compositions with the phrase, "To God Be the Glory." His portraits reveal a solemn face surrounded by an imposing wig. His sons sometimes referred to him as "the old peruke," or "wig." Like boys of any other age, they sometimes regarded their father as old-

49

fashioned, and this view was held by others of the time. They thought Johann Sebastian was a fine organist but somewhat behind the times as a composer. After all, the composers in early eighteenth century Germany were thinking about the opera and about sonata form which influenced piano music so much. Bach had no interest in the opera, and he preferred the old musical forms of the seventeenth century to the new ones of the eighteenth.

His preference in instruments was for the old. When Bach visited the court of Frederick the Great in Potsdam, Frederick took delight in inviting the great musician to play his new piano. Bach tried it but made it clear that he preferred his own clavichord, a preference which Frederick and Bach's son, Carl Philipp Emmanuel, Frederick's court musician, found it difficult to understand.

But "Old Bach," as Frederick called him, was ahead of his time in many ways. He was one of the first to see the necessity of "equal temperament" and the first to write music demonstrating the practicability of equal temperament. The first volume of *The Well-Tempered Clavichord* was completed in 1722, and it contains Preludes and Fugues in each of the twelve major and minor keys.

Equal temperament means a system of dividing the octave into twelve equal semitones, a division which we accept as a matter of course, so that on our piano keyboards F-sharp and G-flat, for example, are sounded by the same key. Before Bach's time, however, F-sharp and G-flat were not considered to be the same tone and music played on the harpsichord was limited to a few keys. Bach's idea of tuning was adopted by the builders of keyboard instruments, making it possible for musicians to play in any of the keys and to modulate, or move, from one key to another with ease.

Bach was also ahead of his time in his method of using the hands at the keyboard. In his time keyboard instruments were played with the four fingers in a flat position and the thumb was rarely used. Bach taught his children and his pupils to curve the hand with finger tips above the keys so that the thumb was used along with the fingers. This led to modern piano techniques.

Very little of Bach's music was published during his lifetime, and most of that small proportion he engraved with his own hands. One of these compositions, the *Musical Offering*, a trio for flute, violin, and clavier, was written for Frederick the Great, who was quite proud of his ability to play the flute.

First acquaintance with Bach's music prompts some listeners to say that "it has no tune." More careful listening reveals, however, that it is really all "tune," for every part has a tune of its own and the combination of three, four, or five independent tunes makes

50

wonderful music if they are Bach's tunes. Such music is known as "contrapuntal" from the word "counterpoint," which means the combination of two or more independent melodies. Bach made much use of the musical form known as "fugue." In a fugue, certain melodies, known as the "subject" and "countersubject," are heard again and again in an interweaving of melodic lines throughout the composition. An excellent example is Bach's *Little Fugue in G Minor*. While Bach wrote towering works of complexity such as the *Toccata and Fugue in D Minor*, he also wrote simple little minuets and gavottes, such as are found in the *Notebook*, written for his second wife, Anna Magdalena, and the *Klavierbuchlein* (Little Clavier Book) written for his son, Wilhelm Friedemann.

The German name, "Bach," means "brook," and so Johann Sebastian Bach, the brook that was not taken seriously in his own day, became the mighty sea to which all music and musicians are today indebted.

QUESTIONS

1. What great composer is responsible for Bach's recognition as a genius?
2. Tell something about Bach's early musical training.
3. Name several positions Bach held and state what was accomplished in each.
4. How did the German chorale or hymn tune influence Bach in his work?
5. What happened when Bach visited the court of Frederick the Great?
6. What is meant by "equal temperament" of the scale?
7. How did Bach change the method of using the hands at the keyboard?
8. Name some of his greatest compositions.
9. Name several of Bach's contemporaries; include one statesman, one composer, and one organist who figured in his musical life.
10. Bach wrote four settings of The Passion of Our Lord, based on the gospels of St. Matthew, St. Luke, St. Mark, and St. John. What does this music describe?

LISTENING SUGGESTIONS

Air for the G String
Brandenburg Concerti 1-6
Any Chorales arranged by Bach
Any of the Chorale-Preludes for
 Organ
Come, Sweet Death (Komm, Süsser
 Tod)
Concerto in D Minor for Two Violins
Fantasy and Fugue in G Minor
Italian Concerto
Jesu, Joy of Man's Desiring

Little Fugue in G Minor
Magnificat
Mass in B Minor
Partitas, 1-6 (any)
Passacaglia and Fugue in C Minor
Passion According to St. John
Passion According to St. Matthew
Sheep May Safely Graze
Suites for Orchestra
Toccata and Fugue in D Minor
Well-Tempered Clavichord, The

51

George Frederick Handel (1685-1759)

George Frederick Handel was born in the Saxon town of Halle (Hahl-leh) in 1685, which was also the year of Johann Sebastian Bach's birth. The native towns of Bach and Handel were less than a day's journey apart, but the two great composers never met.

The lives of these two distinguished composers had many contrasts. Bach lived a quiet, orderly life with his large family and his many pupils, while Handel, who never married, roamed all over Europe during the course of a stormy, adventurous life. Bach had nothing to do with the stage, but Handel's life was largely bound up with the theatre. Bach came of a family of musicians and was expected to follow music; Handel became a musician only because he was strong-willed enough to defy family objections.

Handel's father, a successful physician, was sixty-three years of age when his famous son was born. He decided upon a legal career for his son, but little George lost no time in getting acquainted with musical instruments. When he was only eight he showed such skill at the organ keyboard that the Duke of Saxe Weissenfels practically ordered Dr. Handel to see that this remarkable boy was given musical training. The doctor reluctantly complied, and Handel studied theory and several instruments. In due time George entered the University at Halle, but his university career was terminated when he was offered the post of organist at the Halle Cathedral.

Handel's restlessness began to assert itself, and from Halle he went to Hamburg, playing in the opera orchestra and writing operas. After three years he went to Italy, the home of opera. He was fascinated by the operatic performances he heard in Florence, Naples, and Venice. In Rome, where opera was then banned, he was impressed by the church music and by the instrumental music in the palace of Cardinal Ottoboni. These influences had a marked effect upon Handel's own music composed thereafter.

When Handel was twenty-five, he was appointed Kapellmeister at the Court of Hanover. The Prince, known as the Elector, regarded Handel highly and gave him permission to visit England. At that time Italian opera was a veritable "rage" in London, but the performances were not of high standard. Handel thought he could do better and proceeded to write an opera, which was produced at the Haymarket Theatre. The opera, *Rinaldo*, proved to be a hit, and Handel, already famous as a performer on the harpsichord and organ, became a social lion in London. Upon returning to Hanover, he soon missed the exciting life of London, and after a little more than a year was back in London, ready to undertake another operatic venture. Again the

52

English were cordial to the composer. His operas were successful and Queen Anne bestowed a lifetime pension upon him.

Handel's failure to return was quite displeasing to the Elector of Hanover and when, in 1715, Queen Anne died and the Elector became George I, King of England, the composer was placed in an uneasy position, from which he extricated himself, according to the story, by composing the famous *Water Music* which found such favor with the King that Handel was forgiven.

The story of Handel's successes and failures in the operatic field is too long to recount here. For some years he produced the operas he composed. These were hectic years, devoted to settling quarrels between prima donnas, holding off creditors, and trying to meet the fickle tastes of English theatre-goers. Handel made and lost two or three small fortunes. All this turmoil had its effect, even upon Handel, a man of strong will and splendid physique, and in 1737 he suffered a stroke of paralysis. Upon his recovery he made another attempt at an operatic comeback. This failed, and he turned his full attention to oratorio.

Handel had already experimented with oratorios, or sacred dramas, and London audiences seemed favorable to them. Their interest had turned away from the worldliness of opera to the more serious oratorio, and Handel found that people would attend these dramatic sacred works in the concert hall. He chose to set to music such stories as *Samson, Saul, Israel in Egypt,* and finally the *Messiah.*

To millions of people, Christmas is hardly Christmas unless they have heard a performance of the *Messiah,* in church or the concert hall or on the air. And this masterpiece, so long admired by music-lovers, was written in the amazingly short time of twenty-four days. Moreover, it was composed when Handel was struggling to regain his health, after he had lost his fight to control the operatic theatre. He was fifty-six years old, heavily in debt, and forgotten by most of his former friends, yet this indomitable man had the courage and energy to compose this great work.

The first performance of the *Messiah* took place in Dublin, Ireland. London was not interested at the time. At this first performance, in a rather small hall, it is recorded that ladies were asked to come without hoops in their skirts and the gentlemen were asked to leave their swords at home. This, in that day of fashion, was truly a concession to the importance of the work and its composer.

Eventually England accepted the work, and at the first London performance King George was so affected by the singing of the "Hallelujah Chorus" that he rose to his feet, thus establishing a tradition which prevails to this day. Handel himself probably regarded the *Messiah* as the favorite of his many works. He is said to have told his servant, after completing the "Hallelujah Chorus," that "I think I did see all heaven before me and the great God himself."

The demand for performances of the work grew so rapidly that, even in Handel's lifetime, the *Messiah* earned a great deal of money. He conducted benefit performances of it for the Foundling Hospital, his favorite charity, earning more than eleven thousand pounds, a considerable sum in those days. Having no wife and children of his own, Handel gave thought to the children who had no fathers and mothers. He gave much money to the Hospital, and at Christmas time he sent treats to the boys and girls. It seems fitting that his last public appearance was made to conduct the *Messiah* at a Foundling benefit. He conducted the performance, for he had continued to play the organ and conduct, although he had been blind for eight years. A few days after this performance in Covent Garden, still a famous theatre, Handel passed away, on Good Friday, at the age of seventy-four.

Thus passed the greatest musician in English history — a man who spoke English with a heavy German accent, and who, though he early became an English citizen, was always regarded by some Englishmen as a foreigner. Handel's oratorios encouraged the English, and later the Americans, to form choral societies, and his *Water Music* and *Fireworks Music* and other instrumental music influenced later English musicians. His church music and his songs and arias helped to shape the music of those who followed him. His operas are largely forgotten, but many of their tunes are not. The celebrated "Largo" from *Xerxes* is a fine example of the noble sort of melody that Handel could write. It was a love song from an opera and not sacred music, though today it is often heard in churches, sung to sacred words.

It is not surprising that the *Largo* and such other melodies as *I Know that My Redeemer Liveth, Where'er You Walk,* the "Air" from the *Water Music,* and many others have endeared Handel to music-lovers. Such tunes are straightforward and speak directly to everyone.

QUESTIONS

1. Where and when was George Frederick Handel born?
2. Compare the life of Handel with that of the composer Johann Sebastian Bach, who was born in the same year. How were they different and how alike?
3. Describe Handel's early life and tell how he decided to make music a career.
4. How did his visit to Italy influence his composing?

54

5. What was the result of his experience as Kapellmeister at the court of Hanover and his visit to England?
6. Give titles of some of Handel's operas and relate some of his experiences in composing and producing them.
7. Why did Handel turn to the writing of oratorio?
8. Tell some interesting facts concerning the writing of the *Messiah* and its first performance.
9. How did Handel use the proceeds from numerous performances of the *Messiah?*
10. Name several well-loved melodies that Handel composed.

LISTENING SUGGESTIONS

"Angels, Ever Bright and Fair" from *Theodora*
"Care Selve" from *Atalanta*
Concerti for Organ
Concerti Grossi for Strings (any)
Faithful Shepherd Suite
"Hallelujah Amen" from *Judas Maccabaeus*
The Harmonious Blacksmith

"Largo" from *Xerxes*
The *Messiah* and separate parts, such as "Hallelujah Chorus," "And the Glory of the Lord," "He Shall Feed His Flock," "Pastoral Symphony."
Royal Fireworks Music
Water Music Suite
"Where'er You Walk" from *Semele*

Christoph Willibald von Gluck (1714-1787)

Christoph Willibald von Gluck (Glook) is remembered as a composer who did much to improve opera. He was born in 1714 in the section of Europe once known as Bohemia and his musical education was received in Prague, Vienna, and Milan. As we have seen in the career of Handel, the Europeans of the eighteenth century were enthusiastic patrons of the opera, and especially of the Italian opera. During the greater part of the eighteenth century, composers, even Handel, followed the Italian pattern of opera, which was a succession of songs and choruses connected by declamatory passages, known as recitatives (ray-see-ta-teevs').

Gluck had won fame in Italy and in Austria as an operatic composer, and from Vienna he went to Paris, then the operatic capital of the world. And in 1776, when the American Colonies were fighting for their independence, an operatic war was being waged in Paris between a group of Italian style opera adherents headed by Nicolà Piccinni (Pee-chee'nee) and Gluck and his followers who believed that an opera should be a carefully thought-out setting of a dramatic story rather than a succession of arias provided to display the vocal talents of singing stars. Gluck's ideas eventually triumphed, and his principles were followed by Mozart and others who came after him.

Gluck had stood high in the court at Vienna, and one of his pupils was Marie Antoinette, daughter of the Emperor of Austria. When she afterward married the heir to the throne of France and moved to Paris, she remembered the music teacher of her childhood and was a factor in helping him to obtain recognition in Paris.

Gluck's operas are not often heard today as stage works, but much of their music, with its classic grace and beauty, is played by orchestras. Gluck lived in a time when Europe was much interested in the culture of the ancient Greeks, and most of his operas, such as *Alceste* (Al-chest'eh), *Orfeo e Euridice* (Or-fay'o, Yu-ree-dee'cheh) and *Iphigenia in Tauride* (If-ee-gay-nee'a in Tau'ree-deh) were based on Greek myths.

QUESTIONS

1. What was Gluck's chief contribution to music?
2. Tell something concerning the "operatic war" that was waged by Gluck and the Italian composer Piccinni.
3. How did Marie Antoinette assist Gluck?
4. Name one of Gluck's operas.

LISTENING SUGGESTIONS

Ballet — *Don Juan*　　　　　　　Overture to *Alceste*
Ballet Suite — Gluck-Mottl　　　　Overture to *Iphigenia in Aulis*
Dance of the Happy Spirits

FRANZ JOSEPH HAYDN (1732-1809)

Franz Joseph Haydn (Hy'den) and George Washington, the illustrious father of our country, were both born in the year 1732. Haydn was born in lower Austria in the heart of a settlement of Croatians, and the folk music of these people made such an impression on him that later in life when he started to compose he incorporated some of these tunes in his works.

As with many of our famous composers, Haydn's parents were poor, and their family large. Haydn's mother was a cook, and his father a carriage-maker. The father was uneducated, but he had a fine tenor voice and played the harp by ear. Haydn inherited his father's fine voice, and when he was but six years of age he seemed to possess so much talent that he attracted the attention of a relative who was visiting the family. This man, named Frankh, offered to take the little fellow home with him and start his musical education. Frankh was a school teacher and a choirmaster in a nearby town. He was an exacting and sometimes a cruel master, but he was a conscientious teacher, and at the end of two years he had given Haydn an excellent musical foundation. The boy had been taught to sing the Mass with the choir, and he had acquired a fine technique on both the violin and the harpsichord.

At this time the choirmaster at the great Cathedral of St. Stephen, in Vienna, was searching for talent, and after hearing Haydn sing offered him a position in this choir. The church school connected with the cathedral where these young singers were supposed to receive their education was not well managed, and Haydn was forced to spend lonely and weary hours struggling with his school books and his musical compositions. Often he was both cold and hungry. After nine years at St. Stephen's, his voice changed at the age of seventeen, and his younger brother was hired to take his place. Perhaps the church authorities would have felt inclined to help him on his way, but even during the dreary days at the choir school, he had begun to show his mischievous disposition and his love of fun. This led him to play practical jokes, and he even went so far as to offend the Empress herself.

After leaving St. Stephen's, Haydn found himself quite destitute. He felt that should he return home he would only prove an added burden to his parents, and since he was determined to go on composing, he continued to wander about looking for some way to earn his living. During his pilgrimages he met an old acquaintance who offered to share his humble quarters with Haydn, and later he met another friend who gave him the money to hire an attic room of his own. He was able to earn a meager living by arranging music for special events, and by playing at balls, weddings, and other functions. His patient efforts gradually brought him to the notice of people of importance, and among them was a poet by the name of Metastasio (Meh-tah-stah′zee-o).

The poet brought him to the notice of the fashionable Italian singing teacher, Porpora. Haydn agreed to play accompaniments for this man, and to act as his personal servant and valet. This association added to his prestige, and he met people of wealth and position.

At this time a Bohemian baron was looking for someone to conduct his orchestra, and Haydn was happy indeed to accept this post. The baron had stipulated that he was not to marry, but Haydn fell in love and decided to defy this ruling. His romance was cut short, however, because the girl of his choice decided to become a nun. The girl's father urged Haydn to marry the older sister, and because of his accustomed good nature and easy-going ways, he agreed to oblige the family! As might be expected, the marriage was anything but a happy one.

The real turning point in the life of this famous man came when he was hired as assistant director of music by Prince Paul Anton Esterhazy (Es'ter-haht'zee). The Esterhazy princes controlled a large number of towns and villages and were wealthy and powerful. They were great lovers of music and employed a large orchestra and a fine body of singers. Haydn had been in their employ but a few years when Paul Anton Esterhazy died, and Prince Nicholas, who succeeded him, promoted Haydn and made him head of all musical activities. Prince Nicholas built a palace comparable to Versailles. This place with its extensive grounds and beautiful gardens recalled the famous palace in France, and Haydn was delighted because Prince Nicholas loved pomp and ceremony and entertained many royal personages. Haydn wrote music for all these occasions.

He lived happily at this court for twenty-eight years. Being relieved of all primary wants, he was free to compose, and what was still better, he had a group of court musicians at hand to perform his works. It was here that he wrote most of his symphonies and his chamber music, and during this time he perfected the grouping of the symphony orchestra. He arranged it in sections — strings, wood-winds, percussion, etc. — much as we find it today. During his latter years he visited England, where he was most cordially received. Oxford University conferred a doctor's degree on him.

His interest in oratorio was inspired by his admiration for Handel's works which he heard in England. When he returned to Vienna he composed two oratorios following Handel's style. These were *The Creation,* and *The Seasons.*

Mozart and Beethoven both studied with Haydn and profited by this contact, and both freely acknowledged their debt to him.

Haydn's works reflect his good nature and love of fun. His *"Surprise" Symphony* gets its name from a sudden unexpected loud chord in a soft passage, an effect which Haydn is supposed to have said would "wake up the old ladies." In his *"Farewell" Symphony* the members of the orchestra gradually drop out of the playing and leave the stage until only a single violinist is left. Haydn also wrote a symphony for strings and toy instruments with cuckoo calls, bird whistles, and other amusing effects, quite like the rhythm band pieces often played in the primary grades of our schools of today.

Haydn's publishers often nicknamed his symphonies, and they are still known as *"The Clock," "The Military," "The Oxford," "The Drum Roll," "The Schoolmaster,"* and so on. Some of his quartets also have similar appellations.

Fortunately for music lovers, Franz Joseph Haydn enjoyed a long life and never ran out of tunes. His creative output gave us one hundred and four symphonies, sixty-one string quartets, twelve Masses, many songs, and a host of other instrumental works.

One of Haydn's string quartets deserves special mention. It has the nickname, *"The Emperor."* It is a series of variations on a patriotic tune which Haydn had written in 1797 at the request of the Austrian Court. This tune can be found in any hymnbook with the words, "Glorious things of Thee are spoken," and it is one of the most singable patriotic songs that any country ever had. In writing it Haydn went back to the simple Croatian people with whom he had his origin, for the tune was originally a Croatian folk melody. The story is told that five days before his death Haydn asked to be carried to his piano where he played this "Emperor's Hymn" as a final salute to his beloved Austria and as a gesture of defiance to Napoleon, whose armies were then bombarding Vienna.

QUESTIONS

1. Where was Haydn born?
2. What type of folk music did he incorporate in his works?
3. Describe several incidents in his early life.
4. Who was Porpora?
5. Tell about Haydn's association with the Esterhazy princes.
6. What great oratorios did Haydn compose?
7. What two well-known musicians were pupils of Haydn?
8. Name some of his famous symphonies.
9. Tell some interesting facts concerning the Emperor's Hymn.
10. What were some of the musical forms Haydn perfected and standardized?
11. Give some idea of the extent of his creative output.
12. Why was he called "Papa Haydn"?

LISTENING SUGGESTIONS

Concerto for Trumpet
The Creation
Emperor Quartet
Any other Haydn String Quartets
"The Heavens are Telling" from *The Creation*
Mass in Time of War
Saint Cecilia Mass
Symphony No. 92 in G Major (Oxford)

Symphony No. 94 in G Major (Surprise)
Symphony No. 100 in G Major (Military)
Symphony No. 101 in D Major (Clock)
Symphony No. 104 in D Minor (London)
Other symphonies
"With Verdure Clad" from *The Creation*

Sonata Form

In the time of Bach and Handel the prevailing pattern for instrumental music, either for solo instruments or the orchestra, was the "suite" (sweet). It consisted usually of an overture, or opening number, followed by a series of dances in varying rhythms, such as the minuet, gavotte, sarabande, and gigue (zheeg). In writing his symphonies and quartets, Haydn modified the suite idea until it became a series of four movements. The first movement, usually in allegro, or fast-moving, tempo, presented certain musical ideas which were worked out with the composer's finest skill. The second movement was slow and song-like with emotional appeal, while the third was usually dance-like, often a minuet. The final movement was again in rapid tempo with a brilliant conclusion.

Since Haydn is often referred to as the "father" of the sonata, the symphony, and the string quartet, it might be well to acquaint ourselves with the general plan and the structural design on which these works are based.

The first section is the most important movement of the sonata or symphony and one of the most interesting. This first section is written in what is termed as "sonata form." It usually opens with a few introductory measures and then the first theme or "subject" is announced. This first theme is often more rhythmic and more vigorous than the second one, which is more tender and melodic. In fact, these two subjects are sometimes referred to as the "father" and the "mother" themes.

The second theme is usually set forth in a different key from the first, and when a composer goes from one key to another — we say he is "modulating." There must be a smooth and pleasing connection between these musical ideas, and these connecting measures are referred to as the "bridge." After both themes have been announced, the composer then likes to develop his musical ideas and reshape the material in many different ways. These themes are developed in the key of the second theme or subject. Just as a preacher states his text, and then proceeds to enlarge on his ideas, the composer discusses his musical subject matter with us. In fact, he shows his real genius in this way. This middle section of the first movement is called the "development" section.

In the third division the composer restates his original themes and this time both themes are presented in the original key. This fact gives a feeling of unity and solidarity to the entire first movement. The closing measures are usually brilliant and are known as the "coda." This coda brings this first movement of the sonata to an end.

60

The technical names for these three sections of the first movement of a sonata are the "exposition," the "development," and the "recapitulation."

The second movement of a sonata or symphony is slow and romantic and contains two contrasting themes. Because it is so melodic and expressive, it is often the movement that meets with the greatest favor and understanding from the listener.

The third movement of the sonata — the *minuetto* — is the only one to carry over a dance movement from the suite. As the name implies, it is written in the form of a minuet and gives the feeling of grace and elegance which characterized this old dance. Beethoven is credited with turning this section of a sonata into a *scherzo* (a lively piece), but Haydn anticipated this idea and was the first to use the name, *scherzo* (skairt'so).

The last or fourth movement of the sonata may follow the pattern of the first movement and be written in sonata form, or it may be written as a *rondo* in which the principal theme alternates with one, two, or three secondary themes.

A theme with variations may take the place of any of these forms and may appear as the first, second, third, or fourth movements of a classical sonata. The first and last movements of a sonata are usually fast moving, and are generally marked "allegro." The second movement, as has been stated, is an "andante" or "adagio." Someone is quoted as saying that in the first movement the composer tries to show how much he knows, in the second, how deeply he feels, and in the last, how glad he is to be through.

Sonata form is used not only in solo sonatas, but in string quartets and chamber music combinations, the symphony, and the modern concerto. A symphony has been called a "college-bred" sonata. It is written for orchestra, and all the classic symphonies follow the design of the sonata.

Starting with Beethoven's more mature period of writing, the sonata and symphony became more and more free in design and structure, and latter day composers have broken away almost entirely from the old forms. The symphonic poem and the modern suite, two types of "program music," have given them an opportunity for more effective and dramatic expressions of their ideas. Present-day composers have written for very large orchestras, and in many cases their compositions call for players who are endowed with great virtuosity.

In Haydn's time it was customary to maintain a balance of contrasting keys. Thus in the first movement of the *"Surprise" Symphony,* theme number one is in G major, while theme number two is in D major, and the first or exposition section ends in D major. When

61

Haydn comes back to the two themes in his recapitulation, both are heard in G major and the first movement ends in that key.

This musical pattern known as "sonata form" was followed by Mozart, Beethoven, Schumann, Schubert, and many others who came after Haydn, but, from Beethoven on, composers used more freedom with the structure until today composers do not follow it closely, and many of their compositions are not affected by its rules. This brief explanation may, however, be of some aid to those who listen to the music of the eighteenth and nineteenth centuries.

QUESTIONS

1. Why is the first section of a sonata so important?
2. Compare the first theme of the first movement with the second theme of the first movement.
3. What is the middle section of the first movement called?
4. Describe the general characteristics of the second movement of a symphony or a sonata; the third movement; the fourth movement.
5. What changes took place in the sonata and symphony during Beethoven's period of writing?

LISTENING SUGGESTIONS

Any symphonies, sonatas, or string quartets listed under Haydn, Mozart, Beethoven, Schubert, and Mendelssohn

WOLFGANG AMADEUS MOZART (1756-1791)

Mozart (Moht'zart) was another beloved and renowned Austrian composer. He was born in Salzburg, Austria, and the old house that was his birthplace still stands at the foot of a rocky slope and has been preserved as a Mozart museum. To one who has visited Salzburg and attended one of the famous Salzburg music festivals, it seems that Mozart's genius still pervades this quaint city and inspires both performers and listeners.

Mozart was doubtless the most famous child prodigy the world has ever known. His baby hands hovered over the piano keys when he was less than four years old, and he made remarkable attempts at composition when the notes made by his tiny fingers resembled mere blobs of ink.

Mozart's father, Leopold Mozart, held the position of court composer and assistant Kapellmeister under the archbishop of Salzburg. He was an excellent violinist and a good teacher, but as a composer he was quite mediocre. He was imbued with a driving ambition, and when he discovered that his son was a child wonder, he decided to travel

62

to the great music centers of Europe and exploit the talent of this unusual boy.

Wolfgang had a musical sister who had been given instruction from the time she was very young, and so the father planned an extensive tour for the two children. From the time that little Mozart was six years old until he was eleven, he and his sister were taken from one musical center to another. In Vienna, Empress Maria Theresa was much impressed with the boy prodigy, and while the two children were at this court Mozart's favorite playmate was Marie Antoinette, who was then a girl of seven.

Mozart's youthful genius also astounded musical Paris, and he was cordially received at the court of Versailles during the reign of Louis XV. Later he visited London where the Order of George III was bestowed upon him. In Italy Mozart heard his first opera. This was an experience he could not forget, and he immediately felt the urge to turn to this form of expression. Upon visiting Rome his musical experience was further enriched by hearing some of the great church music. He arrived just in time for the celebration of Holy Week, and it was then that he heard the Papal choir sing the famous *Miserere* by Allegri. This musical work was considered so sacred by the church authorities that no one was allowed to remove the manuscript from the chapel, nor was anyone permitted to copy the music. Mozart was so deeply impressed with this work, and listened so intently, that he was able to return home and copy down on paper what he had heard. The *Miserere* is arranged alternately for four and five-part choruses, and ends with a nine-part chorus. Imagine anyone possessing a musical memory that would make it possible to perform such a feat!

When his mother heard about what he had done, she feared that her son would be punished for his presumption. However, she had nothing to fear. The score was checked for accuracy by a member of the Sistine Chapel Choir, and was found to be a perfect reproduction of the original. Mozart was not only never reprimanded for this act, but the Papal Order of the Golden Spur was later bestowed upon him.

Mozart's later travels consisted of a series of contrasts. When he could no longer attract attention as a boy prodigy, he found it difficult to impress the dignitaries in the courts of Europe. The musical world seemed either unable to appreciate great music, or unwilling to pay for it. He was also confronted with many petty jealousies and prejudices. He and his parents found themselves often in need of money, and during those days they each suffered many severe illnesses. Mozart's father was very dictatorial, and had taken such complete

63

charge of Wolfgang's plans during his early life that when the young man became of age, he was at a loss to know how to manage his own affairs.

Mozart's marriage was a happy one, and both he and his wife loved fun but were gay and impractical. When times were good they would live luxuriously, and when their funds gave out they would be forced to borrow money. When they asked their friends to assemble for musical evenings, Franz Joseph Haydn was often included as one of the guests, and it was on such occasions that much of Mozart's chamber music was performed.

Like Beethoven, who was to follow this great composer, Mozart was never one to write poor music for the sake of bringing in money, and he was not one to court favors from influential people. Since Mozart's father had done all the bargaining in the early days, the young man had never learned to curb his tongue or cater to those in power. For this reason his last days were tragic, and as his health failed he sorely needed both friends and money. Mozart's lack of financial success was not due to the fact that he was lazy. He was unsystematic, and anything but provident, but he was always busy. He taught many pupils, gave concerts, and worked incessantly at composition.

Unlike Haydn, his music bore little relation to his environment or to his surroundings. In fact, Mozart wrote some of his most inspired compositions when he was ill, unhappy, and financially worried. His works are famous for their perfection of form and beauty of melody. Mozart lived in an age when the ruling and the educated people placed great emphasis on style and elegance. Clothing for both men and women was embellished with many frills and furbelows, conversation was marked by flowery speeches, and the art of the day was distinguished by elaborate decoration. The boy Mozart, traveling from one European court to another, absorbed these influences, and his music has at all times a refinement and an elegance.

Mozart's music is of his own time, but it is more — it is music for all time. It may be considered the finest example of "pure" music; that is, music which does not express personal, philosophical, or descriptive ideas, but which concerns itself purely with musical ideas, with beauty of melody and harmony. It is for this reason that we call Mozart a true classical composer. His music is not essentially German, Italian, French, or of any country. It is music for music's sake. Many people think of "classical" music as any music which is not in the popular style, but its real meaning is to refer to music of the classical period of Haydn, Mozart, and Beethoven. Of the three, Mozart's best represents the true meaning of "classical," for Haydn

64

often used folk music and descriptive music, and Beethoven was often deeply concerned with expressing through his music his own personal emotions.

If you look at a published copy of one of Mozart's compositions, you are likely to see a notation K. No. 478 or K. No. 532. These refer to the numbers in a catalog of Mozart's works compiled by an Austrian scholar, Dr. Ludwig Köchel (Ke[r]sh'el), who listed in chronological order the amazingly large list of Mozart's compositions. It seems incredible that a man who died at the age of thirty-five could have produced so much music. His output included twenty-two operas, forty-nine symphonies, twenty-three concertos for piano, twenty-three concertos for other instruments, twenty-four string quartets, and hundreds of compositions for voice, chorus, piano, orchestra, chamber groups, and individual instruments.

The works for which he is best known are his three great operas, *The Magic Flute, The Marriage of Figaro* (Fee'gah-ro), and *Don Giovanni,* and his three great symphonies, No. 39 in E flat Major, No. 40 in G Minor, and No. 41 in C Major (the "Jupiter"). These three symphonies, incidentally, were written within two months in the summer of 1788 at a time when Mozart was beset by debt and illness in his family. There is no hint of this in the music, however.

Mozart died in 1791 while at work on his famous *Requiem Mass.* He had been commissioned to write this work by an unscrupulous nobleman who intended to present the work as his own. Mozart probably did not know this, and while forcing himself to complete the work, he became so ill that he wrote a friend, "It is my death song." He died before he could finish the *Requiem* but his dear friend, Süssmayer, took notes as he sat at Mozart's bedside and was able to complete the score. Mozart was buried in a pauper's grave, and no one today knows its location. Everyone, however, knows the music of this genius, and it lives as an imperishable monument to his memory.

QUESTIONS

1. Tell something about Mozart's family.
2. What is a "child prodigy"?
3. What incident in Rome proved Mozart's musical genius?
4. Where did Mozart hear his first operas?
5. Name two musical centers that were visited by the elder Mozart and his two talented children.
6. What were some of the reasons that Mozart had a difficult time to earn enough money to keep him out of debt?
7. What were some of the characteristics of Mozart's music that made it truly great?

8. What are his most famous operas?
9. Name one of his greatest symphonies.
10. How many symphonies did he write?
11. Upon what great work was he engaged at the time of his death?
12. How did Mozart's music reflect the customs of the times in which he lived?

LISTENING SUGGESTIONS

Ave Verum
"Dove sono" from *The Marriage of Figaro*
Any Mozart Horn Sonata
"Il mio tesoro" from *Don Giovanni*
Minuet from *Don Giovanni*
Overture to *Don Giovanni*
Overture to *The Magic Flute*
Overture to *The Marriage of Figaro*
Any Mozart Piano Concerto
Any Mozart Piano Sonata

Quintet for Clarinet and Strings
Requiem Mass
Serenade, *Eine Kleine Nachtmusik*
Any Mozart String Quartet
Symphony No. 40 in G Minor
Symphony No. 41 in C Major (Jupiter)
Any other Symphonies
Turkish March
Any Mozart Violin Sonata

๙ 9 ๕

GERMAN COMPOSERS — XIXTH CENTURY

LUDWIG VAN BEETHOVEN (1770-1827)

LUDWIG VAN BEETHOVEN (Bayt'ho-fen) was born in the university town of Bonn on the Rhine River, in 1770, and during his lifetime much transpired in this country and in France that was of historical importance. Before the turn of the century, the American Colonies had won their freedom from England, and France had been stirred to her very depths by revolution and political upheaval. Perhaps these restless times had their effect upon Beethoven, for it has often been said that his independence of thought and action seemed a reflection of the days in which he lived.

Beethoven's family on his father's side was musical. Both his father and grandfather were hired by the Elector at Bonn to sing in the chapel choir. Beethoven's mother had been a cook, and she was a kind and gentle woman, and much beloved by all who knew her. The father was an ambitious and unscrupulous man, and when he discovered that Ludwig possessed great musical talent, he immediately made plans to develop a "child wonder" and feature the little boy as Mozart's father had done with Wolfgang. He started to teach Ludwig himself and later turned him over to a teacher who boarded with the family.

Whereas Mozart had been taught with love and understanding, Beethoven's first masters were cruel and often whipped the boy. They made him practice long hours, and sometimes they would awaken him at night and force him to go to work. Young musical prodigies are "born and not made," and although Beethoven was heard in public when he was only six years of age, his playing did not cause a real stir. From time to time Beethoven's father arranged for a change of teachers, but it was not until he was placed in the care of Neefe, the court organist and director of the theater orchestra at Bonn, that he found one who was kind and understanding. At this point his musical studies became a real joy to him.

When Beethoven was 17, the Elector of Bonn arranged for him to go to Vienna to study with Mozart. An introduction was arranged, and when Beethoven played for Mozart, the latter did not seem too impressed. He thought that Beethoven had spent many hours perfecting a "show piece," and was not complimentary in his comments to the lad. This aroused Beethoven's anger, and he demanded that Mozart give him a theme on which he could improvise. Mozart complied with this request and was so astounded by the genius that the boy displayed that he remarked to guests who had gathered in an adjoining room, "Keep an eye on this young man. Someday the world will hear of him!"

Since Mozart had long been an idol of Beethoven's, you can imagine what it meant to him to receive this encouragement. Before arrangements could be completed for Beethoven to start his lessons with Mozart, Beethoven was recalled to Bonn for several years. After losing his mother, whom he loved devotedly, his home life became miserable indeed. Because of intemperance his father lost his good voice, and his position at court, and Beethoven's music became his only solace. It was in this period of his life that he formed the habit of taking long walks, and it was when communing with nature that Beethoven found the inspiration for some of his most profound musical ideas. He kept a notebook, and when these themes came to his mind, he would jot them down.

Haydn had doubtless heard of this promising young man, but up to this time they had never met. When Haydn was returning from a trip to England he stopped in Bonn, and it was there that he offered to teach Beethoven if he would come to Vienna. Beethoven accepted his offer, and at the age of twenty-two, he returned to this great musical center where he spent most of the remainder of his life. After lessons began with Haydn, Beethoven was not entirely satisfied with his new teacher. Beethoven already felt a desire to depart from the strict formal writing of this period, and for this reason he and Haydn were not in agreement about many things. He finally decided to break away from his tutor, for he was critical of Haydn and blamed him for being careless in checking his mistakes. In those days teachers received the equivalent of about twenty cents a lesson, so they could hardly be blamed for displaying some lack of interest and enthusiasm toward their pupils. Later in his life Beethoven spoke with appreciation and affection of his old master, and he dedicated a number of his early piano sonatas to Haydn.

Beethoven's career in Vienna made steady progress. Influential friends in Bonn made it possible for him to meet important people in Vienna, and he was accepted in the most aristocratic circles. Among these friends were the von Breuning family and Count Waldstein, who were devoted to him throughout his lifetime. Beethoven sorely needed

68

the prestige that these people brought to him, because he lacked most of the social graces and refused to accept any favor from those in high position. He was careless about his dress, and his manners were often crude and unethical. He was supersensitive, proud, and given to sudden outbursts of temper. Because of his temperamental ways, he often cut himself off from those who wanted to help him. However, many friends remained faithful, and with their help, in spite of his many personal handicaps, he became a great favorite in musical circles.

He gave his first public concert in Vienna when he was twenty-five years old and met with the same enthusiastic appreciation which attended his entire career. Never before had anyone played the piano with such expressiveness and emotional fervor. Beethoven played the piano while Mozart used both the harpsichord and the piano. The piano as we know it today was fast becoming perfected, and in 1818 Broadwood & Sons, an English firm still in existence, sent Beethoven one of their finest instruments. By this time the piano pedals had been perfected, and the improved instrument gave Beethoven an opportunity to display his vitality and dramatic power.

During the years that followed, Beethoven received so much financial help from wealthy patrons that he was able to devote most of his time to writing. It was at this period in his life that he composed his first three symphonies, twenty piano sonatas, and some of his best chamber music.

Before Beethoven was thirty years old, he began to lose his hearing, and at the age of fifty, his hearing was entirely gone. This tragic loss, plus the fact that a nephew on whom he had showered love and devotion turned out to be worthless and unappreciative, saddened and embittered the last years of his life. In spite of this, however, Beethoven poured forth some of his most sublime music.

Prematurely old at fifty-six, and after a most dramatic life — one filled with hardships, struggles and intense activity — Beethoven died in Vienna in March, 1827.

Beethoven's works are often referred to as the connecting link between the formalism of the early composers and that of the "Romantic School" of writing. His compositions retained much of the perfection of form and the grace and elegance of the eighteenth century period of formal writing, but, because of his highly imaginative and emotional nature, he blazed new trails.

We have already mentioned that Beethoven was a great artist at the keyboard, and it was here that "he tried out" his themes and his harmonizations. His literature written for this instrument consisted of thirty-two sonatas and five piano concerti. Hans von Bülow called his

69

piano sonatas "The New Testament of piano literature." Beethoven's favorite means of expression, however, was the symphony orchestra. He bestowed upon the musical world nine of the greatest and most beloved symphonies ever written.

His *Third Symphony,* known as the *"Eroica"* or *"Heroic,"* was originally dedicated to Napoleon. Beethoven, always a champion of the masses, believed that Napoleon was fighting to free people from imperialism, but when he realized Napoleon's true ambition, he tore up the sheet which bore the dedication.

The best-known and most-beloved of all his symphonies is the *Fifth* — often referred to as the *"Fate" Symphony.* We have already referred to Beethoven's habit of taking long walks in the woods, and his *"Pastoral Symphony"* (No. 6) was inspired by his love of nature. In this symphony can be heard the rippling brooklet, the songs of birds, and the sounds of the storm. It is often called the first "program" symphony.

Nature provided many musical suggestions and others he obtained from another basic source — the "music of the people." Some of his finest works contain themes taken directly from or based on folk music. One of his best symphonies (No. 7) is built almost entirely on folk tunes, including, in the Finale, a lively Irish dance tune.

In a preceding chapter we have spoken of the "Scherzo" — a third movement of the symphony which Beethoven used in his later works to replace the more formal "Minuetto." This departure was only one of many which he used to free the symphony from the very formal style followed by former composers. Probably his greatest departure was his choral setting of Schiller's *Ode to Joy* in his colossal *Ninth Symphony.* Beethoven wrote only one opera, *Fidelio,* for which he wrote four different overtures. He wrote only one oratorio, *Christ on the Mount of Olives,* but composed several excellent Masses.

Beethoven's compositions did not flash across his mind and were not conceived in short periods of time. He spent days and months and even years writing and rewriting his music, and his intellectual processes were different from those of Mozart, who composed rapidly and seldom had to change a note. As a result Beethoven reached heights which had not been attained by his predecessors. No one had a greater capacity for taking pains. Beethoven's sketchbooks, which have been preserved, show where he worked over his ideas time and again, sometimes in as many as eighteen versions of the same work.

Some biographers feel that too much stress has been placed upon the unhappy phases of Beethoven's life. He had many troubled days, but some were of his own making. Had he been a better business man, he might have been free of financial difficulty, for no composer up to this time had been so well appreciated during his lifetime. Beethoven's compositions began to be published when he was only thirteen, and many of them were highly successful. Although he never married, he had several ardent love affairs with charming and high-born women, and he was highly respected by the truly great people of his time.

One biographer has called Beethoven "the man who freed music." It is an apt description, for this composer liberated music from its old status as a pastime for the rich and titled, and made of it a possession for all people, a truly democratic art which all might enjoy. His imagination freed music from the strict rules which had theretofore governed it, and he made music a means of expression for the emotions as no other musician had done. His music stands as the first great expression of social and intellectual freedom — a statement of ideals toward which the world has slowly struggled.

Beethoven also "freed" musicians, for his career proved that they need not be "hired servants," kept for the amusement of wealthy patrons. He, more than any other, succeeded in elevating the professional musician to a place of respect. His own personality, reflecting his reverence for God and his love for men and for nature, became a guiding light for the creative musicians who have succeeded him.

QUESTIONS

1. What was the spirit of the time in which Beethoven was born?
2. Tell something of his early life.
3. What was Mozart's opinion of Beethoven when Beethoven was still a young musician?
4. Who were some of Beethoven's influential friends?
5. What were some of Beethoven's less fortunate characteristics?
6. What were some of his fine ideals?
7. How did the development of the piano affect Beethoven's compositions?
8. What are the outstanding characteristics of his music?
9. How many symphonies did he write?
10. Name some of the other fields of composition in which he excelled.
11. What was the name of his one opera?
12. How did Beethoven dignify the profession of musician?

LISTENING SUGGESTIONS

Concerto in E Flat, No. 5 for Piano (Emperor)
Concerto for Violin
The Heavens Resound
Minuet in G

Missa Solemnis in D
Overture to Egmont
Leonore Overture No. 3
Sonata No. 21 in C for Piano (Waldstein)

Sonata No. 23 in F Minor for Piano   Any String Quartet
  (Appassionata)   Any of the Symphonies (1-9)
Sonata Op. 27, No. 2 for Piano   "Turkish March" from *Ruins of*
  (Moonlight)   *Athens*

CARL MARIA VON WEBER (1786-1826)

Carl Maria von Weber (Vay'bair) is of interest to us as the first composer who gave voice in his music to the German national spirit. Bach, Handel, Mozart, and Beethoven thought in terms of the world, not one country. Weber was proud of the growing strength of Germany as a nation and as a cultural force, and his music often employed German folk melodies and German legends.

Weber's father and mother were identified with the theatre, and Constance Weber, his cousin, became Mozart's wife. Exposed from childhood to the experiences and impressions of the theatre, it is not surprising that Carl Maria was absorbed in the opera. Much of his short life was spent in composing and producing operas. They were more serious than the prevailing taste and were usually confined to German subjects. As a result, many of his early ventures were failures. Eventually, however, his *Der Freischütz* (Fry'sheetz) — based on German legends — was acclaimed in Berlin and Vienna, and shortly before his death his last opera, *Oberon,* achieved success in London.

Weber, despite his travels and frequent ill health, managed to write a great deal of music in addition to his operas. One of his piano pieces, *Invitation to the Dance,* is often heard today, both as a piano solo and in its orchestral arrangement.

QUESTIONS

1. Why is von Weber of especial interest to the musical world, and especially to the Germans?
2. Why was he particularly absorbed in opera?
3. Name one of his most famous operas.
4. Name his best known composition for the piano.

LISTENING SUGGESTIONS

Invitation to the Dance   Overture to *Der Freischütz*
Overture to *Euryanthe*   Overture to *Oberon*

FRANZ PETER SCHUBERT (1797-1828)

Can you whistle or hum Schubert's *Serenade* or the themes of his *Unfinished Symphony?* Or do you know his songs, *Who is Sylvia?,*

72

The Erl-King, Ave Maria, and *Hark, Hark, the Lark?* If you do not know them and you really like music, you will want to add them to your repertoire.

Franz Schubert, composer of these and many other immortal songs, has been acclaimed the creator of the "Art Song." To understand this term we must realize that there are two ways to set a poem to music. One is in the manner of a folk song in which the melody is the same for each verse. This is sometimes called a "strophic" song. The other method of setting a poem to music is to change the melody as the meaning of the words change, fitting the music to the mood of the poem. This style is sometimes called "through-composed."

It was the latter style which Schubert followed to give the world some of its greatest masterpieces, which we know as art songs. This gifted young composer achieved the real union of words and music in a way that none had attained before and few have approached since. Schubert's songs not only match the mood of their poetry but go far in painting pictures in tone. Listen to the hoof-beats in the triplet accompaniment of *The Erl-King,* the running brooklet accompaniment in *Whither?,* and the dashing to and fro of the fish in *The Trout.*

Bach, Handel, Haydn, and Mozart were busy with instrumental music, church music, opera, and oratorio, and such solo songs as they wrote do not represent their best inspiration. But to Schubert the "lied" (leet), as the Germans called the solo song, was all-important. He was fortunate in having excellent poetry at hand, for Goethe (Geh'teh), Heine (Hy'neh) and others in his time were enriching German literature, and in these German poems Schubert found a rich mine. Schubert once sent some of his settings of Goethe's poems to the elderly poet, who unfortunately had not the grace to acknowledge them, although it is said that later, after Schubert's death, Goethe appreciated their beauty.

Like many Germans, Schubert had a high regard for William Shakespeare, and some of his finest songs are settings of Shakespearean lyrics. Two of these are *Who Is Sylvia?* and *Hark, Hark, the Lark.* And still another of his most beloved songs was inspired by an English text, the "Ave Maria" from Sir Walter Scott's *Lady of the Lake.* This poem is not a translation of the Latin *Ave Maria* so often sung in Catholic churches.

Schubert was too modest for his own good in an age when musicians had to fight hard for recognition, and especially for financial reward. Beethoven, a more forceful character, was able to realize considerable money from his works, but poor Schubert was underpaid for the masterpieces he produced. There were no copyright laws in his time,

73

and a composer had to be a good businessman. Since Schubert was not a shrewd bargainer, the publishers frequently took advantage of him and purchased his works for the proverbial "song." It is said that while Schubert received less than $3,000 for all his compositions, his publishers made nearly $15,000 in a few years from one song alone, *The Wanderer*. In defense of the publishers, it may be said that doubtless few of them could anticipate the universal appeal of Schubert's songs and other works.

From his seventeenth year until his death at thirty-one, Schubert composed more than six hundred songs. But his magnificent gift for melody was not limited to songs. During these same years he produced eight symphonies, numerous operas and Masses, and much chamber music, to say nothing of a large amount of piano music. His eighth or *Unfinished Symphony* is a favorite with music-lovers. Its melodies have been used in the operetta *Blossom Time*, which has told the story of Schubert to thousands of theatre-goers. Why the Eighth Symphony was left unfinished will probably always be a mystery, though in the real sense it is not unfinished, for the two beautiful movements have a satisfying completeness. Another mystery lies in the fact that it lay in manuscript and unheard for forty years after the composer's death.

This tremendous outpouring of music from one man came from a young man who was the thirteenth child of a schoolmaster living in a suburb of Vienna. Franz's talent was recognized by his father, who did what he could to foster it. Fortunately for Franz, others recognized his gifts, and he spent at least five useful years in the Konvikt School in Vienna, where he had much musical training and experience and was chosen to sing in the Emperor's choir.

At sixteen Schubert could no longer sing in the choir, his voice having changed, and he had his own way to make. He had no taste for business, the army turned him down, and there seemed to be no musical opportunities. He therefore followed his father's profession of schoolmaster for a few years. It was uncongenial work, and doubtless the pupils did not learn too much from this dreamy young man whose mind was inventing melodies. At twenty Schubert gave up teaching and gave himself wholly to music.

It is fortunate for the world that Schubert had friends who loved him and appreciated his talent to a degree that caused them to make sacrifices of their own in order to help Franz. In his schooldays there had been Joseph von Spaun, part of whose allowance went regularly to buy music paper for Schubert. And there were Schober, Schwind, Mayrhofer, and the noted singer, Vogl, who began to interest audiences in Schubert's songs. These men looked after

74

Schubert, raised the money to publish his first compositions, and supported the composer when he had no funds of his own. The circle was known as the "Schubertians" and their meetings as "Schubertiades."

Schubert greatly admired Mozart and Beethoven. Like Mozart, the music of Schubert goes serenely on its way, largely untroubled by the turmoil of the world, although it often has echoes of the folk songs and dances of Austria. It does not have the emotional excitement of Beethoven's music, and it differs again in that Schubert had really more good melodies than he needed while Beethoven would develop an entire composition from a theme of a few notes.

Shortly before his death, Beethoven is said to have encouraged the young Schubert, and at Beethoven's funeral Schubert was one of the torchbearers. He and his friends little realized that less than two years later Schubert would be laid to rest near Beethoven.

QUESTIONS

1. Name several compositions of Schubert that are general favorites.
2. What is meant by the term "Art Song"?
3. What was the German name for the solo song?
4. What well-known poets provided Schubert with the poetry for many of his songs?
5. How many songs did Schubert compose?
6. Name some of his other compositions.
7. Tell something about Schubert's profession after his voice changed.
8. Who were some of his friends and how did they come to his aid?
9. How did Beethoven influence Schubert?
10. Give an instance of how Schubert employed the descriptive powers of music.
11. What would you consider Schubert's greatest contribution to music?

LISTENING SUGGESTIONS

Ave Maria
Death and the Maiden
The Erl-King
Hark, Hark, the Lark
Any *Impromptu*
Marche Militaire
Any *Moment Musical*

Rosamunde — "Ballet Music"
Serenade
Symphony No. 5 in B Flat
Symphony No. 7 in C
Symphony No. 8 in B Minor
  (Unfinished)

FELIX MENDELSSOHN-BARTHOLDY (1809-1847)

Most composers started life as poor boys, but Felix Mendelssohn, as the son of a wealthy German banker, was more fortunate. There was

75

always music in the Mendelssohn home in Berlin, and Felix and his sisters, Fanny and Rebecca, and his brother, Paul, sang and played together. His father encouraged him to become a musician, although he did not try to exploit him as a prodigy in the fashion of Mozart and Beethoven. And when Felix had become of age, his father did not endow him, but expected him to make his way as a musician. And this the young Mendelssohn was quite able to do, for he was a musician of many talents.

We know Felix Mendelssohn as the composer of the celebrated "Wedding March" and the other *Midsummer Night's Dream* music written for the Shakespeare play. His oratorio, *Elijah,* his "Spring Song" and the other *Songs without Words* have added to his luster as a composer. Mendelssohn had other talents, however, for he was one of the most distinguished orchestra conductors of his time and one of the first to conduct with the baton. Before his time conductors usually conducted from the harpsichord or piano.

Mendelssohn was at the same time a capable business man, for he took the Gewandhaus (Geh-vahnd'hous) Orchestra in Leipzig, and made it not only an artistic but a financial success. He proved his administrative talents likewise in the reorganization of the Conservatory at Leipzig, making of it an important school with an influence which lasted far beyond his time.

As might be expected of one who had every advantage in life, the music of Mendelssohn always has an elegance and a refinement. We hear it in the·*Midsummer Night's Dream* music, in his much played and justly esteemed *Violin Concerto,* and in his other works. Favored with a background of money and influence, he was still in touch with the music of the people and folk influences are found in much of his music. His *"Scotch"* and *"Italian"* Symphonies are colored with the folk music idioms of their countries. Many of his compositions were inspired by his travels, which took him throughout Europe.

Some of Mendelssohn's most important compositions were in the realm of sacred music. The great choral societies of England inspired his splendid oratorios, *Elijah* and *St. Paul,* and in one of his symphonies, the *"Reformation,"* he makes extensive use of the celebrated Lutheran chorale, *A Mighty Fortress.* Every year at Christmas we sing one of Felix Mendelssohn's melodies to the words, "Hark, the Herald Angels Sing." Like some other tunes, this one was borrowed for the Christmas season, since the composer wrote it for a cantata celebrating the invention of printing.

Like another famous German musician, George Frederick Handel, Mendelssohn spent much time in England and was highly regarded by the English people. A versatile musician who excelled as pianist, organist, composer, and conductor, Mendelssohn was always ready to recognize the music of others. While still a youth of eighteen, he organized and presented a performance of Bach's great *St. Matthew Passion,* which had been neglected for more than seventy years. Mendelssohn also encouraged young English musicians and throughout his short life labored unselfishly for the cause of music.

Highly respected in his own time and for many years afterward, Mendelssohn's music came to be regarded, early in our century, as somewhat superficial and old-fashioned. Music-lovers now are inclined to cherish many of his compositions for their beauty and finish, even though they may not have the depth of the music of Bach and Beethoven.

QUESTIONS

1. How did Mendelssohn's childhood differ from that of other composers?
2. What were some of Mendelssohn's talents other than composing?
3. What influences are felt in the music of Mendelssohn?
4. Name several of his symphonies.
5. What well-known oratorio did he compose?
6. How would you describe the music of Mendelssohn?
7. How did Mendelssohn happen to write the music to Shakespeare's comedy *Midsummer Night's Dream?* Can you find out what each part describes?
8. What great composer's music did he revive and immortalize for future generations?
9. What Christmas melody do we owe to Mendelssohn?

LISTENING SUGGESTIONS

Concerto in E Minor for Violin
Concerto in G Minor for Piano
Elijah — any choruses or solos
Hebrides Overture
On Wings of Song
Overture to *Midsummer Night's Dream*
Rondo Capriccioso
Ruy Blas Overture

Scherzo from *Midsummer Night's Dream*
Any of the *Songs without Words*
Symphony No. 3 in A Minor (Scotch)
Symphony No. 4 in A (Italian)
Wedding March from *Midsummer Night's Dream*

ROBERT SCHUMANN (1810-1856)

Robert Schumann shared with Schubert a great love for poetry and the art song, and he had, in common with Beethoven, an independence of spirit which he expressed in his music and in his critical writings.

Born in the Saxon town of Zwickau (Tsvik-ow), Schumann was the son of a bookseller from whom he inherited a love for literature and the urge to write. As a young man, Robert Schumann was for a time undecided as to whether he should be a poet or a musician. He resolved to become a great pianist and in his zeal invented a device to strengthen one of his fingers. It did not strengthen the fourth finger as he had hoped but stiffened it for life, and the aspiring pianist turned to composition.

He began to write music for the piano and also to edit a musical magazine. He was thus probably the first composer to make his mark as a music critic. His judgments usually proved to be sound. He was outspoken against dull or showy music, of which there was far too much in the early nineteenth century, and he gave recognition to music of merit, as when he saluted Frederic Chopin in the *New Journal* with the phrase, "Hats off, gentlemen — a genius!"

Schumann did everything in an intense, exuberant fashion. This was partly because he always had positive ideas and in part because of his high-strung temperament. His was a brilliant mind which finally gave way under overwork and worry, with the result that the composer spent the last two years of his life in a mental sanitorium. His impetuosity, revealed first in his zeal for piano practice, is heard in his music and is seen in the way he worked. One year he would write nothing but symphonies, the next year it might be choral music or chamber music.

The year 1840 was Schumann's "song-year." It was a year of great happiness for him, for he was at last able to marry Clara Wieck (Veek), daughter of his first piano teacher, Friedrich Wieck, who opposed the marriage. Clara Schumann was one of the finest pianists of her day and a truly remarkable woman, who was able to teach, give concerts, raise a large family, and look after an erratic and often ailing husband. She was a source of real inspiration to Robert and also to the young Johannes Brahms, whom she and her husband befriended.

Robert Schumann and his music provide probably the best example of what is known as the "Romantic Period" in the history of music. His flights of imagination, his penchant for doing the unexpected in music produced compositions which are really poems in tone. In his songs the piano accompaniment is always important, sometimes so important that it has the chief melody and the voice has a supporting part. He was at his best in music for the piano. His one *Piano Concerto* (in A Minor), his *Carnaval* and *Fantasy Pieces* have long been favorites with pianists. One of the latter, entitled "Whims," is well named and typical of its composer. In it, the rhythm is quite as

78

irregular, with emphasis on the off-beats, as in the jazz music of today.

Schumann loved children, and he and Clara had seven of them. Like Bach, he wrote little piano pieces for them, especially in his *Album for the Young*. As a young man he had also written the *Scenes from Childhood*, a collection of short pieces which contains his beloved "Traumerei" (Traum'er-eye). He was one of the few great composers who really thought in terms of music for children.

Schumann is known also for his four symphonies, two of them subtitled as the *"Spring"* and the *"Rhenish"* (from the River Rhine) Symphonies. Although he made little use of actual folk material, his symphonies and many of his other works contain evidences of his love for German folk music. He sometimes made effective use of a folk tune, as in his song *The Two Grenadiers*, which tells the story of two of Napoleon's soldiers and ends with the stirring *Marseillaise*.

Robert Schumann is important in our story of music not only because he wrote beautiful music, but because he encouraged musicians, and artists in general, to become more imaginative and less formal in their artistic creations.

QUESTIONS

1. Why did Schumann become a composer instead of a great pianist?
2. What did he accomplish as a music critic?
3. Why do you think Schumann's wife was a help to him?
4. Name several of Schumann's well-known piano compositions.
5. Which of his compositions showed that he loved children?
6. How many symphonies did he compose?
7. With what important cultural development of the early nineteenth century was Robert Schumann associated?

LISTENING SUGGESTIONS

Carnaval
Concerto in A Minor for Piano and Orchestra
Fantasy Pieces
The Lotus Flower
Quintet in E Flat for Piano and Strings

Scenes from Childhood
Symphonic Etudes
Symphony No. 3 in E Flat (Rhenish)
Traumerei
The Two Grenadiers

RICHARD WAGNER (1813-1883)

Richard Wagner was brought up back-stage, which is to say that his early life was influenced by the theatre and people of the theatre. His own father died shortly after Richard's birth, and his stepfather,

79

Ludwig Geyer, was an actor and producer of plays. And while Richard was still a small boy two of his older sisters had stage careers. It is small wonder, therefore, that this German boy should turn to the stage, and when he did, he contributed to it new ideas. Indeed, Richard Wagner's music and ideas of stagecraft have provoked so much discussion that it is said that more than eight hundred books have been written about him.

If you have seen a picture of Richard Wagner, you have noted the firm set of his jaw and you probably have concluded that here was a man of independent spirit. And so he was. He liked his own way, and if he didn't like the rules, he broke them. For a time he was enrolled in the St. Thomas School in Leipzig, where Bach had presided a century earlier, and his teachers here and elsewhere found that if he liked a subject he soon mastered it; if he didn't like it, he ignored it.

Of short stature and frail physique, Wagner perhaps exercised this independence as a compensating factor. He refused to yield to editors who wanted him to write "potboilers," no matter how badly he needed money, nor how earnestly his poor wife, Minna, pleaded with him. And his zeal for espousing unpopular political causes frequently caused him trouble. At one time he had to stay in exile in Switzerland for twelve years.

Wagner was far from an admirable character. He borrowed money from his friends and often neglected to repay them. He was often domineering and arrogant, and his relationships with other people were often broken off by these defects of character; but in his devotion to his art there never was any wavering of his loyalty.

Richard's boyish efforts at dramatic composition were distinguished by wild flights of imagination, as in his first drama, where all forty-two characters died or were killed by the end of the fourth act and he had to bring back some of them as ghosts. The play did not survive, but fortunately the author learned to discipline his imagination, with the result that we now have the music-dramas for which he is known to all the world.

Wagner greatly admired Beethoven, who, in Wagner's time, was generally considered a musical radical. Perhaps it is significant that there was a bond between these two independent spirits, even though Beethoven died when Wagner was a boy of fourteen. When Wagner undertook serious composition on a large scale, he soon began to break with operatic traditions. His first opera, *Rienzi*, the overture of which is very well known, is quite conventional, but in the others we see the development of the ideas which Wagner always cherished.

80

In *The Flying Dutchman, Tannhäuser* (Tahn'hoy-zer), and *Lohengrin* (Lo'en-green) are the first hints of the "leit-motiv" (light-moteef) and the "eternal melody" which were to make *Tristan and Isolde* (E-sold'eh) and the four music-dramas of the "Ring" cycle different from other operas. The "leit-motiv" is a short melody or theme which Wagner uses to identify a character or an element in his story. One theme announces the appearance of Siegfried (Zeeg'freed); another is associated with the Sword, and still another with the Magic Fire. Through the use of these themes, Wagner accentuates the relation of persons or things to the development of the story. While Gluck and Weber had used the "leit-motiv" idea before him, it remained for Wagner to make the most effective use of it.

The "eternal melody" idea was the conception of a scene in a drama as one continual piece of music, not a succession of solos, duets, and choruses as early operas had been. After *Lohengrin,* the music in Wagner's music-dramas flows on through each scene until that scene is finished. Sometimes, indeed, it flows on too long for the tastes of opera-goers. But his music has such beauty of melody and its harmonies are so lovely and ever-changing that his operas, despite some scenes which lack action, have won millions of admirers.

In his later works the voices are merely parts in the orchestra. Brunhilde (Broon-hild'eh) is not a soprano accompanied by the orchestra; she is really a part of the orchestra, even though she has words to sing, and sometimes she has a less important voice than the violins or flutes. Strangely enough, Wagner, who played no instrument but the piano, and that badly, was a master of orchestration. He learned much from studying the scores of Beethoven and Weber and his imagination did the rest.

Another original idea of Wagner's was the combination of the arts. He believed that the ideal art came about through a harmonious fusion of language, music, decoration, and stagecraft. He wrote his own librettos (a libretto is the book and lyrics of an opera or musical play). He felt that the music should grow out of the words and, having considerable poetic ability, he was able to accomplish his ideal union of words and music. He gave personal attention to details of stagecraft and is said to have been the first to insist that the stage curtain divide in the center and pull to each side instead of rolling up. He placed his orchestra in a deep pit where it would not interfere with the view of the stage. His ideals for the theatre were finally realized, after many long and discouraging years, in the building of the Festspielhaus (Fest'shpeel-house) or Festival Playhouse in Bayreuth (By'royt) and it was there that the first great Wagner Festival

81

was held in 1876. Many festivals have been held there since that year and today they are in the charge of his grandsons.

Wagner believed strongly in a national music, and nearly all his works deal with German subjects. An exception is *Tristan and Isolde* which deals with a Celtic legend. In *Tannhäuser* and *Lohengrin* and *Die Meistersinger*, Wagner recreates for us the people of medieval Germany with knights and ladies, and the guilds of artisans and workmen. "Hail, Bright Abode," the stirring chorus in *Tannhäuser*, offers a picture of an early German tournament of song and *Die Meistersinger* presents historical personages. From these works came some of Wagner's most beloved melodies — "The Bridal Chorus" from *Lohengrin*, the "Pilgrims' Chorus" and "O Thou Sublime, Sweet Evening Star" from *Tannhäuser*, and the "Prize Song" from *Die Meistersinger*.

In his later works Wagner found his stories in the heroic folk-legends of Germany — the stories of Wotan (Voh'tahn), Brunhilde and Siegfried from the ancient Teutonic mythology. These four massive music-dramas — *Das Rheingold* (Rhine'golt), *Die Walküre* (The Val-key'reh), *Siegfried*, and *Götterdämmerung* (Get-ter-dahm'er-ung) known as *Twilight of the Gods,* are called *The Ring of the Nibelung*. His last work, again based on legend, was *Parsifal*, the story of the Holy Grail.

Wagner was thus conscious of his people and of their music. While he did not often use actual folk tunes, as had many other composers, he always wrote a folk tune of his own when the occasion called for it.

As a young man Wagner had an excellent start when he was appointed court conductor at Dresden. His outspoken political views, however, banished him to Switzerland. There he was befriended by numerous people who had begun to discern Wagner's genius. One of these friends was Franz Liszt, who performed Wagner's music-dramas and befriended him throughout his life. Liszt's daughter, Cosima, became Wagner's second wife, and it was for her and their son, Siegfried, that Wagner composed the beautiful *Siegfried Idyll*, offering it as a combined Christmas and birthday present to his wife.

One of Wagner's patrons was Ludwig, King of Bavaria, sometimes referred to as the "Mad King." He was sufficiently sane, however, to appreciate the genius of Wagner, and he determined to help the composer. In the preface to the "Ring" cycle, Wagner had written, "Is the Monarch to be found who will make performance possible?" The score with this preface caught the attention of Ludwig, who sent for Wagner, then in hiding because of his debts. Ludwig built a home for the composer and aided him otherwise, financially. Their plans for a great national theatre at Munich were not realized, but others were flocking to the Wagner banner and the theatre was erected at Bayreuth.

Wagner, like Handel, refused to accept defeat but kept to his course when Paris laughed at *The Flying Dutchman* and hissed *Tannhäuser*. He was to live to see his music triumph, and he died in 1883 in Venice, greatly honored and living in the luxury which had been denied to him in his early years.

QUESTIONS

1. How did the theatre influence Wagner?
2. Tell some interesting facts concerning his character.
3. What is the "leit-motiv" and in which operas was it used?
4. How did Wagner become a master of orchestration?
5. What is a libretto?
6. Who wrote the librettos for Wagner's music-dramas?
7. Tell something about the Festival House in Bayreuth.
8. From what sources did Wagner receive the inspiration for his opera stories?
9. What did Franz Liszt do for Wagner?
10. In what way did Ludwig, King of Bavaria, aid Wagner?
11. Name several of Wagner's early operas.
12. What are the four operas in the "Ring of the Nibelung"?
13. Why did Wagner have the right to say how his works should be staged?

LISTENING SUGGESTIONS

"Good Friday Spell" from *Parsifal*
"Magic Fire Music" from *Die Walküre*
"O Thou Sublime Sweet Evening Star" from *Tannhäuser*
Overture to *Rienzi*
Overture to *Tannhäuser*
"Pilgrims' Chorus" from *Tannhäuser*
"Prelude and Love-Death" from *Tristan and Isolde*

Prelude to Act I — *Lohengrin*
Prelude to Act III — *Lohengrin*
Prelude to *Die Meistersinger*
"Prize Song" from *Die Meistersinger*
Ride of the Valkyries
Siegfried Idyll
"Siegfried's Rhine Journey" from *Götterdämmerung*

JOHANN STRAUSS, JR. (1825-1899)

Johann Strauss, Jr., was the "Wayne King" of his day — in other words, the "waltz king" of his time, which was the middle of the nineteenth century. Johann was the eldest of three brothers, all of

83

whom were composers and conductors. The names of Eduard and Joseph are still known for some of their waltz tunes, but it was Johann who immortalized the waltz and made it a popular dance throughout the world. Johann the Elder, father of the brothers, had popularized the waltz throughout Europe and Johann the Younger made it fashionable in America, conducting concerts in Boston and New York.

So universally known and accepted are the Strauss waltzes that they have practically become folk music. Millions of people have played, whistled, hummed, and danced to *On the Beautiful Blue Danube, Tales from the Vienna Woods, Artist's Life, Vienna Life,* and the *Emperor* waltzes, and their graceful melodies and infectious lilting rhythm will long endure.

The Strausses were "playing-conductors." All of them played the violin and in conducting their orchestras they alternated between beating time and playing along with the orchestra. The bulk of the work in their dance orchestras was done by the strings, for the saxophones had not then attained the importance they have in dance orchestras today.

Johann Strauss, Jr., also made a great name for himself as a composer of operettas, establishing a tradition in musical shows which has since been carried on by Victor Herbert, Oskar Straus, Emmerich Kalman and others. One of the Strauss operettas, *Die Fledermaus* (Flay'der-mouse) is frequently performed at the Metropolitan Opera in New York and has also appeared in film versions.

QUESTIONS

1. Who was Johann Strauss, Jr.?
2. How did the waltz become popular?
3. Name several well-known Strauss waltzes.
4. What operetta was written by Johann Strauss, Jr.?
5. Why did Vienna seem to lose much of its gaiety when Johann Strauss died?

LISTENING SUGGESTIONS

Artist's Life	*Perpetual Motion*
On the Beautiful Blue Danube	*Pizzicato Polka*
Emperor Waltz	*Roses from the South*
Die Fledermaus	*Tales from the Vienna Woods*
The Gypsy Baron — Overture	*Voices of Spring*
One Thousand and One Nights	*Wine, Woman and Song*

JOHANNES BRAHMS (1833-1897)

A familiar picture in music studios and music stores depicts a heavy-set man with a long, flowing beard, seated at the piano with a large cigar in his mouth. This is Johannes Brahms in perhaps his best-known pose. For Brahms it was not a pose, however, since he was not given to pretense and indeed was sometimes considered brusque to the point of bad manners. He did not enjoy drawing-rooms and small talk, but he was still able to pay a nice compliment to a lady and to recognize other composers, as on the occasion when he autographed the fan belonging to the wife of Johann Strauss with the first bars of *The Blue Danube Waltz* and the words, "Unfortunately not by Johannes Brahms."

Brahms was born in Hamburg, Germany, in 1833, the son of a double bass player. He struggled with poverty as a youth and when still very young earned his way by playing the piano in restaurants. Eventually he found his way to Vienna, which he loved so much that he spent the greater part of his life there.

A pianist of great ability, Brahms, at the age of twenty, toured Europe as accompanist for the Hungarian violinist, Remenyi (Reh'-men-yee), and this association doubtless led to Brahms' interest in gypsy music, the inspiration for his famous *Hungarian Dances*. In these dances Brahms used some gypsy folk tunes and some tunes modeled on folk melodies.

Brahms was a thoughtful, serious-minded composer who proceeded calmly with his work. Although his talent was recognized when he was still young, he waited until after he was forty to write his *First Symphony*, and he took ten years to work it out. He composed four symphonies, and they have now been for many years among the most favored repertoire of symphony orchestras.

Brahms was a "down-to-earth" person, never far away from the common people. It is not surprising, therefore, that he often made use of folk tunes and that his own melodies frequently have the character of folk songs. In his symphonies and chamber music you will frequently hear simple, folk-like tunes, often used with great skill in a complex musical pattern, but still melodies that are essentially folk-like. One of his most successful uses of actual folk tunes is in his *Academic Festival Overture*, written as a gracious response to the English University which conferred a doctor's degree upon him. In this he employed the songs known to the students of his day. One of them, "Gaudeamus Igitur," may still be found in some American songbooks.

A bachelor throughout his life, Brahms must have loved children, for he composed a song which many consider the most beautiful of all lullabies. His songs have a freedom, expressiveness, and tenderness which hold them in high esteem among singers. He was, in fact, a worthy successor to Schubert in the great art of song-writing.

Brahms was a most versatile musician, turning his attention to many forms. A skilled pianist, he wrote well for the instrument, and his two piano concertos are among the world's great concert pieces, but his *Violin Concerto* and his *Concerto for Violin and Cello* (Double Concerto) are equally acclaimed. In other works he employed the horn or the clarinet as a solo instrument with great success.

Brahms gave considerable thought to choral music and one of the great choral works now heard at festivals is Brahms' *A German Requiem.* He wrote many fine smaller choral works, some of which are familiar to school and college choirs today. At one time he conducted a women's chorus, and having difficulty in finding the music he needed, he proceeded to write his own, just as Bach, over a century before, had composed much church music from necessity.

So highly regarded did Brahms become that many refer to him as one of the "Three B's," the other two being Bach and Beethoven. Brahms thought deeply about music, and his larger works have such a wealth of musical ideas that each new hearing of them seems to reveal something one has not heard before. He was fond of the musical form known as "theme and variations," and his ingenuity in presenting a melody in various transformations has won the admiration of music-lovers. An example of this skill is his *Variations on a Theme by Haydn,* often played by symphony orchestras. While he could be profound, Brahms, like other great musicians, knew the value of simple things and gave us tunes like the *Lullaby* and the *Hungarian Dances* which anyone can like and understand. Anything Brahms undertook was done conscientiously, and his music impresses us with its sincerity and its nobility.

QUESTIONS

1. Where was Brahms born?
2. Tell something about his early life.
3. What was the inspiration for his *Hungarian Dances?*
4. State other interesting facts concerning his symphonies.
5. Why did Brahms hesitate to write a symphony and how long did it take him to compose *Symphony No. 1?*
6. In what composition did he use folk music and why was it written?
7. What famous choral work did Brahms compose?
8. How do his songs differ in style from those of his predecessors?
9. Name several of his well-known songs.

86

LISTENING SUGGESTIONS

Academic Festival Overture
Concerto in D Minor for Piano
Concerto in B Flat for Piano
Concerto for Violin
Concerto for Violin and Cello
German Requiem, A

Any of the Hungarian Dances
Liebeslieder Waltzes
Lullaby
Any of the four Symphonies
Variations on a Theme by Haydn
Any of the Waltzes for Piano

RICHARD STRAUSS (1864-1949)

Richard Strauss was a Bavarian, born in Munich, and was not related to the Austrian Strausses of waltz fame who came from Vienna. Richard's father, Franz, the finest horn-player of his time, saw to it that the boy was given excellent musical instruction and taught him to revere Mozart and Beethoven. As a young man he became an admirer of Liszt and Wagner. For a time he held Liszt's old post as Court Conductor at Weimar and he also held important conducting positions in Munich and Berlin. His real interests, however, were in composition, and he achieved a distinguished name in the creative field.

Everyone who listens to a symphony orchestra has been impressed by the contributions which Richard Strauss has made to the orchestra as a medium for expressing sound. Richard Wagner made the orchestra a rich, full, and elaborate means of making music, but Richard Strauss went beyond Wagner to make the orchestra an even more complex and more expressive medium, with tonal effects which even Wagner had not thought of.

Richard Strauss composed symphonic poems, following in the lead of Liszt, in which the music is suggested by literary ideas. One of the Strauss tone poems tells the story of Don Juan, another the tale of Don Quixote (Key-ho'teh). One of his best known works is *Till Eulenspiegel's Merry Pranks* (Oy'len-shpee'gel's), based on the exploits of a mischievous legendary character of early Germany. Others, like *Thus Spake Zarathustra* (Tsah'rah-toost'ra) and *Death and Transfiguration* have a basis in certain philosophies. All of these tone poems are what we call "program music," in that they tell definite stories.

Strauss is also known as a musical "realist" because of the detail with which he depicts his musical stories. Thus in *Don Quixote* one hears the bleating of the sheep and the creaking of the windmill (for which he used a wind-machine). The hanging of the rogue, Till Eulenspiegel, is realistically depicted in the music, and there are many similar realistic effects in his works. He could also use folk songs, and

87

German tunes are heard in *Till Eulenspiegel* and in a piece he wrote about Italy we encounter *Funiculi-Funicula.*

Richard Strauss became very successful early in life, and he considered himself an important composer. He did not have the modesty of Schubert nor the humility of Bach, and one of his longest tone poems, *Ein Heldenleben* (Hel'den-lay'ben) (A Hero's Life), is frankly all about Strauss himself, with numerous quotations from his other works. Another orchestra piece, his *Sinfonia Domestica,* has to do with Strauss and his family.

Strauss was a shrewd business man and creative musicians can thank him for his firmness in always insisting that the composer should share adequately in the profits resulting from his works.

Some beautiful songs and numerous operas are included in the long list of Strauss compositions. One of the operas, *Der Rosenkavalier,* has become a favorite. Produced in 1911, it is the only important work which Strauss produced after he was thirty-five years old. Although he wrote much music in later life, it never achieved the success met with by the tone poems and songs written as a young man. Thus he contrasts with composers such as Wagner and Verdi who did some of their best work late in life.

QUESTIONS

1. What do we mean by program music?
2. Name one composition by Richard Strauss that would come under this title.
3. Why is Strauss known as a musical "realist"?
4. Name one of his most successful operas.
5. Why do you think Strauss' later works are not as successful as the earlier ones?

LISTENING SUGGESTIONS

Also Spake Zarathustra
Death and Transfiguration
Don Juan
Don Quixote

Ein Heldenleben
Rosenkavalier, Der (any part)
Rosenkavalier, Der, Waltzes
Till Eulenspiegel's Merry Pranks

OTHER GERMAN AND AUSTRIAN COMPOSERS

The list of notable German and Austrian composers is long, and there is not space here to discuss more fully the others who have contributed to music. The Austrian, Anton Bruckner (1824-1896), wrote nine massive symphonies, some of which are still played. In all of them he used the brass instruments extensively. His friend, Gustav Mahler (1860-1911), born in Bohemia, wrote ten symphonies, in some of which he used a chorus of voices, as had Beethoven. Mahler was a famous conductor and presided over both the Metropolitan Opera and the New York Philharmonic Orchestra for brief periods.

To Engelbert Humperdinck (1854-1921) we owe one of the most delightful of all operas, *Hansel and Gretel*, which, in simplified form, is probably more often given than any other children's operetta. Many of its tunes came from German folk music. Also in the late nineteenth century lived Max Bruch (1838-1920) and Max Reger (Ray'ger) (1873-1916), distinguished teachers and capable composers. In a more recent period there have been Arnold Schoenberg (Shane-bairg) (1874-1951) and Paul Hindemith (1895-   ). A distinguished teacher as well as composer, Hindemith spends most of his time in America. Schoenberg, who died in 1951, devoted much of his life to advocating the use of the twelve-tone scale and "tone-rows." In constructing a "tone-row" it is necessary to use each of the twelve semitones without repeating any. Many musicians consider it a sort of musical mathematics, and it is still a highly controversial musical invention.

Germany and Austria have also produced some great performers. Fritz Kreisler (Krice'ler) is known the world over as a celebrated violinist, and as the composer of such favorite violin pieces as his *Caprice Viennois* (Vee-en-wah') and *Liebesfreud* (Lee'bes-froyd). Bruno Walter, famous orchestra conductor, who has appeared many times in this country, was born in Berlin, while Erich Leinsdorf, like Kreisler, was born in Vienna. Felix Weingartner, Wilhelm Furtwangler, and Otto Klemperer have won fame as orchestra conductors, while Walter Gieseking and the late Artur Schnabel have attained great prominence among the world's finest pianists. There also have been great singers from these countries. One who often appeared at the Metropolitan Opera in New York and in concert is the soprano, Lotte Lehmann (Lay'mahn).

QUESTIONS

1. What popular German opera is based largely on folk music? Who composed it?
2. Give a distinguishing characteristic of Anton Bruckner's symphonies.
3. What composer gave much attention to the twelve-tone scale?
4. What famous musician of Austrian birth became noted in this country as a violinist and composer?
5. Name a celebrated conductor of German birth.

LISTENING SUGGESTIONS

Caprice Viennois — Kreisler
Concerto for Violin in G Minor —
  Bruch
Hansel and Gretel (any part) —
  Humperdinck
Liebesfreud (Love's Joy) —
  Kreisler
Matthias, the Painter — Hindemith
Old Refrain, The — Kreisler

Prelude to *Hansel and Gretel* —
  Humperdinck
Symphonic Dances — Hindemith
Any Symphony by Bruckner
Any Symphony by Mahler
Transfigured Night (Verklärte
  Nacht) — Schoenberg
Virgin's Slumber Song — Reger

The British Grenadiers

Traditional (about 1690)

English Song

Some talk of A - lex - an - der,
Of Hec - tor and Ly - san - der,

and some of Her - cu - les,
And such great names as these.

But of all the world's brave he - roes

There's none that can com - pare,

With a tow row row row_ row row row, To the Brit-ish Gren-a - diers._

THE BRITISH ISLES

To the world's inexhaustible storehouse of folk songs and folk dances, the British Isles bring some of the richest contributions. It is surprising for countries so tiny in area to produce such a veritable gold mine in quality and quantity, but this is due in part to the diverse character of the four countries and to the differing temperaments of the people.

However, there are many racial qualities in common which we may well consider. The English, Irish, Scotch, and Welsh are all sturdy peoples, fond of nature, devoted to their own hearth fires and determinedly staunch in their beliefs, religious and political, which may be regarded as good reason for the maintenance of separate borderlands. Although a certain "family" spirit underlies their association with each other, their friendly relationships are made possible because each group has its own separate home.

England

During World War II when the existence of England was threatened, someone wrote a song and called it *There'll Always Be an England*. Whatever the future may hold for England, the past shows very definitely that for more than a thousand years there "has been" an England that was important in the affairs of the world. In the past her holdings were found in every clime and country. Her inborn love of the sea is shown in her many folk songs which reflect the freshness of salt spray and the rhythmic beat of waves breaking on the coast — rugged magic showing the strong fibre and background of its people. Such songs as *Nancy Lee,* and *Sailing,* and sea chanteys such as *Blow the Man Down* are well known to all of us.

The lure of the hunt has ever proved irresistible to a real Briton, from early times to the present day. When we listen to an old hunting song, such as *John Peel*, with its echoes of hunting horns and galloping horses, we can easily imagine a gay array of scarlet-jacketed lords and ladies, full of the joy of life and the zest of the hunt.

It would be an incomplete picture of English life in past centuries were we to fail to mention its appreciation of ale and good roast beef. Many are the drinking songs dedicated to the nut-brown ale and the feeling of conviviality brought out by its combination with tables loaded with rich meats, puddings, and sauces. Baronial halls have echoed and re-echoed to the sound of voices raised in loud and joyous accents. *To Anacreon in Heaven* was one of these famous convivial songs with a fine stirring melody. It is to this tune that we Americans sing our national anthem, *The Star-Spangled Banner*.

The English as a rule do not "wear their hearts on their sleeves." In their love songs they are more dignified and restrained than, for instance, the Irish, although equally genuine. They enjoy singing of the charms of milkmaids and buxom village maidens and extolling their virtues, but seldom in melodies or harmonies drenched with emotional feeling. There is ever a bit of reserve, which seemingly acts as the hard shell of the chestnut, a glimpse of whose inner sweetness we are occasionally allowed to see. In such songs as *Drink to Me Only with Thine Eyes* (not a "drinking song" by the way) and *Oh, No, John!* we find some weakening of this reserve.

Very early there existed in all of the British Isles a class of musicians known as "bards," or wandering minstrels. They were the direct means of spreading folk music and tales, as their travels took them far and wide over the country. Many towns and many noble families maintained their own staffs of minstrels. In the latter instance these bards would sing or recite, to their own accompaniment, long ballads, often inspired by knowledge of the family's history. The village and household bards held a more honored position, and their lives were more stable than those of the traveling bards, who, on the other hand, enjoyed a more varied selection of literature by the very reason of their ramblings.

At all seasons the minstrels and fiddlers served on occasions which called for music, but never to better effect than at the Yuletide. At this time, their old carols and madrigals rang out on the clear frosty air and snow-blanketed lawns of rich and poor. The feelings of good will and charity engendered by these wandering carolers, or "waits," were the most vital feature of the occasion. Usually at the close of the singing in the courtyards, the doors would be opened to the minstrels and they would be invited to warm themselves before the open fire and partake of Christmas goodies. This old custom of carolling still lives to some extent and has found its way to some localities of America.

Singing societies flourished in England, glees (a term from which our "glee club" originated), madrigals, and folk songs providing the singers with rich outlets for their musical expression. The best-

93

known and enjoyed folk dances were the morris dance, hornpipe, reel, and anglaise (on-glehz). The Canaries (perhaps from the Canary Islands) was a popular dance during the reign of Queen Elizabeth. As we picture these old dances of England, we seem to see also the Maypole dancers "on the green" reaching for vari-colored streamers, gaily keeping time with their feet to the lively tunes played by the fiddlers and pipers.

English folk songs usually give the impression that the unknown authors and composers really felt that England was the best of all possible countries — a place to be proud of and to fight for. English tunes are straightforward and vigorous with a fine, broad melodic sweep. You feel this in singing or hearing such melodies as *The British Grenadiers, Rule Brittania,* or *The Vicar of Bray.* They are the living expression of Gilbert's lines in *H. M. S. Pinafore:*

> *For he himself hath said it*
> *And it's greatly to his credit,*
> *That he is an Englishman.*

Gilbert said it humorously, but the lines are quite faithful to the spirit of English music. Those English traditional songs gave many ideas to the immortal collaborators, William S. Gilbert (1836-1911) and Arthur Sullivan (1842-1900), whose operettas are as popular today as when they were new. English-speaking people everywhere love *H.M.S. Pinafore, The Pirates of Penzance, Patience, The Mikado,* and the others in the series. They have had countless performances in theatres and are today standard repertoire in many American high schools and colleges. Fame and fortune came to Gilbert and Sullivan, and both were knighted at Great Britain's court. The two often quarrelled, but their joint labors resulted in musical entertainment which does not seem to grow old, in contrast to so many musical plays and operettas.

All of us know at least a few English folk songs but only the folk song specialist knows the extent of the great treasure chest of British folk music. It has been stated that Cecil Sharp, one of Great Britain's foremost collectors of folk music, gathered together forty-five hundred folk songs and five hundred folk dances. And there are many which do not appear in his collections. English tale and legend has inspired many a poet and composer. Robin Hood and his merrie men have been often celebrated in music. Our American composer, Reginald De Koven, used this traditional story very effectively in an opera. William Shakespeare used the stories and traditional songs of Britain in some of his great dramas, and his verses have been the inspiration

94

of many a composer — not only in England, America, and other English-speaking countries, but in Italy, Germany, and other countries.

THE MUSIC OF SHAKESPEARE'S TIME

Shakespeare's time was a period of great musical and literary culture in England. English rulers in the sixteenth and seventeenth centuries were interested in the arts, and some were accomplished musicians. King Henry the Eighth was a composer and performer, and Queen Mary and Queen Elizabeth were excellent musicians. The latter was an accomplished performer on the virginal, a small keyboard instrument popular with the young ladies of the day. William Byrd (1543-1623) was Queen Elizabeth's teacher and friend, and to him and Thomas Tallis she granted an exclusive license for printing music.

Byrd composed some of the finest church music of all time, and is also known for his madrigals and keyboard arrangements of traditional English music, such as *Greensleeves*. That England had a high regard for William Byrd is shown by the fact that although he was a Roman Catholic at a time when England was strongly anti-Catholic, he was respected by all, and throughout his long lifetime he continued to write fine music for both the Catholic and Anglican (Church of England) services.

William Byrd is said to have been a serious-minded, austere sort of man and his religious music is profound, with an other-worldly beauty which is best appreciated in performances in a large church or cathedral. It is in some respects comparable to the music of his famous Italian contemporary, Palestrina. Byrd is important in the story of music for another reason in that he was the first composer to give important attention to music for the keyboard, played on the harpsichord and its little predecessor, the virginal. These keyboard pieces of Byrd's were published as long ago as 1611 in the Parthenia Collection and existed in manuscript in such collections as *My Ladye-Nevells Booke* and the *Fitzwilliam Virginal Book*, which were published much later.

Byrd deserves to be remembered also as the composer who first developed the idea of the theme with variations where a tune is presented in various forms with harmonic, rhythmic, and melodic changes. Byrd used this scheme many times, employing his own melodies and sometimes folk tunes for the basic themes. Later composers, especially Bach, Mozart, Beethoven, and Brahms often used the theme with variations idea.

Still another area in which William Byrd pioneered was in music for strings. Before his time the stringed instruments were viols, the

95

ancestors of our violin. Byrd was probably the first to write music for violins, viola and cello and thus pointed the way to "chamber music," the term which we use to designate music for string trios and quartets, a type of music to which composers from the eighteenth century to the present time have devoted some of their best inspiration. In view of his important accomplishments, it is not surprising that the English people of his own time referred to William Byrd as the "Father of Musick."

England prospered during the reign of the first Queen Elizabeth (1558-1603) and with this prosperity came a lively interest in the fine arts. Almost everyone in England seems to have loved music. Singing madrigals, catches, and rounds was a favorite after-dinner pastime. We still sing rounds in our music classes at school, including some that were sung in Queen Elizabeth's time. A "catch" is a humorous round, and a good example is *Three Blind Mice,* which was well known in Elizabeth's time.

In sixteenth century England a man waiting his turn in a barber shop would often be offered a cittern (a sort of guitar) with which to amuse himself. Perhaps the idea of "barbershop quartet" singing originated then also. When Englishmen went abroad they took musicians with them, and it is recorded that Sir Francis Drake, the great explorer, always carried a group of musicians and that his crew did much singing on their voyages.

This was the time of William Shakespeare and other gifted playwrights, and Shakespeare himself, on several counts, may be considered a musician. He seems to have had considerable knowledge of music, and certainly no one has ever used the English language in a more musical fashion. His poetry has been set to music by many composers, and in his plays music was often employed to heighten effects of mystery and solemnity or to accompany love scenes and ceremonial occasions.

One of Shakespeare's good friends was Thomas Morley, composer of *Now Is the Month of Maying* and many other madrigals. Morley composed some of the songs in Shakespeare's plays and became one of England's foremost composers in this period, which is known as England's "Golden Age of Music." Morley was a graduate of Oxford with a degree in music, for England was probably the first country to award university degrees in music. For some years Morley was organist in London's famed St. Paul's Church.

In the music of Morley's time each voice had an independent part and the sopranos, altos, tenors, and basses had each a melody to sing and the combination of these melodies made splendid music. This kind of music is called "contrapuntal" and differs from the style we know today where each voice sings a note in a chord. If the song had a sacred text it was called a "motet," and if it had secular words, it was termed a "madrigal."

Morley wrote many madrigals and edited and published several collections of them, one of which, *The Triumphs of Oriana,* was dedicated to Queen Elizabeth. Another famous composer of the time of Morley and Shakespeare was Orlando Gibbons, composer of *The Silver Swan.* One of the poets who supplied verses for the music of Gibbons was Sir Walter Raleigh — the same Sir Walter who had a part in the development of the colony of Virginia and whose name became a synonym for gallantry. In this "Golden Age" England probably had more good composers than at any other time in her history. They cannot all be named here, but one we shall note because of his very British name of Dr. John Bull.

HENRY PURCELL AND LATER COMPOSERS

Toward the end of the seventeenth century came Henry Purcell (Pur'sell) (1659-1698) who left such a wealth of music during his short life that Englishmen often regard him as England's most distinguished composer. When Purcell was still very young he was made organist at Westminster Abbey, an important post, and throughout his life he was prominent at the Court, serving under Charles II, James II, and William and Mary. He wrote much ceremonial music for official functions and much music for the stage, often on British subjects such as the story of King Arthur. Purcell was also a teacher and his opera, *Dido and Aeneas,* was written for the girls of the boarding school where he taught.

Samuel Pepys (Peeps), whose Diary is so famous, refers frequently to Purcell and his royal patron, Charles II, noting that Purcell wrote lively anthems which pleased His Majesty, a gay character who kept time to the music as it was sung in the services.

After Purcell, English music declined. England was busy expanding the Empire, and the musical life of the country was centered in London, where for a long period in the eighteenth century George Frederick Handel completely overshadowed the native-born composers. One Englishman of this period, Thomas Arne, should be remembered as the composer of one of the most British of all tunes, *Rule Britannia.*

During the first half of the nineteenth century another German-born composer, Felix Mendelssohn-Bartholdy, dominated the English scene. No great native composer appeared, although much church music was produced, some of which we sing today. The English have always loved the organ and most of their nineteenth century composers gave much attention to the organ and church music. Sir John Stainer, composer of the often-performed cantata, *The Crucifixion,* was one of these musicians, and another was Samuel Sebastian Wesley.

Since 1900 English-born composers have again come to the fore. Sir Edward Elgar (1857-1934) attained renown for his choral and orchestral works. His *Pomp and Circumstance March No. 1* has guided thousands of young graduates in their school commencement marches. It is one of a set of four marches which he composed for the coronation of King Edward VII. His oratorios, *The Dream of Gerontius, The Apostles,* and others have been often performed in all English-speaking countries. Elgar, like some of the early English composers, was fond of the variations idea and one of his best known orchestral works is the *Enigma Variations.*

Ralph Vaughan Williams, born in 1872, is a prominent present-day English composer. Few musicians have been so deeply interested in folk music. As a young man Vaughan Williams took many trips through the English country districts where he noted down the folk songs he heard. He has made good use of them in such works as the *Fantasia on Greensleeves* and the *Fantasia on Christmas Carols.* In his *London Symphony* this composer gives us some of the sounds of London and the familiar Westminster Chimes may be heard, suggesting the tones of the famous old clock, Big Ben, in the London Tower.

Frederick Delius (1862-1934) was sent as a young man to manage his father's orange groves in Florida. The love of music was too strong, however, and Delius finally had to give up business in favor of music, returning to England and finally moving to France. He too loved English folk-music and reproduced its accents in such works as *Brigg Fair* and *On Hearing the First Cuckoo in Spring.*

Still another Englishman who loved the folk music of his country was Gustav Holst (1874-1934). He was impressed by the quaint scales of British folk music and arranged many English and Welsh folk songs for choral singing. A versatile musician, he was also deeply interested in the music of such Eastern countries as India. As a trombone-player Holst was interested in band music and was one of the first composers to write for the modern band. Like Purcell, he taught in a girls' school in London, and Holst's *St. Paul's Suite* was written for his pupils.

William Walton (1902-   ) is known to many for his oratorio *Belshazzar's Feast* and for his music for Sir Laurence Olivier's films, Henry V and Hamlet. Benjamin Britten (1913-   ) is perhaps the latest addition to a long series of distinguished British composers.

98

His opera, *Peter Grimes,* has been performed in this country and his *Ceremony of Carols* is highly esteemed in this country and in England. Many young Americans know his *Variations on a Theme by Purcell* through hearing it played in the film, The Young Person's Guide to the Orchestra.

England may take pride also in her interpreters of music. Among conductors there have been Sir Adrian Boult, Sir Henry Wood, Sir Malcolm Sargent, Sir Thomas Beecham, and Eugene Goossens (for many years conductor of the Cincinnati Symphony Orchestra). It will be noted that England generally confers the "Sir" of knighthood on her distinguished men. Upon Myra Hess, whom many consider the greatest woman pianist of our time, the Crown bestowed the title of Dame, equivalent of knighthood for a man.

Associated with British music also is the Australian-born pianist who has done so much to acquaint us with the folk music of Great Britain, Percy Grainger (1882-   ). His *Country Gardens, Shepherd's Hey,* and *Molly on the Shore* — all of them folk tune arrangements — have pleased many American audiences. Long active in America, Grainger eventually became a citizen of the United States.

The story of English music is to an important degree the story of the folk music of England. For four hundred years English composers, from Byrd and Gibbons, who reproduced the Street Cries of London in their compositions, to Holst and Vaughan Williams, who depended so largely on English country songs, the composers of England have listened closely to the simple folk songs and dances of their people.

QUESTIONS

1. What countries comprise the British Isles?
2. Why have these four small countries been able to contribute so many and such varied folk songs and folk dances?
3. What four characteristics do these countries have in common?
4. Enumerate four or five types of songs which can be found among English folk songs.
5. Name three English folk dances.
6. Do you know any songs by Gilbert and Sullivan?
7. During the reign of certain rulers in England music flourished. Name one of these and tell something about the music of that period.
8. Who was William Byrd? Why was he important in the history of piano (keyboard) music?
9. In what ways may William Shakespeare be considered musical?
10. Tell something of interest concerning Henry Purcell.
11. What foreign-born composers influenced English music?
12. What celebrated march was written for the coronation of a king and who composed it?

13. What modern English composers have based much of their work on folk song?
14. Name a famous English woman pianist.
15. How have the English honored many of their distinguished musicians?

LISTENING SUGGESTIONS

Brigg Fair — Delius
British Grenadiers, The
Ceremony of Carols, A — Britten
Country Gardens — Grainger
Drink to Me Only with Thine Eyes
Enigma Variations — Elgar
Folk Song Suite — Vaughan Williams
Gondoliers, The
Greensleeves
H.M.S. Pinafore
Henry VIII Dances — German
John Peel
London Symphony — Vaughan Williams
Mikado, The

Molly on the Shore — Grainger
Music from *Hamlet* — Walton
Music from *Henry V* — Walton
Now Is the Month of Maying — Morley
On Hearing the First Cuckoo in Spring — Delius
Peter Grimes (any part) — Britten
Pirates of Penzance, The
Pomp and Circumstance No. 1 or *No. 4* — Elgar
Rule Britannia — Arne
St. Paul Suite — Holst
Shepherd's Hey — Grainger
Young Person's Guide to the Orchestra, The — Britten

SCOTLAND

Scotland calls to mind bagpipes, heather, and thistles, and lads in plaid "kilties." In some respects Scotland is similar to our own New England with its rocks, hills, and lakes. The Scottish soil yields reluctantly to the toil of the Scottish farmer, who must expend relentless effort to wrest a living from the land. Since most of Scotland's people depend upon the land, they are of necessity a thrifty, hard-working people, forced to make the most of their resources. They look upon life with canny eyes and a shrewdness not so marked in other dwellers in the British Isles. This, no doubt, has given rise to the many "Scotch jokes" based on a reputation for stinginess. Those who know Scotland, however, know that this reputation is unfounded and that Scottish people are as friendly and generous as any others.

Scottish folk literature celebrates the surpassingly beautiful lakes, rills, and "braes," and the Scottish people, being largely country dwellers, have turned to the beauties of nature and the rural scene. *Comin' thru the Rye, Loch Lomond, My Heart's in the Highlands, Flow Gently, Sweet Afton, Ye Banks and Braes o' Bonnie Doon,* and many others are the folk songs of nature-loving people. In the folk music of Scotland we hear the saucy tunes of piping herdsmen, the

100

martial pibrochs (pee'brahks) of the warriors, the simple croons of the tillers of the fields, and the eerie, mournful tunes which toll of the "cauld blasts" which sweep over the moors and heaths. These varied and romantic ingredients combine to form a most interesting folk music.

Scottish folk songs are often associated with Scottish history. Such songs celebrate famous battles or popular heroes, as in the case of *Charlie Is My Darling*. The "Charlie" of this song was Prince Charles (Bonnie Prince Charlie) whom the Scots of two hundred years ago hoped might regain the throne of Scotland. Years of strife between Scotland and England gave rise to warlike songs such as the stirring *Wi' a Hundred Pipers*.

In the early days, Scottish tunes were not associated with any definite set of words, and the same tune often served for several poems of widely varying character. More than two hundred years ago the poet, Allan Ramsay, collected many of the tunes and fitted to them the appropriate traditional poems and ballads. This work was continued by the famous Robert Burns, who loved his country's tunes and knew its folklore. To these tunes Burns set touching love ballads and poems depicting the hardships and simple pleasures of poor people. Other Scottish people helped to collect the folk music of their country. Sir Walter Scott, author of *Ivanhoe* and many other historical novels, helped in the collection and publication of Scottish songs, and one of the best loved of all Scottish songs, *Annie Laurie*, was composed by a Scotswoman, Lady John Douglas Scott.

The character of the music of any country is inevitably affected by the musical instruments of that country, and this has been true of the music of Scotland. The harp and especially the bagpipe were the popular instruments of early Scotland. Many of the bagpipes could not play the major scale of seven tones which we know so well, but played only five notes. A five-note scale is known as a pentatonic scale. There are several varieties of the pentatonic scale, but you can easily play the most common one by sounding in succession the five black keys of the piano.

Many Scottish tunes are constructed from pentatonic scales. *Comin' Thru the Rye* is a good example. This tune also exhibits another distinctive characteristic of Scottish folk music — the "Scotch snap." This is a syncopated rhythmic figure, usually a sixteenth note followed by a dotted eighth, which gives a sort of "kick" to the movement of the music.

Still another peculiarity of Scottish music is the "drone bass." This comes directly from the bagpipe. When a piper plays, he produces the melody with his right hand while with his left hand he holds certain keys, or "drones," which may sound continuously throughout the piece. Usually these drones are the keynote and the fifth, or dominant, of the scale in which the instrument is playing. This two-tone combination is known as an "open fifth." You hear it also when a violinist tunes up and plays A and E or D and A together. The drone bass is heard in folk music of other countries where the bagpipe is played, such as France, Ireland, and Hungary.

Because of these unique qualities Scottish folk music has interested many great composers. Felix Mendelssohn wrote a "Scotch" Symphony and his *Fingal's Cave Overture* has echoes of Scottish folk music. Haydn and Beethoven arranged Scottish folk songs and Beethoven and Chopin wrote *Ecossaises* (Ek-o-says'es) or *Scotch Dances* for piano. Camille Saint-Saëns (Sa[ng]-Sahns) has a fine Scotch dance in his *Henry VIII Suite*.

Scotland may not have given the world a Bach or a Beethoven, but it has produced some imperishable melodies. Scotland's best composers are the unknown musicians who gave us such melodies as *Loch Lomond* and *The Bluebell of Scotland* and such sturdy hymn tunes as *Dundee*.

QUESTIONS

1. In what respect is Scotland similar to our own New England?
2. What are some of the characteristics of the Scottish people?
3. Why have the Scottish poets and musicians so often turned to nature for their inspiration? Name at least two songs inspired by nature.
4. Why did Scottish people like the song *Charlie Is My Darling*? About whom was it written?
5. What was unusual concerning the Scottish tunes of the early days?
6. What great poet wrote famous poems and ballads to fit these tunes?
7. What unusual musical instrument is associated with Scotland?
8. What is the pentatonic scale?
9. Give an example of a song using the five-tone scale.
10. What is the Scotch "snap"?
11. Name one Scotch song where this is used.
12. What do we mean by "drone" bass?
13. Name one composer who has written music employing some of the unique qualities of Scottish music?

LISTENING SUGGESTIONS

Annie Laurie
Auld Lang Syne
Any Bagpipe music
Campbells Are Comin,' The
Charlie Is My Darling
Comin' thru the Rye

Hebrides Overture — Mendelssohn
Loch Lomond
Scotch Symphony — Mendelssohn
Scots Wha Hae
Scottish Fantasy — Bruch
Wi' a Hundred Pipers

102

The Harp That Once Thro' Tara's Halls

THOMAS MOORE   Irish Air

The harp that once thro' Ta-ra's halls The soul of mu-sic shed,

Now hangs as mute on Ta-ra's walls As if that soul were fled.

So sleeps the pride of— for-mer days, So glo-ry's thrill is o'er.

And hearts that once beat high for praise

Now feel that pulse no more.

IRELAND

It has been said that "all the world loves an Irishman." His careless gaiety, quick wit, happy-go-lucky ways, and generosity win friends for him on every side. Beneath these happier characteristics lies an undercurrent of wistfulness which, like a subterranean stream, may gush forth unexpectedly from the tranquil surface. These major and minor moods are presented just as contrastingly in his folk music, with lilting, jolly strains suddenly changing to somber, melancholy airs that are most haunting. The Irish peasant folk were a child-like people in their beliefs and reactions to old superstitions, fairy lore, and supernatural beings. An Irish mother lulling her child to sleep often called for protection for the wee one against "banshees" and other evil spirits. Irish folklore has many references to fairies and leprechauns (lep're-kons). These are recalled in the recent musical show, *Finian's Rainbow,* in which a leprechaun is one of the principal characters.

Like Scottish people, the Irish for the most part turned to nature and their daily occupations for song material. Their melodies are often less angular and less vigorous, rhythmically, than the Scottish but are equally joyous. The broad melodic sweep of many Irish tunes appears in such examples as *Believe Me, If All Those Endearing Young Charms* or *The Minstrel Boy.* For sheer beauty of melody, Irish folk tunes cannot be surpassed, in the opinion of many musical authorities. A fine illustration of this beauty may be heard in *The Londonderry Air.*

Irish folk music also has many lively dances, the best known being the reel and jig. Such jig tunes as *The Irish Washerwoman* and *Garryowen* will always make our toes tingle and our faces smile. The contagious rhythms and saucy tunes of these dances have been used to good advantage in compositions by Victor Herbert, Fritz Kreisler, Percy Grainger, and others.

Composers of other lands have long admired Irish music and have frequently drawn upon it. The "hit tune" of the opera *Martha* is an Irish folk tune, "The Last Rose of Summer," which the composer, Friedrich von Flotow, liked so well that he interpolated it in his score. Beethoven liked and arranged Irish songs and used an Irish dance tune in the finale of his Seventh Symphony.

Irish music had an influence on the rest of Great Britain, and in some degree in Europe. Civilization and an interest in the arts seem to have developed in Ireland at an earlier day than in the rest of Britain. In the earlier times, before St. Patrick brought Christianity to Ireland in the fifth century, the Druids used music in their

104

services. Early writers report that Irish monks sang in a primitive kind of harmony as early as the sixth century and contests in harp-playing were held as early as the sixth century in "Tara's Hall," celebrated in the famous song, *The Harp That Once through Tara's Halls.* Irish bards and harpers traveled widely in Europe and left an influence on the folk music of Denmark, France, and the other parts of Great Britain. Even the great poet, Dante, writing in Italy in the thirteenth century, speaks of the Irish harp and its music, and Queen Elizabeth employed an Irish harper.

Obviously, music of such ancient origin must have been quite different from the music we know today, and some of these ancient characteristics have persisted in Irish folk music. For example, a genuine Irish tune in the minor mode never employs the raised seventh degree which we expect in the minor. The Irish minor scale may be demonstrated at the piano by playing from A to A on white keys alone. Some of these quaint "modal" aspects of Irish tunes came from the influence of early church music, and some were brought about by the character of Irish instruments, the bagpipe having its effect, as it did in Scotland.

A collector of folk tunes once estimated that there are at least 5,000 different Irish folk melodies. Whatever the number, music-lovers will always be indebted to "The Little Green Isle" for its rich musical storehouse.

QUESTIONS

1. In what ways are Irish folk tunes like the Scotch and in what ways are they different?
2. What are two favorite Irish dances?
3. What was the legendary instrument of Ireland?
4. What famous composer was born in Ireland and then came to this country while still a young man?
5. Name one composer who admired Irish music and who made use of it in some of his compositions?
6. How did Irish bards influence the music of other countries?
7. How many folk tunes are said to have been collected from Ireland's rich storehouse?

LISTENING SUGGESTIONS

Galway Piper, The
Garryowen
Girl I Left Behind Me, The
Harp That Once Through Tara's Halls, The
Has Sorrow Thy Young Days Shaded
Irish Rhapsody — Herbert

Irish Washerwoman
Last Rose of Summer, The
Londonderry Air
Low-Backed Car, The
Meeting of the Waters, The
Minstrel Boy, The

WALES

Wales is the smallest country in the British Isles, but its musical area is important. The Welsh, like the Irish, began to develop the art of music at an early day. There are records dating back as far as 60 A.D. which detail lists of "bards," as their musicians were called, but while the names of the bards and their rules are thus preserved, there is nothing to show the style and character of their early songs. We know that the Welsh sang in harmony hundreds of years ago and were very likely the first people to sing in four-part harmony as we know it today. A twelfth-century writer speaks of the Welsh as follows: "In their musical concerts they do not sing in unison like the inhabitants of other countries, but in many different parts."

In Wales, as in Ireland, the bards were a powerful influence in the early development of music. They sang songs for every occasion of Welsh life and their stirring national songs, such as *Men of Harlech* and *Forth to the Battle* inspired generations of Welshmen to resist oppression. The influence of the bards upon their people was so great that Edward I of England gave particular attention to suppressing the bards and their music in his conquest of Wales. While much of the early Welsh music was, therefore, unfortunately lost, no conqueror was able to destroy the Welsh love of singing, and many beautiful folk songs have come to us from Wales. Among them are vigorous marching songs (*Men of Harlech*) and lovely tender melodies (*All Through the Night* or *Suo Gan*). Welsh tunes usually follow bold melodic lines with a greater compass and more frequent skips between notes than is characteristic of much other folk music. *The Ash Grove* is a typical example of the style of Welsh folk music.

In common with the Irish and Scottish people, Welsh musicians have always had a marked fondness for the harp. It was the instrument with which the ancient bards accompanied their songs, and the attention which Welshmen gave to this instrument has emphasized its importance in the development of Welsh music. Welsh harpers were in demand in Eighteenth Century England as household musicians in the homes of wealthy families. John Parry, a blind harper, attained much fame in England and is said to have been highly regarded by the composer, Handel. Parry was probably the first musician to collect the folk music of Wales, publishing a volume of Welsh songs in 1742.

For many hundreds of years the Welsh people have preserved a unique musical institution in their "Eisteddfod" (Eye-steth'vod) or music festival. There is mention of Eisteddfods as early as the seventh century A.D., and these competition-festivals are held each year in Wales. They serve as contests of skill for singers, instrumentalists, composers, and choral groups, and the Eisteddfod may be considered to be the ancestor of our school competition-festivals in the United States. Medals and prizes are awarded and the decisions are made by distinguished musicians from all over Great Britain and sometimes from America. Welshmen who came to America brought with them the Eisteddfod tradition and Welsh communities in Ohio, Pennsylvania, Wisconsin, and Canada continue to hold their Eisteddfods. As a result, any community which includes a considerable number of people of Welsh descent is likely to have flourishing choral groups and excellent church choirs.

The Welsh harpers and bards bequeathed much beautiful folk music to music-lovers. Welshmen of a more recent period (the nineteenth century) have contributed some of the finest tunes to be found in the hymnbooks of the Protestant churches. These have the same strength that may be noted in Welsh folk tunes. These hymn tunes are now so well liked that they often serve as the tunes for several hymns. Thus *Hyfrydol* (Uv-ruh'dul) may be the tune for the hymn, *Praise the Lord, Ye Heavens Adore Him* and also for *Come, Thou Long-Expected Jesus*. Other favorite Welsh hymn tunes are *St. Denio* (St. Dane'yoh), *Aberystwyth* (Ah-ber-ist'with) and *Cwm Rhondda* (Coom Rahn' dah).

An interesting Welsh musical custom is "penillion" singing. This is a form of musical improvisation in which music is composed "on the spot," as it were. In South Wales the harper plays a well-known tune and the penillion singer must make up words and a counter-melody which will fit the tune and be in strict time. In North Wales the procedure is even more difficult. The singer improvises the harmony parts and the words, but he must not begin until after the melody has started and he must end with the harper.

These and other interesting manifestations of a deeply-rooted love for music have given the Welsh a justly deserved reputation as a musical people.

QUESTIONS

1. Did the Welsh develop music at an early date? How early?
2. In what way did the bards of Wales exert a powerful influence in ancient days?
3. Name some of the characteristics of Welsh folk music that differentiate it from that of other countries.
4. Name two well-known Welsh folk songs.

5. Tell something of the history of the Eisteddfod and the reason it is so important.
6. Describe "penillion" singing.
7. See how many Welsh hymn tunes you can find in a hymnbook.

LISTENING SUGGESTIONS

All Through the Night
Ash Grove, The
Captain Morgan's March
David of the White Rock
Deck the Halls

Land of My Fathers (Welsh National Air)
March of the Men of Harlech
Suo Gan
Any Welsh Hymn Tune

Shepherds, Shake Off Your Drowsy Sleep

Traditional

Besançon Carol

mf

1. Shep-herds, shake off your drow-sy sleep,
2. Hark, ev - en now the bells ring round,

Rise and leave your sil - ly sheep,
Lis - ten to their mer - ry sound.

An - gels from heav'n a - round loud sing - ing,
Hark! how the birds new songs are mak - ing,

Ti - dings of great joy are bring-ing, Shep-herds the
As if win - ter's chains were break-ing,

cho - rus come and swell! Sing No - ël! O sing No - ël!

≫ 11 ≪

FRANCE

THE FOLK MUSIC OF FRANCE is closely linked with her interesting and stirring history. Long before the Renaissance there was in France a large body of poet-musicians, known in Provence (Provahns') and the South of France as troubadours and in the North of France as trouvères (troo-vairs'). The word "troubadour" has continued in use to the present day to describe a singer of songs, particularly of romantic songs. One of Verdi's best known operas is entitled "The Troubadour" (*Il Trovatore*) and deals with the unfortunate career of Manrico, a Spanish troubadour. Other countries followed France's lead in troubadour music.

The troubadours flourished from 1100 to 1300 A.D. They were usually men of noble birth, sometimes even kings. Richard the Lion-Hearted of England was a troubadour. At first the troubadours sang their own songs, but later their songs were usually sung by traveling musicians known as "jongleurs" or "minstrels." These itinerants made it possible for the songs of the troubadours to become widely circulated, for of course this was before the days of printed music.

The songs themselves were usually devoted to love, nature, or religion. The poetry had the spirit of the Age of Chivalry, and Frenchmen of that day apparently enjoyed the same reputation for gallantry for which the French are known today. The tunes were composed by the troubadours, but they were strongly influenced by two sources — folk songs and the music of the church. The jongleurs who sang these songs were poorly rewarded, and they lived with the servants and peasants. These contacts kept alive the folk music of France far more effectively than if it had had to depend upon the court appearances of the jongleurs.

The names of many of the troubadours have come down to us, but we shall note but one — Adam de la Hale (Hahl), because of his play, *Robin and Marian,* which was the first comic opera and was presented in 1285. Into this musical play, de la Hale introduced some of the popular songs of the day.

The Crusades had a marked influence on the culture of France, as on that of other European countries. Oriental musical ideas and

110

instruments came to France and Spain because of the Crusades. It is believed that the famous tune we know as "For He's a Jolly Good Fellow" came from Arabia and was brought to France and England by returning crusaders. In France it is sung to the words "Marlbrough s'en va t'en guerre" (Marlborough is going to the war). It was a favorite tune with Napoleon Bonaparte and several composers, notably Beethoven, borrowed it.

The folk songs of Northern France were usually serious and frequently religious in character. In the Southern provinces they tended more toward a gay or sentimental style. The folk songs of Brittany are bold and vigorous, not unlike the Welsh, while the songs of Provence are gay and polished. In Normandy the songs are simple and concerned with the everyday affairs of the peasants. From Eure and Burgundy come drinking songs, and Burgundy is known also for its Christmas songs. In Southwest France, where the Basque people live, we find still another type of French folk song, strongly similar to the music of bordering Spain. Rural and city dwellers had their folk songs, and the popular street songs of the cities came to be known as "voix-de-ville" (voices of the city). From this term came the word "vaudeville," a type of entertainment well known to the older generation of Americans.

For hundreds of years after the time of Charlemagne, the French were a highly religious people, and the music and customs of the church had a profound influence upon the lives of the people. French mystery plays celebrating the birth of Christ date back to the twelfth century, and the French adopted the custom initiated in Italy by St. Francis of Assisi of centering their Christmas ceremonies about the "crèche" (cradle). They danced and sang around the crèche, thus originating the practice of "caroling" which we know today.

These French carols are known in their own country as "Noëls" (a word meaning "news") and the term is often used in this country. French Noëls are simple and easy to learn and usually bright and lively. Some widely-sung examples are *Bring a Torch, Jeannette, Isabella* and *Shepherds, Shake Off Your Drowsy Sleep*. One of the best known French Christmas songs — *The March of the Three Kings* — is said to be seven hundred years old.

French folk songs are nearly always simply constructed. Often they consist of a two line verse and a refrain common to all verses. The refrain may be made up either of nonsense syllables similar to the tra-la-las we often hear, or imitative sounds such as are in the French Christmas song, *Pat-a-Pan*. French folk music has always reflected closely the life and thoughts of the people. Social customs can be traced in the music; thus the courtly festivals of the eighteenth

111

century in France are remembered because of the considerable number of French folk songs known as "Bergerette" or Shepherdess Songs. These songs sprang up during the time when the French nobility took delight in enacting rustic pageants in which shepherds and shepherdesses were the chief characters.

MUSIC AT THE FRENCH COURT

France had her composers from the time of the troubadours on, but the first really great composer in France was, strangely enough, an Italian. Jean Baptiste Lully (Loo'lee) (1632-1687) was born in Florence, but in every other way he was a Frenchman. He came to France as a boy of fourteen and for several years was a kitchen servant in the household of Mlle. de Montpensier, cousin of Louis XIV. Eventually the King discovered Lully and made him a member of the "Violins du Roi" (The King's Violins), a group of twenty-four players of stringed instruments which furnished music for the court. Lully's talent was such that he was not long in becoming director of the group and the principal composer for the court. His duties at first were to compose the royal ballets. France, then as now, loved the ballet, and Louis XIV himself delighted to act in these ballets, which were usually devoted to accounts, in no subtle way, of his greatness as a king.

In collaboration with the great French dramatist Molière (Mohl-yair'), Lully expanded the ballet to a form which included not only music for dancing but songs for soloists and chorus. From this it was but a step to French operas, modeled somewhat after Italian operas which had originated in Lully's native Florence. Lully was thus the founder of French opera, a form which became especially important in eighteenth and nineteenth century France and gave the world numerous operas which continue to hold the stage today.

Shortly after Lully's time came two other noted composers, François Couperin (Coop'er-an) (1668-1733) and Jean Phillipe Rameau (Rahm-oh') (1683-1764). Couperin, like Johann Sebastian Bach, was the most famous member of a family of distinguished musicians, for there were several Couperins who served as organists, violinists, and harpsichordists at the French Court in the seventeenth and eighteenth centuries. François, known as "Couperin Le Grand," was a gifted organist and a fine performer on the harpsichord. He wrote an instruction book for the harpsichord which influenced the style of Bach's keyboard compositions. Couperin's compositions for the harpsichord are frequently played today by performers on the harpsichord and by pianists. They invariably reflect the wit and elegance of the French of their time.

Rameau was born in 1683, two years earlier than Bach and Handel. He became important as a writer on musical subjects. His *Treatise on Harmony* was a landmark in the theory of music and exerted a great influence on later musicians. He composed extensively, especially in the operatic field, and eventually became Lully's successor as the most important composer at the court. He was a student of tone color, and his ideas, often considered daring in his time, have had great influence, even though his music is largely forgotten. Rameau was the first Frenchman to appreciate the possibilities of the wood-wind instruments, and ever since his time French musicians have been noted for their skillful and expressive use of the flute, oboe, and clarinet.

Rameau and Couperin were pioneers in another field — that of "program music." Until the time of Beethoven musical ideas were formal and abstract, concerned with tonal combinations but not with outside ideas. Beethoven greatly increased the emotional content of music, but it was not until the mid-nineteenth century that the idea of program music became established and composers such as Liszt and Berlioz began to use music as a means of painting a picture or telling a story. Yet, more than a hundred years before Liszt's time there was program music in France in the little keyboard pieces of Couperin and Rameau, many of them of a highly descriptive character. In one of Rameau's harpsichord pieces, *The Hen,* it is not at all difficult to hear the "cut-cut-ca-da-cut" of the busy little fowl.

History reveals the time of Louis XIV and his successors as a period of great luxury and elegance during which imposing palaces and gardens, such as those at Versailles (Vair-sye'), were created and artistic achievements of all kinds were fostered. The ballrooms and gardens of the nobility were often the scene of musical pageants and ballets in which dancers, dressed in satins and laces and adorned with white wigs, took part. Such dances as the *minuet* and *gavotte* were in favor, and these dance forms influenced later composers. In such a society the opera, with its pomp and glamour, was certain to flourish, and one finds that French society during most of the eighteenth century devoted much attention to the opera. At one time there were rival factions, one supporting the operas of Gluck and the other the operas of Piccinni, and Parisians and their newspapers followed the news of this contest with something like the interest which Americans now give to the World Series.

Curiously enough, the composers who supplied the stage works for France during much of this operatic period were foreign-born; the Italians; Piccinni (Pee-chee'nee), Cherubini (Kay-roo-bee'nee), and Spontini (Spon-tee'nee); the German, Christoph von Gluck

113

(Glook); and the Belgian, Andre Grétry (Gray'try). The French Revolution, during the closing years of the eighteenth century, wrought great changes in the social fabric of France, but it did not long affect the Frenchman's fondness for opera, and during the regimes of Napoleon Bonaparte and his successors opera continued to flourish. And again the operas were produced by composers from other countries. For many years the French operatic stage was largely dominated by the works of the Italians, Cherubini and Rossini, and the German Meyerbeer. A few French operas were heard, such as *Mignon* (Meen-yohn) by Ambroise Thomas (Toh'mah) and some works by Mehul (May'ool) and Auber (O'bair), but it was not until the last half of the nineteenth century that Frenchmen really began again to appreciate the work of French composers. The French attitude was much like that of many Americans who felt, until a comparatively recent time, that the best music and musicians come from foreign sources.

The Frenchmen of a hundred years ago wanted their grand operas to be really "grand" in the sense of being spectacular. And the operas of Meyerbeer, which delighted them, were distinguished for spectacular scenes as lavish for their time as some of the famous stage productions which Florenz Ziegfeld produced in America years later. This insistence upon display persisted for many years in France, and no opera could succeed without a sumptuous ballet. Richard Wagner revised his *Tannhäuser* as a concession to the Parisians, but since he refused to interpolate a full-fledged ballet, the French audience provoked a veritable riot and this celebrated music-drama had to be withdrawn and taken to more receptive theatres.

SOME FRENCH COMPOSERS

When, a century after the time of Rameau, France had produced another musical genius in Hector Berlioz (Bair'lee-ohs) (1803-1869), she treated him rather badly. Preoccupied with the opera, France for the most part ignored his compositions for orchestra, although he did succeed once in winning the coveted Prix de Rome. He was, however, primarily a man of the theatre, and it was a source of great disappointment to him that none of his operas was a success in France. He was more successful, during his lifetime, in other countries, but after his death, as often happens, his native country realized that he was a composer of importance and his orchestral works were widely played, as they are to this day. His *Symphonie Fantastique, Roman Carnival Overture,* and other works are loved by orchestra conductors because of the skill with which every tonal resource of the

114

symphony orchestra is utilized. Berlioz, in fact, expanded the tonal language of the orchestra to such a degree that not much has been added to it since his time. He wrote a book on orchestration which was a guide to composers for many years and is still often quoted as an authority.

Those who know his music do not find it difficult to reconstruct the personality back of it. His life and his music reveal violent contrasts and always a highly developed sense of the dramatic, or perhaps the word should be "theatrical." He found, perhaps, his greatest inspiration in Shakespeare, who, in Berlioz' words, "struck him like a thunderbolt."

Where Berlioz loved the theatre but found his triumphs in the concert hall, there were other nineteenth century Frenchmen to whom the operatic public showed greater kindness. Charles François Gounod (Goo-noh) (1818-1893), after a couple of failures, produced the opera which has probably been performed more often than any other French opera. *Faust* was given first in March, 1859, and since then it has had well over two thousand performances at the Paris Opera alone. Like Liszt, Gounod had a deep interest in religion and at one time intended to become a priest. He devoted himself, by turns, to the writing of operas and music for the church. His oratorios and Masses gained wide acceptance, and excerpts from these, such as *Unfold, Ye Portals, Lovely Appear, Send Out Thy Light,* and the "Sanctus" from the *St. Cecilia Mass* have been standard repertoire for church choirs and school groups. Especially well known is his *Ave Maria* for soprano, a melody superimposed upon Bach's "First Prelude in C Major." Gounod was himself a choral conductor of considerable renown.

Like Handel and Mendelssohn, Gounod found a welcome in England. His first recognition as a composer occurred when sections of one of his early Masses were performed in England before they were heard in his native France. Gounod lived in England for some years and found in Shakespeare's story, *Romeo and Juliet,* the inspiration for his opera of that title.

Another opera of which France may be justly proud is Georges Bizet's *Carmen.* Based on a Spanish subject and filled with perhaps more good tunes than can be found in any other opera, *Carmen* is today a world-wide favorite. "The Toreador Song," the "Habanera," the "Flower Song," and "Micaela's Song" have all endeared themselves to lovers of melody. In its music Bizet (Bee-zay') immortalized the spirit of Spanish folk music.

Bizet (1838-1875) is also known to us for his lovely music written for *L'Arlesienne* (Lar-lays-yen) (the Woman of Arles), a play by

115

Alphonse Daudet (Doh-day'). The play is largely forgotten, but the music lives on in the form of two suites for orchestra. In one of these the composer made excellent use of the old French Christmas song, "March of the Three Kings." Saxophone players will be interested to know that the *L'Arlesienne Suites* mark the first use of the saxophone in symphonic works, a step which was to be followed by other French composers. The "Carillon" in the *L'Arlesienne* music is perhaps the most skillful use any composer has ever made of bell-effects. The entire orchestra seems to be a chiming of bells.

Charles Camille Saint-Saëns (1835-1921) was an illustrious figure in French music during the late nineteenth century and the twentieth century. Frail as a child, he surprised the doctors by living to be eighty-six. Throughout his long life he composed incessantly. His first song was written when he was six years old, and he was still full of ideas when an old man. Many Frenchmen are satisfied to live out their lives in France, but not Saint-Saëns. He loved to travel, and visited many countries. He died away from home, on a trip to Algeria in 1921. When he was eighty years old he came to the United States (for the second time) and represented his government at the Panama-Pacific Exposition in San Francisco where he played the organ and conducted his compositions. When he was eighty-five he appeared as a soloist in Paris.

His love of travel and tireless interest in the whole world made Saint-Saëns a composer who is less French in expression than many of his countrymen. When he visited England he dug up old music in museums and followed its style in his opera, *Henry VIII*. When he visited Algeria he recorded for us the local color of that country in his *Algerian Suite*. From the Orient came musical ideas which he used to excellent advantage in his best opera, *Samson and Delilah*. The "Bacchanale" (Bahk-ah-nahl') from this opera sounds most oriental in rhythm and melody, yet the tunes, with one possible exception, are those of Saint-Saëns.

With all this versatility of style, however, there is about the music of Saint-Saëns a clean precision and a finesse which mark it the work of a Frenchman. And one reason to remember Saint-Saëns is that he was, on occasion, a genuine humorist in music. His *Carnival of the Animals* is full of delightful touches. He describes in tone many of the animals of the zoo, including among them "Pianists." It is from the *Carnival of the Animals* that we get the lovely melody, "The Swan," for which Saint-Saëns is so well known.

Saint-Saëns loved to describe things in music and thus contributed importantly to "program music." His *Danse Macabre* (Ma-kahb'), with Death tuning his weird fiddle, is a good example of the de-

116

scriptive powers of this composer, and this skill is further illustrated in *The Spinning Wheel of Omphale* (Ahm-fahl'eh) and *Phaeton* (Fay'eh-ton). Saint-Saëns also wrote much "pure" music — not concerned with descriptive or emotional ideas, but music for its own sake — such as his symphonies and his numerous concertos for violin, piano, or cello.

Jules Massenet (Mahss'en-nay') (1842-1912) like other nineteenth century French composers, except Saint-Saëns, thought largely in terms of the opera, although he also produced numerous suites for orchestra. That he knew and loved the traditional music of France is revealed in much of his work which has the characteristics of French folk music. Many of his operas were successful in his time, and *Manon* (Mah-nohn) is still a favorite with opera-goers. Some of his operas are now remembered for perhaps one outstanding tune. From *Thaïs* (Tah-ees) came the lovely melody known as "Meditation," much played by violinists, while baritones everywhere like to sing "Vision Fugitive" from Massenet's *Hérodiade* (Ay-rohd'i-ahd).

France has given the world an important share of its best operas, and it has contributed importantly to another phase of music — the music for organ. For several centuries the French have given much attention to the organ, in their churches, and as a concert instrument. Many of the world's great organists were born in France. Alexandre Guilmant (Gheel'mahn), Charles Marie Widor (Vee'dor), Joseph Bonnet (Bahn-nay), and Louis Vierne (Vee-ern) are a few of the men who have made French organ playing and French organ music highly regarded throughout the world. Still others are Marcel Dupré (Du-pray), active today in France and the United States as recitalist and teacher, and César Franck (Frahnk), greatest of them all as a composer.

Born in Belgium, César Franck (1822-1890) was taken to Paris when very young. His father intended him to be a concert pianist, but the glamour of the concert hall was not for César Franck. His sincere, unassuming character was almost unworldly and it shines in his music, which has a nobility about it, without the faintest touch of showiness or theatricalism. It was a style well suited to the organ and to sacred music. And it was in church music that Franck excelled, although his one symphony (in D Minor) is regarded as a masterpiece. The Frenchmen of his own time heaped scorn upon his symphony, for Franck did not have the adulation that was given in his time to Gounod, Saint-Saëns, and the others. His operas were never even produced, but now he has come to be recognized in France and elsewhere as a truly great musician.

Franck's life was an example of unselfishness and of sacrifice to

117

attain ideals. He arose at five o'clock in the morning in order to have an hour or two for composing before his busy round of teaching. His time for composing was so limited that most of his best works were not written until after he was fifty, and his symphony was written when he was sixty-four. His symphony, like all his works, owes some of its beauty to the constantly changing tone colors resulting from its shifting harmonies. He was also fond of the device known as "canon" in which a second voice or instrument repeats, note for note, a tune which has been announced by the first voice or instrument. An example often heard is his *Panis Angelicus* (O Lord Most Holy). The same thing happens when we sing rounds such as *Three Blind Mice* or *Row, Row, Row Your Boat*.

César Franck deserves distinction as one of the world's greatest music teachers. His pupils revered him, and for good cause, for he gave himself untiringly in their behalf. Among those who owed much to Franck were Emmanuel Chabrier (Shah'bree-eh), composer of the orchestral rhapsody, *España* (Es-pahn'ya), Ernest Chausson (Show-son), Vincent D'Indy (Dan-dee) and Gabriel Pierne (Pyer-nay).

In the late nineteenth century France produced two composers who are remarkable for their fertility of imagination and their capacity to extend the descriptive and expressive power of music. Claude Debussy's father planned that his son would become a sailor, perhaps an admiral, but the son's love for music early asserted itself and a musical career was not to be denied. The young Claude did love the sea, however, and wrote wonderful music about it, even though his longest voyage was across the English Channel. Many of his compositions were inspired by nature: *The Sea, Clouds, Moonlight* (Clair de Lune), *Gardens in the Rain,* and *The Afternoon of a Faun.* These compositions evoked the atmosphere of their subjects, rather than always being directly descriptive, and Debussy came to be known as a musical "impressionist," with a feeling in his music somewhat similar to that noted in the paintings of such French artists as Monet (Mo-nay) and Renoir (Ray-nwahr).

As a student, Debussy (1862-1918) was the despair of his teachers because he would not follow the rules. He was always hearing, and writing, new chords which did not follow the established precepts of conventional harmony. Some of them resulted from his use of the whole-tone scale (C-D-E-F sharp-G sharp-A sharp-C). These revolutionary ideas made the music of Debussy different from that of anyone else. Debussy never forgot that he was a Frenchman, however, and often demonstrated, in the turn of a musical phrase, his love for the early music of France. He signed his name "Musicien Français."

His orchestral pieces, *La Mer* (The Sea), *The Afternoon of a*

118

Faun, Iberia, and *Festivals* are often played today, and he is also highly regarded for his one string quartet and his opera, *Pelleas und Melisande.* As might be expected, this opera is altogether unlike other French operas. Its orchestra is always mysterious and other-worldly and its singers chant a form of song-speech instead of singing in the usual operatic style. Debussy is also remembered for a delightful set of children's piano pieces, *The Children's Corner,* written for his little daughter.

Maurice Ravel (1875-1937) had some elements in common with Debussy. The teachers frowned on him, and he was never able to win the Prix de Rome, which all talented French composers were expected to win. Debussy finally won it on his fourth attempt — with a work in which he took no great pride. Like Debussy, Maurice Ravel explored the descriptive possibilities of music in such works as *Jeux d'Eau* (Zhoo-doh') (The Fountain), a celebrated piano piece. Unlike Debussy, Ravel chose to preserve in his music some of the classic elements of French music. An example is *Le Tombeau de Couperin* (At the Tomb of Couperin) in which he pays tribute to the eighteenth century French composer. Ravel was an innovator, but his explorations were more in the direction of finding new tonal resources in the orchestra than in new harmonic combinations. On a commission from Serge Diaghileff (Dee-ahg'ee-leff), the celebrated choreographer (ballet director), Ravel composed the ballet *Daphnis and Chloe.* Two suites for orchestra, taken from this ballet, are much played by symphony orchestras and are regarded as models of orchestration. Also immensely popular is the *Bolero,* written as a ballet for Ida Rubinstein. This work and others, such as *Rapsodie Espagnole* and the *Mother Goose Suite,* have won the admiration of musicians the world over as examples of the skillful use of the orchestra.

The list of French composers of the nineteenth and twentieth centuries is a long one. Paul Dukas (Doo-kass) (1865-1935) won renown with the celebrated descriptive piece for orchestra, *The Sorcerer's Apprentice.* Gabriel Fauré (Foh-ray') (1895-1924), one of Ravel's teachers, wrote much beautiful music in various forms, and his *Requiem* has been widely performed by choral groups. Jacques Ibert (Ee-bair), Arthur Honegger (Ohn'egger), Darius Milhaud (Mee-yoh), Francis Poulenc (Poo-lank), and Jean Francaix (Frahn-say) are French composers actively at work today. Honegger is remembered for his noisy *Pacific 231,* an orchestral picture of a steam engine, but he is also esteemed as the more serious composer of such large works for chorus and orchestra as *King David* and *Joan of Arc at the Stake.* Milhaud has lived in California for some years, where he teaches at Mills College. He has written a great variety of music,

119

in many forms, and frequently uses folk music. In various compositions he has employed the folk music of France, Brazil, and, recently, of Kentucky.

We owe to France some of the most distinguished musical interpreters of the present day: Lily Pons, born in Cannes, France, has won fame in opera and radio; Robert Casadesus (Cahs'a-day-soo') ranks among the foremost pianists of the day, and Alfred Cortot (Cortoh) is recalled as a brilliant pianist by many concert-goers. Pierre Monteux (Mohn-tyoo'), born in Paris in 1875, is a beloved figure among orchestra conductors in America. He conducted the Boston Symphony Orchestra for several years, and from 1935 to 1952 was conductor of the San Francisco Symphony Orchestra. The present conductor of the Boston Symphony Orchestra, Charles Munch, is likewise a native of France. One of the great music teachers of our time, Nadia Boulanger (Boo-lanh-zheh) is a Frenchwoman. She has been a source of help and inspiration to numerous Americans, among them Aaron Copland, Virgil Thomson, and Roy Harris.

The story of what France has meant to music extends beyond the accomplishments of the composers and performing musicians native to France. France provided leadership in the development of the opera and the ballet and its church musicians figure prominently in the history of the organ and its music. The concert halls and conservatories of France have played a most important part in the careers of many musicians who were not French.

Paris, noted for many things, is a distinguished musical city because of the opportunities it has given to creative and performing musicians to obtain recognition. Composers from the time of Lully, at the court of Louis XIV, to Stravinsky of our own time have built their reputations in at least some degree upon Paris performances of their works.

Music students from all over the world have found inspiration and instruction in the music schools of France. Most celebrated of all these schools is The Paris Conservatory of Music, founded in 1795. This school has included many fine musicians among its directors and teachers. Their contributions in the form of teaching materials have been noteworthy. The American boy or girl who practices Arban studies for the cornet, Klose studies for the clarinet or Kreutzer etudes for the violin is learning from material prepared by teachers at the Paris Conservatory.

France was one of the first countries to develop the idea of scholarships for talented young musicians. Since 1803 the "Prix (Pree) de Rome" has been awarded each year to the best student of composition

120

at the Paris Conservatory. The winners, among whom have been Berlioz, Gounod, Bizet, and Debussy, continue their studies at government expense — partly in France and partly in Rome.

QUESTIONS

1. Tell something about French music in the very early days.
2. Who were the troubadors?
3. What was the general nature of the songs that were sung by troubadors, jongleurs, and minstrels?
4. What influence did the Crusades have on French music?
5. Compare the folk music of the different provinces.
6. Tell something concerning the origin of "caroling" as we know it today.
7. What was the most important contribution that Lully made to French music?
8. What French composer gave special attention to the possibilities of wood winds?
9. What is meant by "program music"?
10. What dances were in favor during the reign of Louis XIV and what influences fostered these court dances?
11. What generally characterized the French grand opera of a hundred years ago?
12. Tell something of interest concerning Berlioz.
13. Who wrote the opera *Carmen*?
14. What famous French composer visited the United States?
15. What effect did Saint-Saëns' travels have upon his music?
16. Name a well-known suite that he wrote which is humorous and at the same time beautiful.
17. Name one famous opera written by Massenet.
18. Tell something of interest concerning César Franck.
19. Can you play the whole-tone scale on the piano?
20. What were some of Claude Debussy's compositions that were inspired by his love of nature?
21. What is meant when we speak of many of Debussy's compositions as being "impressionistic"?
22. Why was Debussy the despair of his teachers?
23. Name a well known composition by Ravel.
24. What characteristics did Ravel and Debussy have in common and in what ways were they different?
25. Name two famous twentieth-century composers of France.

LISTENING SUGGESTIONS

Agnus Dei — Bizet
"Bacchanale" from *Samson and Delilah* — Saint-Saëns
Bolero — Ravel
Carmen — Bizet (any part)
Carnival of the Animals — Saint-Saëns
Children's Corner, The — Debussy
Clair de Lune — Debussy
Clouds — Debussy
Danse Macabre — Saint-Saëns
Daphnis and Chloe Suite No. 2 — Ravel
Elegie — Massenet
España — Chabrier
Faust — Gounod (any part)
Festivals (Fêtes) — Debussy
Fountain, The — Ravel
Funeral March of a Marionette — Gounod
La Valse — Ravel
L'Arlesienne Suites — Bizet
March of the Little Lead Soldiers — Pierne

Mass in G — Poulenc
"Meditation" from *Thaïs* — Massenet
Mother Goose Suite — Ravel
"My Heart at Thy Sweet Voice" from *Samson and Delilah*—Saint-Saëns
Panis Angelicus — Franck
Prelude to *The Afternoon of a Faun* — Debussy
Rapsodie Espagnole — Ravel
Roman Carnival Overture — Berlioz
"Sanctus" from *St. Cecilia Mass* — Gounod
Sea, The (La Mer) — Debussy
Sorcerer's Apprentice, The — Dukas
Spinning Wheel of Omphale, The — Saint-Saëns
Suite Francaise — Milhaud
Symphonie Fantastique — Berlioz
Symphony in D Minor — Franck
"Vision Fugitive" from *Herodiade* — Massenet
"Waltz Song" from *Romeo and Juliet* — Gounod

Marianina

DAVID STEVENS   Italian Popular Tune

Where the Tus-can sun is warm and bright, Dwells a

maid whose laugh is pure de - light; Tho' her charm is

yet un - known to fame, Still I love her just the same.

Ma-ri-a - ni-na, tra la la. Ma-ri-a - ni-na, tra la la!

REFRAIN
f rit.   *a tempo*

O Ma - ria - ni - na!
O Ma - ria - ni - na!

O Ma - ria - ni - na!
O Ma - ria - ni - na!

The wild red rose Was nev - er half so fair.
My Tus - can belle With pop-pies in her häir!

⚜ 12 ⚜

ITALY

ITALY HAS LONG BEEN considered one of the most musical countries of the world. Travelers remember it as a land of sunshine, flowers, and beautiful lakes, with gay gondoliers singing on the canals of Venice and picturesque boatmen and fishermen on the Bay of Naples. It is a country of singers where the art of beautiful singing has been developed in all of its phases.

In such a country it is natural that there should be folk songs of unusual beauty. The Italian people are never happier than when singing and accompanying themselves on the guitar or mandolin. Most of the music is gay and bright, but some is slow and tinged with sorrow. Some of the oldest folk tunes in the world come from northern Italy, and they have inspired many famous composers. The songs differ in various parts of the country, for each section has an expression all of its own. A few most frequently heard throughout Italy are *Tiritomba, Marianina, Santa Lucia, Funiculi Funicula,* and *O Sole Mio.* It is interesting to note that several of these are in reality composed songs, but they have come to be regarded as true folk songs by the people.

There are many folk dances, the most dramatic of them being the *tarantella.* The name was probably derived from the Taranto River in southern Italy. In olden times it was thought that a person who had been bitten by the "tarantula" spider could be cured by dancing this dance until he dropped exhausted. The dance is usually in 6/8 time, starting at a moderate rate of speed and becoming faster and faster until the end. Many composers have made use of this dance form in their compositions, and we hear excellent Tarantellas by Liszt, Heller, Chopin, and others. Other dances that should be mentioned are the *Siciliano* from Sicily and the *pavan,* a slow dance from Padua that was usually followed by a rapid dance called the *saltarello.*

Because schools of music have flourished there since early times, most of Italy's folk music has been absorbed into its composed music and operas. Popular music, as it is whistled or sung on the streets, often includes favorite tunes from the operas. It is said that in Venice special seats in the gallery of the opera house are reserved for the gondoliers in order that they may learn the tunes to sing as they ply their boats on the canals.

Those who have visited Naples have observed the fruit vendor with his cart full of fruit coming down the street, singing at the top of his voice one of the great arias of an opera. He had probably heard it the night before at the magnificent San Carlo Opera House. Or one might be pleasantly awakened by the singing of a familiar aria beneath one's window, and, upon looking out, find it to be the voice of a laborer working on the building. It is in Naples, the "City of Song," that the world-renowned tenor Enrico Caruso (Kah-roo'soh) was born. He is buried there in a beautiful mausoleum on the outskirts of the city.

Several other Italian cities are famous for their unusual contributions to music. From Milan came Ambrose, Bishop of Milan, who in the fourth century collected the old chants and became famous for the Ambrosian Chant named after him. Pope Gregory I later substituted his own system of Plain song, called Gregorian Chant, which is in use today. Milan has other claims to fame with her wonderful cathedral and the beautiful La Scala Opera House, considered by many to be the most famous opera house in the world.

Palestrina and Church Music

Rome, the "Eternal City," has long been associated with the history of the Christian Church and the development of sacred music. Choirs were formed in the ancient churches of Rome as long ago as the time of St. Sylvester, who was Pope during the years from 314 to 335. The famous Sistine Choir was established by Pope Sixtus IV, who built the Sistine Chapel in 1471-84. One of the most celebrated members of this choir was a man who is said to have had a poor voice, but who gained membership because of other musical abilities, particularly his gift for composition. This composer was named Giovanni Pierluigi (Pee-air-loo-ee'gee). In English his name would be John Peter Louis. Ever since his own time, however, he has been known simply by the name of his birthplace, Palestrina (Pahl-estree'na).

Born in 1524 or 1525, Palestrina was sent to Rome as a boy to study music, probably through the influence of a cardinal of the Church who was then Bishop of Palestrina. The young Palestrina became chorister and director in such famous churches as Santa Maria Maggiore and St. John Lateran. He sang in the Pontifical (Sistine) Choir, and Pope Sixtus V eventually made Palestrina "Composer to the Pontifical Chapel."

As a member of the Sistine Choir, Palestrina had listened, with

125

the other members, to a severe reprimand from Pope Marcellus II, who was greatly displeased with the choir and the church music of the time. The choirs then often introduced street songs into the highly elaborate Masses and the music had become so complex that no one could distinguish the words. Palestrina heeded the Pope's admonition and wrote numerous Masses in a simpler and more worshipful style. One of them is still known as the "Pope Marcellus Mass." However, since this Pope held his office but twenty-three days, it does not seem likely that he commissioned Palestrina to write the Mass, as was long popularly believed.

Palestrina produced hundreds of Masses, motets, and madrigals, and published many of them himself, for in his time composers had to do their own publishing. His marriage, late in life, to a wealthy widow helped to make these publications possible. His music is still considered to be among the finest examples of church music. He had a gift for beautiful but simple choral expression, as in his *O Bone Jesu*, and, in a time when church music had become worldly and highly technical, his impresses us with an ethereal beauty.

Italy continued to hold a distinguished position in music throughout the sixteenth, seventeenth and eighteenth centuries. In Venice, in the celebrated St. Mark's Church, Andrea and Giovanni Gabrieli (Gahb-ree-ail'ee) did interesting things with music. Their church music was often written for voices and instruments and more use was made of the organ than in Rome. St. Mark's had, in fact, two organs and two choirs, resulting in a development of the musical style we know as "antiphonal," which means two or more groups singing or playing alternately.

Italians are interested in many kinds of music, and other chapters in this book relate the importance of Italy in the development of the violin and the piano. Two composers who did much to win early fame for Italy in instrumental music were Arcangelo Corelli (1653-1713) and Antonio Vivaldi (1675-1743). Corelli wrote much for the violin and the string orchestra and played and conducted many concerts. He seems to have been more fortunate than most musicians of his time, for he left a large estate, including a valuable art collection.

Vivaldi was known as the "red-haired priest." A Venetian, he became a skilled violinist and composer. Some of his works were highly regarded by Bach, who rearranged them for keyboard instruments. Vivaldi, who took holy orders, spent the last thirty years of his life as director of the Ospedale della Pieta (hospital of the Pieta), a school-hospital where music was given much attention.

Venice had four of these interesting schools which had been

126

founded originally as hospitals to which each year a certain number of girls from poor families were admitted to become nurses. They were instructed in music, and eventually these institutions became conservatories or schools of music. Visitors to Venice in the eighteenth century wrote enthusiastically of the music heard at these schools, and it seems likely that some of the best orchestras of that time were groups of Italian girls of high school age.

Thus Italy long ago provided a forerunner for our high school orchestras, and at the same time pointed out a connection between music and healing — a relationship now emphasized in our country in the attention given to musical therapy, or the use of music in hospitals.

ITALIAN OPERA

Italy was the birthplace of opera, and three cities figured in its beginnings. Mantua, in Northern Italy, probably saw the first attempt at opera in a presentation of *Orfeo* (Or-fay'o), a play with music by Angelo Poliziano (Poh-leet-see-ah'no), produced a few years before Columbus discovered America. The first true opera, as we know the form, was privately presented in Florence in 1597. It was *Dafne*, by Jacopo Peri (Yahk'o-po Pay'ree). In 1600 the same composer's *Euridice* was the first opera to receive public performance.

Peri was a member of a band of music-lovers, known as the "Camerata," who met at the house of Count Giovanni Bardi. Present-day listeners who refer to opera as "long-haired" music may be interested to know that Peri's nickname was "Il Zazzerino" (The Long-Haired). The Florentines who met at Count Bardi's house were interested in reviving the ancient Greek drama, but their activities resulted in the new art-form, the opera. Besides Peri there were in the group two other noted musicians of the time, Giulio Caccini (Jeeool'yo Kah-chee'nee), a composer and singing teacher, and Vincenzo Galilei (Gah-lee-lay'ee), composer, lute-player, and father of the famous astronomer, Galileo.

Venice was the third of the Italian cities which gave opera its start. To this city goes the distinction of building the first opera house for public performance. This was in 1637, and in the following sixty years Venice is said to have built no less than sixteen theatres for opera, indicating the extent to which Venetians were interested in opera.

The man who probably had the most to do with building the first opera house was Claudio Monteverdi (Mohn-tay-vair'dee) (1567-1643). Born in Cremona, town of the famous violinmakers, Monteverdi spent his early years at the Court of Mantua and the latter part of his life in Venice. For his first opera, Monteverdi also turned to the

127

subject of Orfeo. It was presented in Mantua in 1607 and is important in that it was the first opera to use a complete orchestra rather than a few instruments to accompany the voices. Monteverdi's *Orfeo* was recently presented at the Metropolitan Opera in New York with a modernized orchestration.

Monteverdi was the most famous composer of his time, and musicians from Germany, England, and other countries came to Venice to study with him. His imagination did much to expand and develop the resources of the orchestra, and he was also a distinguished composer of madrigals.

Naples soon began to take an interest in opera, and the Neapolitan style developed. It was to have an effect on opera in all of Italy, and the most important early figure in Naples was Alessandro Scarlatti (1659-1725). He was instrumental in setting the style of the "aria," an important type of solo song in the Italian opera. He was a prolific composer, who is said to have written 115 operas. They were, however, simpler and shorter than the operas of the nineteenth century. Scarlatti also wrote hundreds of pieces for solo voice, as well as much music for church use and for instruments. His son, Domenico Scarlatti, was a famous harpsichord player and was one of the first composers to write for the piano.

In more recent times Italian composers have continued to give us operas that seem to be everlasting. Italian ideas of opera prevailed throughout the eighteenth century, and Handel and Mozart were influenced by them. In the nineteenth century Gioacchino Rossini (Gee-ah-kee'no Ros-see'nee) (1792-1868) enriched the operatic stage with forty operas, all written between the ages of eighteen and thirty-eight. These works included the sparkling *The Barber of Seville* with which the fun-loving Rossini has amused many audiences, and the more serious *William Tell*, known to us all for its often-played Overture. The operas of Rossini contain many fine melodies, not always his own, for he sometimes borrowed from Haydn, Mozart, and Beethoven. They also contained the showy arias which were demanded by the prima donnas of Rossini's time.

After *William Tell* Rossini ceased to compose operas and wrote little except for two sacred works, the *Stabat Mater* and a Mass. He had earned a fortune from his operas, which were performed in all the leading opera-houses, such as the Paris Opera, the San Carlo in Naples, and La Scala in Milan. During the last half of his seventy-six years, Rossini was a gentleman of leisure. He loved food and luxurious living and prided himself upon his ability as a cook. He was accused of laziness, but it is probable that the political disturbances in Italy and France, combined with frequent ill health, had much to do with

128

the cessation of his activities. He was very nervous, and it is related that after one ride on the newly invented railroad train he refused ever after to repeat the experience. At his funeral in Paris, part of the music was provided by an ensemble of saxophones, a fitting requiem, perhaps, for a convivial soul.

Rossini overshadowed the numerous other Italian opera composers of his time. Some of them, however, also produced notable operas, such as *Lucia di Lammermoor,* based on an historical novel by Sir Walter Scott and composed by Gaetano Donizetti (Dohn-ee-tzet'ee) (1797-1848). Another nineteenth century favorite was the opera, *Norma,* the work of Vincenzo Bellini (Bel-lee'nee) (1801-1835).

The culmination of the Italian operatic art was reached in the work of Giuseppe Verdi (Vair'dee) (1813-1901), who has given us the greatest number of enduring operas. In contrast to the easy-going Rossini, Verdi was a serious-minded composer whose talent and integrity were such that he wrought much improvement in Italian opera. His works, as his life progressed, had less of the artificial display and more of sound musical merit, so that Verdi did much to improve the taste of opera-going audiences. Always of serious mien, Verdi became even more so after suffering the loss of his wife and two children within a few months. Still under thirty years of age, Verdi vowed to give up music, and opera-lovers may be indebted to Merelli, the manager of La Scala Opera who helped to convince the composer that he should continue with his work.

Music-lovers are well acquainted with the earlier operas of Verdi, especially *Il Trovatore* (Troh-vah-tohr'eh), *La Traviata* (Trah-vee-ah'tah) and *Rigoletto* (Ree-go-let'to). The "Anvil Chorus" and the Tower Scene from *Trovatore* and "Caro Nome" and the famous "Quartet" from *Rigoletto* are known to many people who may never have seen an opera. These operas brought fame and fortune to their composer, but he chose, in preference to the excitements of Rome, Milan, or Naples, the quiet life of the country. He loved his farm at Busseto (Boo-say'to) where he gave much attention to raising horses and dogs.

When he had made up his mind to retire from opera, Verdi was requested by the Khedive of Egypt to compose an opera with an Egyptian setting to celebrate the opening of the Suez Canal. After some deliberation, Verdi consented and wrote *Aida,* (Ah-ee'da) conceded by many to be his most dramatic work, and an opera which impresses with its pageantry as well as its music.

Three years later Verdi wrote the celebrated *Requiem Mass* composed in honor of his friend, the writer Manzoni. He then expected to retire, but another writer, Arrigo Boito (Boh-ee'to) persuaded

Verdi to further effort by offering him two librettos, *Othello* and *Falstaff*, both based on the plays of Shakespeare. They appealed to Verdi, who proved that musical ability may last into old age, since *Othello* was completed when he was seventy-four and *Falstaff* when he was nearly eighty. Musicians consider these his greatest works, although they are by no means as well known as his earlier operas.

Verdi was strong-minded in politics as well as in art. In his early life Italy was not a unified country and much of what is now Italy was controlled by Austria. Verdi, a great patriot, was frequently in trouble with the authorities, for his earlier operas sometimes contained thinly disguised political implications. The scene of his opera, *The Masked Ball*, was laid originally in Naples, but to satisfy the censors it was rewritten with the scene in Boston. When Italy became independent, Verdi was honored by election as a deputy in the first parliament, and somewhat later he was made a senator, thus giving further service to the country he had so well served in a musical way.

Next to Verdi, the more recent Giacomo Puccini (Jahk'o-mo Poo-chee'nee) (1858-1924) is probably the most popular of all Italian composers of opera. He came of a long line of musicians, but unlike his ancestors who were mainly church musicians, Puccini turned to the stage. Like Verdi he was not only musically gifted but also had a fine sense of stage-craft. After a couple of early failures, Puccini achieved success and is reputed to have become a millionaire through the success of such operas as *La Bohème* (Bo-aym'), *Tosca*, and *Madama Butterfly*. *La Bohème*, a story of struggling young artists and musicians, may have appealed to Puccini because of his own hardships as a student in Milan. The conductor of the first performance of *La Bohème* was Arturo Toscanini, who has made much musical history in America. Puccini himself was much interested in America and based his operas *Madama Butterfly* and *The Girl of the Golden West* on American plays.

Two short operas that have brought fame to their composers are *Cavalleria Rusticana* (Kah-vahl-leh-ree'ah Roos-tee-kahn'ha) by Pietro Mascagni (Mas-kahn'yee) (1863-1945) and *I Pagliacci* (Ee-Pahl-yat'chee) by Ruggiero Leoncavallo (Lay-ohn-kah-vahl'low) (1858-1919). Perhaps the most famous excerpts from these two operas are the "Intermezzo," of the former, and the "Prologue" of the latter. Often these operas are given on the same program, for, together, they equal the time of the usual grand opera.

The gifted Ermanno Wolf-Ferrari (Vohlf-Fair-ah'ree) (1876-1948) should not be forgotten. Several of his operas have met with success in both the United States and Europe. *The Jewels of the Madonna* is extremely interesting because of the many Neapolitan folk melodies used throughout the opera. Other modern Italian composers have produced operas which conform to the high ideals of the older composers.

Among the many Italian-born singers who have attained world fame are the soprano Amelita Galli-Curci (Gal-lee Koor'chee), and tenors Beniamino Gigli (Jeel-ye), Giovanni Martinelli, Tito Schipa (Skee' pah), and Ferrucio Tagliavini (Tahl-yah-vee'nee) and the bassos Virgilio Lazzari (Laht-zah'ree) and Ezio Pinza (Peen'zah). Italy has also given us one of the great musical interpreters of all times in the conductor, Arturo Toscanini. Known to millions through recordings and radio, Toscanini's remarkable vitality has enabled him to continue his active career until well into the ninth decade of his life. He was born in 1867 and made his debut as a conductor in Rio de Janeiro when only nineteen. He came to the Metropolitan Opera in New York in 1908 and in 1927 was made conductor of the New York Philharmonic Symphony. In more recent years he has been conductor of the NBC Symphony, and now, through television, thousands of music-lovers have had the privilege of seeing Toscanini conduct.

Among the violinists of Italy and, perhaps, the world, the name of Niccolo Paganini (Pah-gah-nee'nee) (1782-1840) is the most outstanding. He was born in the town of Genoa, Italy, a northern seaport on the Mediterranean, and as a child showed his great talent for music. He was an erratic person but a wizard with the violin. He devised new ways of tuning the violin and invented unusual harmonies. It is said that no one could equal his playing of double stops, harmonics, and pizzicato (plucked strings). He did not compose a large number of works, but his compositions were difficult to play and his playing of them was so flawless that no contemporary violinist would attempt them. Our violinists of today, however, are not afraid of their technical difficulties, and his works are performed by the great artists and attempted by those of lesser note. His *Moto Perpetuo* (Perpetual Motion) which is played from beginning to end without lifting the bow from the strings is a famous exhibition number for violinists.

There is a modern school of instrumental music in Italy and of the several names associated with it, that of Ottorino Respighi (Respee'ghee) (1879-1936) is probably the best known. His symphonic compositions, *The Pines of Rome* and *The Fountains of Rome,* demonstrate his ability as a composer. He also wrote several operas, including *The Sunken Bell.* Francesco Malipiero (Mahl-ee-peeay'roh), Alfredo Casella and Mario Castelnuovo-Tedesco (Cas-telnoo-oh'voh-Tay-des'ko), are other twentieth century composers who have continued the fine traditions of Italian music.

131

QUESTIONS

1. What should the name Italy suggest to our minds?
2. Name several folk songs of Italy.
3. What Italian dance was supposed to have curative properties?
4. Of what does the popular music of Italy often consist?
5. How did Palestrina affect the course of church music?
6. What Italian composers wrote extensively for the violin?
7. Discuss the music schools of Venice and show how they anticipated two musical trends of today.
8. What three cities contributed to the beginnings of opera?
9. Where was the first opera-house built and what great composer was associated with it?
10. To what composer is opera in Naples indebted?
11. Why do you think Rossini quit composing operas?
12. How did Rossini and Verdi differ in temperament and musical output?
13. How did Italy honor Verdi?
14. Name three of Verdi's most popular operas.
15. Which of Verdi's operas are considered his finest?
16. How did America influence the work of Puccini?
17. Which two operas are often given on the same program?
18. Tell something of Italy's greatest conductor.
19. Why was Paganini famous?
20. What recent Italian composer produced important works for the orchestra?

LISTENING SUGGESTIONS

Anvil Chorus (*Il Trovatore*) — Verdi
Ave Maria (*Othello*) — Verdi
Caro Nome (*Rigoletto*) — Verdi
Celeste Aïda (*Aida*) — Verdi
Christmas Concerto — Corelli
Any Concerto Grosso by Vivaldi
Credo (*Othello*) — Verdi
Dance of the Camorrists (*Jewels of the Madonna*) — Wolf-Ferrari
Di Provenza il Mar (*La Traviata*) — Verdi
Fountains of Rome, The — Respighi
Funiculi Funicula — Folk
Grand March (*Aida*) — Verdi
Intermezzo (*Cavalleria Rusticana*) — Mascagni
La Donna é Mobile (*Rigoletto*) — Verdi
Largo al Factotum (*Barber of Seville*) — Rossini

Any Mass — Palestrina
Miserere (*Il Trovatore*) — Verdi
Musetta's Waltz Song (*La Bohème*) — Puccini
O Bone Jesu — Palestrina
O Sole Mio — Di Capua
One Fine Day (*Madama Butterfly*) — Puccini
Overture to *The Barber of Seville* — Rossini
Overture to *William Tell* — Rossini
Pines of Rome, The — Resphighi
Prologue (*I Pagliacci*)—Leoncavallo
Quartet (*Rigoletto*) — Verdi
Requiem — Verdi
Santa Lucia — Folk
Sextette (*Lucia di Lammermoor*) — Donizetti
Sicut Cervus — Palestrina
Stabat Mater (any part) — Rossini
Vissi D'Arte (*Tosca*) — Puccini

132

Minka

J. LILIAN VANDEVERE   Russian Tune

Andante

Min-ka's eyes are sad and tear - y, She must work al -

tho' she's wea-ry. Life it seems, is rath - er drear-y,

Life is sad for Min - ka.

accelerando

Bal - a - lai - kas, gai - ly cry - ing, Set her lag-ging

presto

feet to fly - ing. Danc - ing leaves no time for sigh - ing.

Life is glad for Min - ka.

❧ 13 ❧

RUSSIA

THE MUSIC OF RUSSIA comes to us with a fascination and a strange-
ness that makes us immediately wish to know why these melodies
and harmonies seem so different. The only way to answer our query
is to consider Russia and her people, for an oft-repeated saying is, "As
the people, so their music."

Russia is a vast land nearly three times as large as the United States.
Throughout such an immense territory the climate and geography
vary widely. We might compare it to the contrasts experienced in
going from the Gulf of Mexico, through the United States and Canada,
to the Arctic Ocean. The summer heat extends far northward and
the winter cold far southward.

Before World War I, over four-fifths of the population were
peasants. They had been slaves and serfs, usually unable to read or
write. The Russian peasant had experienced war, revolution, famine,
and continual poverty. Is it any wonder that his songs were sad and
favored the minor modes? Music was his one great comfort in time of
sorrow, and when work became too hard the Russian moujik (moo-
zheek') would sing in his need and sorrow. In a verse of the folk song
called *The Little Cudgel*, a work song of Russia, this idea is expressed. Translated from the Russian, it is as follows:

> *Oh, the English are wise to help labor along,*
> *From water and fire they borrow;*
> *But our Russian moujik, when his work is too hard*
> *Will intone in his need and his sorrow.*

The Russian child had a song for everything: one to get him up in
the morning, one to call him to dinner, and even songs for the various
childhood diseases.

Like the child, the Russian peasant always expressed and idealized
all phases of his existence in song. There was music for every
occasion, whether a wedding, carnival, or the celebration of the
coming of spring. Of the many types of songs, love, war, and work

134

predominate as popular themes. Love is a chosen topic in any country, and war was a much experienced event in the lives of the Russians.

In the past, over eighty per cent of the population were engaged in agricultural pursuits, and we find many occupational songs that mention the sowing of the wheat, the changes of season, and the harvest. Other very popular work songs were sung by the men who pulled the boats up the Volga River. The *Song of the Volga Boatmen* gives us a vivid picture of the Russian serfs as they strained and struggled, singing the famous words "Ei-euck-nyem" (I-ookh-nyem) translated, "Pull, boys, pull." The great Russian bass, Feodor Chaliapin (Shal-yah'pin) often sang this song in his American concerts, for as a lad he was a boatman who helped to pull the barges on the river Volga. The Russians doubtless still love to sing about "Mother Volga" for there are many songs about this famous river. From December until spring, this great river, the longest in Europe, is frozen solid. In the old days it formed a continuous pathway for sledges.

The unique three-horse sleigh, called the *troika*, was often to be seen in the Russia of the past, and Tschaikowsky (Tchi-koff'skee) has given us in his composition *Troika* a wonderful picture of sleigh bells, galloping horses, and the cold white beauty of the frozen countryside. The steppes, cold bleak plains covering much of Russia, are in winter swept by blizzards in the north and terrific dust storms in the south. Their loneliness and vast emptiness have been the inspiration for many poems and songs. Alexandre Gretchaninoff (Gretch-ahn'en-off) has immortalized them in his lovely song called *Over the Steppe*.

In other parts of Russia there are dense, black forests and the country people of the past saw in these forests the creatures of their imagination. Greatly to be feared was the witch, Baba Yaga. Songs were sung about her, and on many a winter evening the peasants gathered round the fire to hear a good story-teller describe her adventures and those of her three messengers, the black, the white, and the red horsemen. These strange tales inspired Anatol Liadow (Lyah'doff) to write his composition entitled *Baba Yaga*. Many other legendary tales were enjoyed by the Russians — tales of giants and god-like heroes. Reinhold Gliere (Glee-air') (1875-   ) immortalized one of these stories in his *Ilya Murometz*, and Alexandre Glazounoff (Glaht'zoo-noff) (1865-1936) and others have told in tone the story of Stenka Razin.

Where the winters were cold and dark, the Russian peasant had to spend much time indoors. His home was solidly built and usually contained a living room heated by a huge pottery stove. At night members of the family would spread their beds on top of this stove.

135

Neighbors and friends often gathered in one of the homes and the long evenings were made pleasant by story-telling, singing, and dancing. The singing was accompanied by one of the many stringed instruments popular in Russia. Perhaps the "balalaika" (bal-lah-ly'kah) should be mentioned first, as it was, and still is, a favorite instrument. The balalaika is triangular in shape and has three or four strings. Balalaikas are made in various sizes, ranging from small ones played like guitars to those about the size of the bass viol, which are held and played like a string bass. The last czar was very fond of this instrument and had his own orchestra, "The Russian Imperial Balalaika Orchestra," which at one time visited the United States. The "gouslee" (goos'lee), another stringed instrument having thirteen to twenty-four strings, and the "bandoura," a sort of lute with many strings, have also been used by the peasants for accompaniment to their singing and dancing.

Russian folk dances are often fascinating in their wildness and seem almost savage in their gaiety, showing us that the Russian thoroughly enjoyed his good times. Especially is this true of the Cossack dances. The Cossacks were a warlike people, skillful as horsemen and were formerly part of the Russian cavalry. They presented a spectacular appearance with brilliant costumes, fur caps and red or black boots. Their dancing was always watched with breathless interest, for they well knew how to manage the most intricate steps. They would thrust their feet forward from a crouching position, then jump into the air with wild yells and down again with heels clicking and whips cracking. The *hopak* (go-pahk') was a popular Cossack dance and one which Moussorgsky (Moo-sorg'skee) has illustrated in his compositions of that name. The *trepak* (tray-pahk') was another dance, and we find a good example of it in Tschaikowsky's *Nutcracker Suite*. We should also mention the *kamarinskaya*, (kah-mah-rin-sky'yah), said to have been the national dance of Russia and originally danced only by men, as it was very wild and barbaric.

The Russian love for dancing also expressed itself in "ballad dances," accompanied by choral singing and called "chorvody." Sometimes they were danced by girls in gay costumes who would join hands and sing and dance in a circle. In the center of the circle stood one girl and she would take up the song after the group stopped singing. In other ballad dances a single couple would dance in the center of a circle of singers. The famous "Polovetzian Dances" in Borodin's opera, *Prince Igor*, follow the traditions of the ballad dance. Such dances were popular in the medieval courts of the Boyars (Russian noblemen), and it is from these dances that the Russians developed their celebrated ballet companies.

136

The Russian Ballet

The ballet is a spectacular dance used as a part of an opera or as an independent stage production. It tells a story through pantomime and dance movements. The Russians, before and since the 1917 Revolution, have been devoted to the ballet and their composers have given the world much fine ballet music. There are splendid ballet scenes in the nineteenth century operas of Rimsky-Korsakoff, (Rim'skee Kor'sa-koff), Moussorgsky, Glinka, Tschaikowsky, and others, and Russian composers have provided many independent ballets, the music of which is known throughout the listening world. The *Nutcracker Suite,* the *Swan Lake,* and the *Sleeping Beauty,* are three of Tschaikowsky's contributions to the ballet stage. From a more recent period have come the ballets of Igor Stravinsky (now living in Hollywood) and the music of *The Firebird, Petrouchka,* and other Stravinsky ballets, is often played in symphony orchestra concerts as well as in ballet performances.

The man who developed the ballet, and especially the Russian ballet, to a high point was Serge Diaghileff (Dee-ahg'ee-leff). Although Russian, he spent much time in Paris and Monte Carlo and organized his famous Russian Ballet in Paris in 1909. Diaghileff's troupe included such celebrated dancers as Nijinsky (Nee-zheen'skee) and Ida Rubinstein, and his activities gave opportunity to many of the foremost composers of the twentieth century. Ravel, de Falla, Prokofieff (Pro-koff'ee-eff), Stravinsky, Milhaud, and many others supplied music for the Diaghileff productions.

The Russian Revolution in 1917 changed many things in Russia but it did not affect the Russian fondness for ballet. Soviet composers give it much attention. Reinhold Gliere in 1927 produced the *Red Poppy* from which comes the popular "Sailor's Dance." Every radio-owner in America has probably heard "The Sabre Dance," from the ballet, *Gayne,* by Aram Khachaturian.

As in Spain and Hungary, we find in Russian folk and composed music the influence of the gypsy musicians. These strange wandering people have contributed importantly to the traditional music of Russia, and such haunting tunes as *Dark Eyes* have been played and sung the world over. Such gypsy songs, not always of Russian origin, have been immensely popular in Russia.

Before the Soviet regime Russian churches were distinguished for the beauty of their music, considered by many to be the loveliest in the world. Based on melodies and chants that are many centuries old, the music of the Russian Orthodox Church derives from the music of the Byzantine (later the Greek Orthodox) Church and from

Hebrew sources. Russian church music is traditionally sung *a cappella* (without instrumental accompaniment) for musical instruments were not allowed within the Russian churches. This music is rich, sonorous and colorful and is written for choirs which often use eight and sometimes as many as ten or twelve voice parts. Since Russia produces extremely low bass voices, it is very common to find the bass part "doubled" (sung an octave lower).

Russian Church music is important to young Americans who are interested in music and particularly to those who like to sing. There are few members of high school or college *a cappella* choirs who have not, at one time or another, sung the *Cherubim Song* by Dmitri Bortniansky. Bortniansky was the first of the Russian Church composers whose compositions are so highly regarded today. He was born in 1751 and conducted the Imperial Chapel Choir during the last years of the eighteenth century.

With the exception of Modest Moussorgsky, practically all Russian composers from the early nineteenth century to the time of the 1917 Revolution contributed to the Russian Church literature. Rimsky-Korsakoff, Tschaikowsky, Anton Arensky and others wrote anthems for the church service which are widely sung in American schools and churches, and they used church themes in their instrumental works. Rimsky-Korsakoff employed old church chants in his *Russian Easter Overture* and Arensky wrote a series of variations for string orchestra on the theme which Tschaikowsky used in his *Legend*. Alexandre Gretchaninoff, for many years a resident of the United States, has written much fine church music. Others whose anthems are often sung are Basil Kalinnikoff, Alexandre Kopyloff, Paul Tschesnokoff, and Sergei Rachmaninoff.

The music of Russian composers has always been closely linked to the story of their country. Napoleon's invasion of Russia and the burning of Moscow seemed to stimulate Russian musicians to a national consciousness. Tschaikowsky felt this patriotism when he wrote his *Overture 1812*, but before his time Russian composers had realized the importance of utilizing in their compositions the traditional folk music and legends of their country. It began with Michael Ivanovitch Glinka (1803-1857), the "father of Russian opera," whose operas *A Life for the Czar* and *Russlan and Ludmilla* brought him much fame.

THE RUSSIAN FIVE

From 1861 until the early years of our century, a group of five Russian composers worked valiantly for the cause of Russian music. They were headed by Mily Balakireff (Bah'lah-kee'reff) (1837-1910) who served Russian music nobly as composer, teacher, and conductor. Curiously enough, the four other members of this group were destined for careers apart from music, although all finally devoted their lives to the art. Nicholas Rimsky-Korsakoff (1844-1908) was a naval officer in early life, César Cui (1835-1918) was an army officer, and Modest Moussorgsky (1839-1881), after a brief army experience, became a civil servant. Alexander Borodin (1833-1887) was a physician and scientist who achieved recognition in the field of chemistry as well as that of music.

The "Five," as these composers came to be known, were always conscious of the folk music and folk tales of their native land, and their music is in a real sense the music of the Russian people. Borodin's famous opera, *Prince Igor*, depicts the long struggle between the Russian people and the Polovtsi, a nomadic people of the twelfth century. The themes in Borodin's symphonies and his *In the Steppes of Central Asia* are closely related to Russian folk music.

Modest Moussorgsky, even more than Borodin, based his music upon the folk music of the Russian people. In the "Coronation Scene" from his opera, *Boris Godunoff* (Go'duh-noff) one hears old church chants, and elsewhere in this opera and his *Khovantchina* (Ko-vahnt'chee-nah) are heard Russian folk songs. Both operas have to do with important phases of Russian history. Born in a rural area, Moussorgsky, throughout his life, kept close to the life of the people, and his songs and operas deal with the people he knew and their history. Among his songs appear such titles as *The Magpie, Gathering Mushrooms, The Ragamuffin, The Hobby-Horse,* and *The Cat and the Bird-Cage*.

Moussorgsky's music was not always polished; in fact, Rimsky-Korsakoff revised some of it, thinking to improve it. Now, however, many people prefer the original Moussorgsky, for they recognize him as a composer who spoke simply and directly about the world in which he lived. He might be called a "realistic" composer. He is interesting from another standpoint in that, although a bachelor, few composers have approached his understanding of children in the songs he wrote about them.

The music of César Cui (Kwee) did not last in favor to the same degree as that of the other four members of this group, but his compositions also contributed to the development of a Russian national music and his work as a writer and critic helped to make the music of Russia known to other countries. Best known of his compositions is the *Orientale*, with its eastern flavor which is characteristic of much Russian music.

Rimsky-Korsakoff's music also emphasizes Russia's nearness to the Orient. You have only to listen to his *Scheherezade* (Sheh-her-azah'deh) *Suite* to hear and feel this Oriental coloring. This composer believed that the Russian was an Oriental at heart, and his music, with its insistent rhythms, its chromatic scales and its fondness for the wood winds, especially the oboe and English horn, is peculiarly fitted to illustrate the stories of the East. These stories he told in such operas as *The Snow Maiden, Sadko, Mlada, Maid of Pskov,* and *Le Coq d'Or* (The Golden Cockerel).

In his autobiography Rimsky-Korsakoff relates that when, as a young man, he was appointed Inspector of Naval Bands, he procured all of the wind instruments and retired to his father's country home until he had learned to play all of them. That he studied them well is indicated by his mastery of orchestration (the use of the instruments in orchestral music). His *Spanish Capriccio, Scheherezade,* and *Russian Easter Overture* have long been admired as examples of how best to use the instruments of the orchestra. His book, *Principles of Orchestration,* has long stood as an authority on the subject.

As professor at the St. Petersburg Conservatory for more than thirty years Rimsky-Korsakoff helped to guide the careers of many other musicians. He helped his brother-composers by editing and orchestrating Moussorgsky's operas, *Khovantchina* and *Boris Godounoff,* and by completing and orchestrating, together with Alexander Glazounoff, Borodin's unfinished opera, *Prince Igor.*

PETER ILYITCH TSCHAIKOWSKY

While the Russian Five were developing their idea that folk song should be the basis of all music, another Russian composer was winning recognition. The music of Peter Ilyitch Tschaikowsky (1840-1893) was regarded by the Five as too eclectic (assembled from many sources) and not sufficiently Russian. The rest of the world, however, gave approval to Tschaikowsky's work, and today most Americans know his music much better than that of any other Russian. Tschaikowsky's melodies have, in fact, been listed on the Hit Parade, for the popular song writers and film producers have frequently appropriated his tunes. The moving picture *Carnegie Hall,* issued a few years ago, helped to popularize Tschaikowsky among American theatre audiences. In this film the scene where Tschaikowsky conducts the orchestra is based on fact, since the composer did visit this country shortly before his death and conducted concerts in New York, Baltimore, and Philadelphia.

No other Russian composer has been so much played in this country, and Tschaikowsky's Fourth, Fifth, and Sixth Symphonies have long been standard concert fare. The same is true of his overture, *Romeo and Juliet,* and his *Capriccio Italien.* His brilliant *Piano Concerto*

No. 1 in B flat Minor has enjoyed a popularity perhaps exceeding that of any other concerto, while his *Nutcracker Suite* is said to have had in recent years the largest sale of phonograph recordings in the entire field of serious music.

Tschaikowsky loved Russian folk songs and used them in such famous compositions as the *Overture 1812* and the *Marche Slave*. The lovely theme of the "Andante Cantabile" of his *First String Quartet* is said to have been a folk song which he heard a workman sing. The first movement of his *Fourth Symphony* employs the Russian folk tune, "In the Fields There Stood a Birch-Tree." His *Trio for Violin, Cello, and Piano* makes extensive use of another Russian folk tune, and his *Second Symphony* is based almost entirely on the folk songs of "Little Russia." In his *Capriccio Italien* we hear an old friend in the tune, *Funiculi Funicula*.

Folk music was only one of the influences which determined the style of Tschaikowsky's music. Like Handel and Schumann, this composer was expected to follow the law, but he soon gave it up for music. In his early years Tschaikowsky was a teacher at the Moscow Conservatory and came to know well the music of the world's great composers. He was particularly attracted by the music of Mozart and Beethoven.

Tschaikowsky was a great reader and often received inspiration from his knowledge of literature. His *Romeo and Juliet* was of course suggested by the Shakespeare play, and in Tschaikowsky's music it is easy to picture Friar Laurence in the church, the feud of the Montagues and the Capulets, and the tender feelings of the two youthful lovers. This composition illustrates Tschaikowsky's fondness for descriptive or "program" music. Other examples of it are his orchestral compositions, *Hamlet* and *The Tempest* (again from Shakespeare); his tone poem, *Francesca di Rimini*, based on Dante's poetry, and *Manfred*, suggested by the poem of Byron. Tschaikowsky's songs and operas resulted from his acquaintance with the poets, especially the German, Goethe, and the Russians, Pushkin and Gogol.

Tschaikowsky's own letters tell us much about his strange personality which was so unpredictable and full of contrasts. He disliked teaching and longed for a quiet country home. This was made possible through a benefactor, Madame Nadejda von Meck, a wealthy widow who bestowed an income on the composer so that he might be free to create. The two are said never to have met in person, but for many years they carried on an extensive correspondence. Once when his benefactress urged him to give more time to symphonic music and less to opera, Tschaikowsky replied, "The stage, with all its glitter, attracts me irresistibly."

141

The quotation is typical of Tschaikowsky, who seemed always restless and undecided. He appeared to like the excitements of concert and opera and was always ready for the many trips which he took to other countries. As soon as he was away from home, however, homesickness beset him and he was ready to return. He seemed to enjoy his one visit to America, although he was awed by the tall buildings of New York City and wrote, "The houses downtown are simply colossal; I cannot understand how anyone can live on the thirteenth floor."

More than most composers, Tschaikowsky wrote his autobiography in his music. Highly emotional, he was likely to be either high up in the clouds or down in the depths. If he felt in a bright mood, the music would have an exuberant joy, as in the Finale of his *Symphony No. 4.* When he was despondent, as he frequently seemed to be, the music conveyed his feelings. We have only to listen to the first and last movements of his Sixth Symphony, which has come to be nicknamed the "Pathetique" (Pathetic), or to such songs as *None but the Lonely Heart.* Like the other Russians he frequently used unusual meters and would have tunes with five beats to the measure instead of the commonly used two, three, or four. Like his countrymen of the old days he delighted in bright and contrasting colors and so in his music we have the brilliance of brass suddenly contrasted with the soft shimmering of strings.

As a young man Tschaikowsky was befriended by two brothers, then very important in Russian musical circles. They were Anton and Nicholas Rubinstein, who encouraged Tschaikowsky to study music seriously and helped him to obtain recognition. Anton Rubinstein founded the Conservatory at St. Petersburg and his brother established the Conservatory at Moscow where Tschaikowsky was a teacher for eleven years. Anton Rubinstein (1830-1894) was considered the greatest pianist of the nineteenth century, with the exception of Liszt. We also remember Anton Rubinstein for some of his much-played piano pieces, especially the *Melody in F* and the *Kammenoi Ostrow* (really the title of a set of twenty-four pieces, rather than the single one which is so widely known).

OTHER RUSSIAN COMPOSERS

The list of Russian composers is lengthy and there are a few others who should be included in our story. One of them performed a splendid service in collecting the folk songs of Eastern Russia. Mikhail Ippolitov-Ivanov (Ee-pol'ee-toff Ee'van-off) (1859-1935) became head of the Music School in Tiflis, a city located in the region known

142

as the Caucasus. He traveled in the Caucasian mountains and the native music he heard there was the inspiration of his *Caucasian Sketches* with its oriental tone coloring in the part labeled "In the Village" and "In the Mosque," and its pompous processional, "The March of the Sardar."

When the Russian Revolutionists overthrew the imperial government in 1917 and established the Soviets, the composers of Russia became divided in their loyalties. Some of them, including Reinhold Gliere and Serge Prokofieff, came to terms with the Soviet government and others, notably Sergei Rachmaninoff and Igor Stravinsky, went into exile.

Sergei Rachmaninoff (1873-1943) was a tall, somber man who combined several careers, for he won distinction as a composer, as a conductor, and, perhaps most of all, as a pianist. When he was a young man, Tschaikowsky befriended him and influenced his style of composition. When he was twenty he composed a set of preludes for piano and one of them, the *Prelude in C Sharp Minor,* made his name a household word throughout the music-loving world. He was constantly asked to play it and finally came to dislike the piece so much that he is said to have remarked that his idea of heaven was a place where the C Sharp Minor Prelude would not be performed.

Music-lovers now have high esteem for Rachmaninoff as the composer of the *Rhapsody on a Theme by Paganini* for piano and orchestra and the four splendid concertos for piano, of which the Second is particularly regarded as a masterpiece. His *The Isle of the Dead* and his symphonies are also in the repertoire of many orchestras, while his numerous songs and church works are often performed.

Rachmaninoff had a friend, Alexander Scriabin (Skree-ah'been) (1872-1915), who was one of the finest pianists of his time and who became the composer of much interesting and unusual piano music. He was an experimenter and invented new chords. He also worked with the idea of synchronizing music and color combinations. Many of his piano compositions are noted for their difficult parts for the left hand. This is said to have resulted from an accident in which he broke his right arm while ice-skating. He practiced diligently with his left hand while convalescing and thereafter wrote passages for the left hand which were easy for him but difficult for other pianists. Thus the course of musical composition may sometimes be influenced by an accident.

Igor Stravinsky (1882-   ), whose important contributions to ballet music have been mentioned, is a Russian by birth, but his interests have gone far beyond his native land. In his youth he was a pupil of Rimsky-Korsakoff. During World War I he lived in Switzerland.

143

Before and after this war he spent numerous years in Paris where his famous ballets were performed. For some years he was a French citizen. Then America attracted him, and since 1935 he has lived mostly in this country. He is now an American citizen and has his home in Hollywood.

Stravinsky is a man constantly in search of new ideas, and his volatile temperament has expressed itself in music of many styles. When his ballet, *Le Sacre du Printemps* (The Rites of Spring) was first performed in Paris in 1913, its wild rhythms and discordant harmonies provoked a veritable riot. At other times he has written music along clear and simple lines, much in the manner of Mozart and the other classical writers. He delights in unconventional combinations of instruments. His *Story of a Soldier* uses clarinet, bassoon, trumpet, trombone, violin, double bass and percussion. His *Symphony of Psalms*, for chorus and orchestra, dedicated to the Boston Symphony Orchestra, uses no violins or violas, and the tone color is thus dark and austere because of the emphasis on the lower-pitched orchestra voices.

America has always interested Stravinsky, and it is related that American jazz so fascinated him on his first visit here that he spent an entire night going from one New York night club to another listening to the dance bands. His lively sense of humor revealed itself in one of his compositions produced in this country. Suggested by a poker game, he called the work *Card Party, a Ballet in Three Deals*. At another time he wrote the music for a ballet to be performed in a circus. His latest work is an opera, "The Rake's Progress."

Mozart was doubtless the most famous child musician who ever lived, but there have been many composers who began their careers at a tender age. Among them was Serge Prokofieff (1891-1953), generally considered foremost among Russian composers who have lived under the Soviet. When he was six years old Prokofieff composed some little pieces, and when he was nine he wrote an opera and performed it with the help of his little cousins. It is interesting to note that when this precocious boy grew up he became a great admirer of Mozart who had been such a famous prodigy. Prokofieff wrote his first symphony in the spirit of Mozart and it became his most-played composition, the *Classical Symphony*, which suggests to many musicians Mozart in twentieth instead of eighteenth century dress.

As a boy and young man Prokofieff was a trial to his teachers. He delighted in breaking the rules and his music was grotesque and highly dissonant but always vigorous. As he grew older his compositions became more conventional, but his independence of spirit caused him to be rebuked on several occasions by the Soviet government for his boldness and originality. His symphonies and concertos have

144

been frequently played in America, but to us he is best known for his *Classical Symphony* and his charming *Peter and the Wolf* — a folk tale for children told by a narrator and the instruments of the orchestra.

Best known among other contemporary Soviet composers are Dmitri Shostakovich (Shoh-sta-ko'vitch) (1906-   ) and Aram Khachaturian (1903-   ). Shostakovich, like Prokofieff, has sometimes been chastised by the Soviets for failure to conform to their cultural ideas. His First Symphony, written when he was nineteen, and his Fifth have found much greater favor than the others of his eight symphonies. Khachaturian, doubtless to his own surprise, produced an American best-seller in the "Sabre Dance," a part of his *Gayne Ballet*. To American concert audiences he is best known for his brilliant *Piano Concerto*. A driving energy characterizes the music of these and other present-day Russian composers.

In the past Russia has produced numerous gifted performers as well as composers. Feodor Chaliapin, the basso, will never be forgotten as one who was among the great singers of the world, and the list of Russian-born violinists and pianists who have attained renown is impressive. In our own time Vladimir Horowitz has been acclaimed as perhaps the greatest master of the piano keyboard and Alexander Brailowsky (Breye-loff'skee) and Benno Moiseivitch (Moy-zeye'-vitch) have achieved international reputations. Earlier in our century Ossip Gabrilowitsch was highly regarded as pianist and conductor. Among violinists Russia has sent us such distinguished performers as Nathan Milstein, Mischa Elman, Efrem Zimbalist and Jascha Heifetz, and the great cellist, Gregor Piatigorsky (Pee-at-ee-gor'skee), is also a native of Russia. From Russia also came Serge Koussevitzky, long the conductor of the Boston Symphony Orchestra.

QUESTIONS

1. How do you think geography and climate of a country affect the general temperament of its people?
2. What occupations and what geographical conditions have inspired Russian folk music?
3. What characteristic instrument is most often used by the Russians?
4. What instrument does it resemble?
5. What differences can be noted between Russian dances and songs?
6. How have wandering tribes of gypsies affected the music of Russia?
7. Why did the Russians tend to develop such beautiful unaccompanied singing in their churches?
8. Name some of the composers who have contributed to Russian church music.

145

9. Who were the "Russian Five"?
10. What are some of the characteristics of Oriental music?
11. What are several compositions in which Rimsky-Korsakoff used these characteristics?
12. Why is the music of Tschaikowsky so well known?
13. Name several of his popular compositions.
14. Name a Russian composer who was inspired by his travels in the Caucasian mountains and one of his compositions.
15. How did the overthrow of the Imperial Government in 1917 affect the Russian composers of that time?
16. Name several careers in which Rachmaninoff excelled.
17. What are some of his well-known compositions?
18. Tell some interesting facts concerning the music of Stravinsky.
19. Why did Prokofieff write his *Classical Symphony?*
20. Name several modern Russian composers and tell something about their compositions.
21. Who are some gifted Russian-born performers of our day?

LISTENING SUGGESTIONS

Anthems by Gretchaninoff, Rachmaninoff, Kalinnikoff, Tschesnokoff, and others

Capriccio Italien — Tschaikowsky

Caucasian Sketches — Ippolitov-Ivanov

Cherubim Song — Bortniansky

Classical Symphony — Prokofieff

Concerto for Piano and Orchestra — Khatchaturian

"Coronation Scene" from *Boris Godounov* — Moussorgsky

Dark Eyes — Folk

Firebird Suite, The — Stravinsky

Flight of the Bumblebee — Rimsky-Korsakoff

Gayne (Ballet) — Khatchaturian

Marche Slave — Tschaikowsky

Nutcracker Suite — Tschaikowsky

Over the Steppe — Gretchaninoff

Overture 1812 — Tschaikowsky

Overture, *Romeo and Juliet* — Tschaikowsky

Overture, *Russlan and Ludmilla* — Glinka

Peter and the Wolf — Prokofieff

Petrouchka (Ballet) — Stravinsky

Piano Concertos (1-4) — Rachmaninoff

Piano Concerto No. 1 in B Flat Minor — Tschaikowsky

Pictures at an Exhibition — Moussorgsky

"Polovetzian Dances" from *Prince Igor* — Borodin

Rhapsody on a Theme of Paganini — Rachmaninoff

Rites of Spring, The (Ballet) — Stravinsky

Russian Easter Overture — Rimsky-Korsakoff

Scheherezade — Rimsky-Korsakoff

Sleeping Beauty, The (Ballet) — Tschaikowsky

Song of India — Rimsky-Korsakoff

Song of the Volga Boatmen — Folk

Spanish Capriccio — Rimsky-Korsakoff

Swan Lake, The (Ballet) — Tschaikowsky

Symphonies (1-9) — Shostakovich

Symphonies (1-6) — Tschaikowsky

Symphony No. 2 — Borodin

146

↘ 14 ↙

SPAIN

SPAIN IS often thought of as a land of romance and poetry, a place of enchantment and mystery. The lover, strumming his guitar and singing a tender love song, the dancer with castanets or tambourine, the toreador, the gypsy, Don Juan and Carmen — each has been a part of this country's legend and romance. Many of the tunes of Spain have an Oriental tinge, and the Moorish architecture which casts its shadows here and there seems to form an appropriate setting. We may pause to wonder why these tunes have this peculiar quality and what has made this country so different from other European countries.

The map of Europe shows us that Spain is a peninsula situated at the extreme southwestern end of Europe and surrounded by high mountains and tempestuous seas. On the tip of Andalusia (An-da-loo'sya), a province in the south, stands the great Rock of Gibraltar guarding the gateway to the Mediterranean Sea.

As we turn the pages of Spain's history, we find that this peninsula has been occupied by different races from time to time. The earliest inhabitants were the Celts and Iberians and Spain is often called the Iberian Peninsula. Not much is known of this early history, but it is thought that as early as 1100 B.C. the Phoenicians established trading posts and colonies on the coast. Spain was under the power of Rome for several centuries and during this time the Christian religion exerted a great influence. With the decline of the Roman Empire, Spain became open to invasion by the barbarians. Various tribes occupied the land, but the most important people to conquer Spain were the Moors and Arabs who entered the country in 711 A.D. In 778 Charlemagne (Shahr'le-mane), an ardent advocate of Christianity, won from the Moors the northeastern part of the country. From that time until the expulsion of the Moors in 1492, there was many a conflict between the Christians and Moslems. Spain was made up of many small kingdoms with the Moors dominating the southern and eastern portions. This had a profound effect on the art,

147

music, and architecture of Spain. The ruins of the Alhambra, the famous palace of the Moorish sovereigns built in 1273 A.D., are a splendid example of this influence. Moorish music was accepted by the Spaniards and developed by them to a point of great beauty. It is this Moorish and Arabic quality which gives so much of the music of Spain its unusual intervals and rhythms. The Moorish princes established universities in Granada, and one of their serious studies was that of harmony. This early training laid the foundation for the music that was to come.

Spain rose to heights of power during the Renaissance. Early in the fifteenth century the small kingdoms of Spain had been united under one rule, and late in this century when Christopher Columbus had set out on his famous voyage, Spain, under the joint reign of Ferdinand of Aragon and Isabella of Castile, was one of the most powerful nations of the world. This supremacy was of rather short duration, however, for in the sixteenth century the defeat of Spain's famous fleet, The Armada, by the English gave England a commanding position in both the Old and the New Worlds.

The folk songs of Spain are charming and beautiful. Some show Moorish or gypsy characteristics, while others are purely Spanish, depending upon the province in which they originate. The "Alborado" (Ahl-boh-rah'doh) or morning serenade is a typical folk song which came from the troubadours, who in olden times sang it to their fair ladies. Castilian folk songs are gay, while those of Catalonia are more somber.

Spain, more than any other country in the world, is renowned for her dancing. Most of the dances with which Americans are familiar make use of the legs and feet in movement. Many oriental dancers use only the arms and hands, while a third type of dancing, where the muscles of the body play a large part, is found in northern Africa and parts of Asia. These three types of dancing are combined in the dances of Spain and they vary in intensity of action according to the part of the country where they are performed. Many of the movements are similar to the classic Greek dances and some show North African influence.

When considering the music and dancing of Spain we must not forget the gypsy who has played such an important part in the colorful life of the people. The gypsies have usually adopted the music and dances of the countries with which they became identified, and this is especially true of the Spanish gypsies, who have kept alive the old dances of Spain. Often in gypsy dancing the audience participates in the dance by rhythmic clapping and stamping mingled with cries of encouragement to the dancers. The gypsy and Spanish

148

temperaments 'seem to be congenial and Spain has been one of the few countries in Europe where, as in Russia and Hungary, the gypsy has felt at home.

The most beautiful folk songs and dances come from Andalusia. Here the people are excitable and display intense feeling in their dancing. The oldest dance found here is the *fandango*; from this dance came the *seguidilla* (sayg-ee-deel'yah). The seguidilla is danced to the accompaniment of guitar and castanets, interspersed with the singing of four-lined verses, called "coplas," by the dancers. The dance ends very abruptly, at which time the performers stand very still in a statue-like pose. The skill of the dancers is often judged by the grace and ease with which these sudden endings are executed. The composition *Seguidilla* by Albeniz (Al-bay'neth) was inspired by this dance, and there is a famous "Seguidilla" in the opera *Carmen*. Other dances popular in Andalusia are the *cachucha, tango,* and *bolero.*

The *jota* (ho'tah), considered the national dance of Spain is especially popular in Aragon and Navarre, though danced in other provinces. It originated in Aragon where the people are more haughty in their appearance, and in the dance less movement is used. The English word "arrogant" is said to be derived from this province. Sarasate (Sar-ah-sah'tay), the great Spanish violinist, composed a *Jota Navarre* in his series of Spanish dances for the violin, and Glinka, the Russian composer, wrote a *Jota Aragonaise* (Ah-rah-go-nays'), based on a folk tune from Aragon. The "bolero" (bo-lay'ro), a Spanish dance in triple time, has interested composers of other countries. The *Bolero* by Maurice Ravel is a famous example.

Many dances with definite Spanish characteristics have originated in the new world, especially in South America and Mexico. The *habanera* (ah-bah-nay'rah), a dance song, owes its origin to Spanish settlers in Cuba and takes it name from Havana where it originated. In *Carmen,* the Spanish opera written by the French composer Bizet (Bee-zay), the gypsy girl, Carmen, sings the "Habanera" in the first act of the opera as she dances and keeps time with her castanets.

Emmanuel Chabrier (Shah-bree-ay') (1841-1894), another French composer, was inspired by his travels in Spain to write a rhapsody, entitled, *España.* In this composition based on Spanish folk tunes he uses the rhythms of the jota and *malagueña* (mah-lah-gayn'yah). The malagueña is a Spanish dance very similar to the fandango and derives its name from the Province of Malaga. Rimsky-Korsakoff, the Russian composer, displayed his interest in Spanish music by composing *Capriccio Espagnol* (Ka-pree'chee-oh Ay-spahn-yohl'), a composition in five movements of which two are based on an alborado, one is a series of variations on a Spanish folk song, another uses a gypsy melody, and the last is a fandango.

Dancing, to the Spaniard, often becomes a sacred ritual when at certain festival times religious dances are performed before the altars and shrines of the churches. At Christmas some carols are sung to the tunes of seguidillas.

The guitar, introduced into Spain by the Moors and troubadours, is used to accompany Spanish dances in the New World and the Old. Castanets and tambourines are added for rhythmical effects. In the time of the Renaissance, the lute was the popular instrument of the country. It had six strings and looked like a pear-shaped guitar. In the sixteenth century, often called "Spain's Golden Age of Music," many compositions for the lute were written. One of the famous composers of that time was Luis Milan, who wrote great lute fantasies.

Even the great composers, Bach and Handel of Germany and Verdi of Italy, composed for the lute and guitar. It is interesting to note that there is a world-famous guitar player living today, Andres Segovia (Say-goh'vee-a), who has given many concerts in Europe and America. And among instrumentalists, we should not forget Pablo Casals (Kah-sahls'), the renowned violoncellist, a native of Spain who has won international fame for his beautiful playing. The piano virtuoso, Jose Iturbi (Ee-toor'bee), is very well known in America, where he has won fame both as a pianist and conductor. His film appearances have made him widely known to motion picture audiences.

In the nineteenth and twentieth centuries, such composers as Felipe Pedrell (1841-1922), Isaac Albéniz (Al-bay'neth) (1860-1909), Enrique Granados (Grahn-ahd'os) (1867-1916), Manuel de Falla (de-Fahl'ya) (1876-1946), and Joaquin Turina (Hoh-ah-keen' Tooreen'ah) (1882-   ) have been identified with a definite Spanish school of music. Pedrell was interested in the true folk music of his country and did much research along this line. He has been called the father of modern Spanish music. Albéniz lived outside of Spain, and, as he spent much time in other countries, he helped to acquaint others with the music of his own country. Granados, another national composer, wrote Spanish dances and the opera, Goyescas (Goyess'cass) which was inspired by the painting of the Spanish artist, Goya. This was performed by the Metropolitan Opera Company in 1916. Granados was present at this performance. While returning to Spain, he lost his life when his ship was torpedoed by the Germans during World War I.

Manuel de Falla was the modern successor of Pedrell. It was his habit to roam throughout his country, spending time with the gypsies

150

and peasants and collecting rare and unusual folk songs. He did not often use these tunes in his own music, but he studied them carefully and his compositions are rich in the flavor of Spanish folk music. He was especially well informed on Spanish gypsy music and reproduced its accents in such works as the ballet, *El Amor Brujo* (El A-mor' Bru'ho). From this ballet comes the often-played "Ritual Fire Dance."

Falla's short opera, *La Vida Breve* (La Vee'da Bray'veh) has been frequently performed, and his reputation was enhanced by his tone-poem for piano and orchestra, *Nights in the Gardens of Spain*, and another ballet, *The Three-Cornered Hat*. In his orchestra music Falla was influenced by his friends, Debussy and Ravel, whom he came to know well during the few years he spent in Paris.

Spain may not have produced world-famous composers to compare with those of some other countries, but acquaintance with her music has meaning for us. Spanish music has been a rich source of musical ideas to composers of other lands and to French composers in particular. The fascinating rhythms and distinctive melodies of Spanish folk music were brought to the New World, where they helped to shape the music of Central and South America and in some degree have affected our own North American popular music.

QUESTIONS

1. Describe the country of Spain.
2. Why were the Moors important?
3. When did Spain rise to power and how was much of her power lost?
4. Name several characteristics of Spanish folk songs.
5. What three types of movement are found in Spanish dancing?
6. What has been the importance of the gypsy to Spanish dancing?
7. Describe the seguidilla. Name some other dances of Andalusia.
8. What is often considered the national dance of Spain? How does the dancing in Aragon differ from that in other provinces of Spain?
9. Name some composers of other countries who have written Spanish dances.
10. What instruments are used to accompany Spanish dancing?
11. Describe the lute and name a famous writer of lute fantasies.
12. What famous composers wrote music for the lute and guitar?
13. Name a prominent guitar player, a famous cellist and a well-known pianist who were born in Spain.
14. Discuss the works of several nineteenth and twentieth century composers of Spain.
15. Have you heard any Spanish music on radio or television recently?
16. What countries in North and South America have been influenced by Spanish music?

151

LISTENING SUGGESTIONS

Capriccio Espagnol — Rimsky-Korsakoff

Clavelitos — Valverde

Dances from *The Three-Cornered Hat* — de Falla

España — Chabrier

"Habanera" from *Carmen* — Bizet

Intermezzo from *Goyescas* — Granados

Malagueña — Albeniz

Nights in the Gardens of Spain — de Falla

Rapsodie Espagnole — Ravel

"Ritual Fire Dance" from *El Amor Brujo* — de Falla

Segovia, Andres, recordings by

"Seguidilla" from *Carmen* — Bizet

Triana — Albeniz

152

Dance Song

Sara Scott

Swedish Dance Tune

1. { Cold win-ter— now is— done, High is— our Mid-night Sun.
   Young kids will leap and play. We too, are— glad as— they.
2. { Hil-dur and— Ka-ren, too, Wear a-prons fine and new.
   Now sum-mer— days are—long. Come, join— the— hap-py— throng.

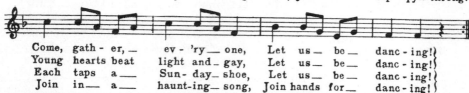

Come, gath-er,— ev-'ry— one, Let us— be— danc-ing!
Young hearts beat light and— gay, Let us— be— danc-ing!
Each taps a— Sun-day— shoe, Let us— be— danc-ing!
Join in— a haunt-ing— song, Join hands for— danc-ing!

Birch trees are green and white. May-poles are tall and—bright.
Mid-sum-mer's Day is here, Best day— of all the— year.

Vil-lage lads come in sight, See them ad-vanc-ing!
Sea-son of joy and cheer, Sing-ing and danc-ing.

≫ 15 ≪

SCANDINAVIA

STORIES OF THE Scandinavian countries, their charm, scenic **beauty**, and exciting tales of adventure, have been sung and resung for many generations. Norway, Sweden, Denmark, and Finland **are** politically independent of one another, but closely united by **ties of** blood and customs. In these countries, as in those of the British **Isles**, there is much in their art, music, and dance that is similar.

Because of the spectacular beauty of the mountainous sections and the cold magic of the far north, we find in Scandinavian music and art a deep poetic feeling and a love of sharp contrasts. Our imaginations are fired with stories of the early Vikings who explored countries near and far, and in many of their songs we hear the call of the sea or an account of brave deeds. Still others are less vigorous and suggest plaintive mountain strains, the weird spell of the midnight sun, or the sweeping, solid stretches of evergreen forests.

The whole world admires the Scandinavian for his sturdiness and vitality, whether he be eking out a scanty existence in a far northern fishing village or tilling the soil in the more fertile farming regions of the southlands. His home is his kingdom, and his family is the very foundation of his life. Because of the long winter months and the dreary rainy season, much of his merrymaking is confined to his own fireside. Here the folk dance of the Scandinavian has full sway, and with enthusiasm he throws himself into the rollicking figures of the dance.

A glance at each of these countries separately, situated as they are in the northern hemisphere, will enable us better to understand the music of these faraway places. They have been called "the brow of the universe: a high and noble brow, crowning the other countries of the world!"

NORWAY

Norway, a country with rugged coast line and many fjords, suggests to our imagination the mighty warriors of days gone by, as well as the peace and beauty of the "Land of the Midnight Sun." Because of her strong national feeling we find within her borders some of the

154

purest and oldest folk songs. There are the sea songs of the fishermen, the songs of the woodcutter and the forester, and, perhaps most romantic of all, the yodel of the herdsman, with its familiar echo, as he calls the cattle home from the mountainside.

Norway's folklore, as well as her music, is influenced by a belief in fantastic, weird creatures, gnomes and elves. This fantastic strain is noticeable in the dances of Norway as well as in her songs. All Scandinavians are born dancers, and the Norwegians have an abundance of good, hearty dances and dance songs. In some places, custom has ruled that the same song cannot be used more than once in one year of dancing. When the dances are very lively, singing is abandoned and a fiddler is called in to play the tune. The *springdans* and *halling* are two favorite Norwegian dances. In the halling the dancers strive to kick high enough to hit the rafters overhead. The more agile dancers turn somersaults in the air and add all sorts of gymnastic feats as they keep time to the steady rhythm of the fiddle. As the dance grows wilder and wilder, the superstitious peasants believe that "Old Nick" or the devil is playing for them. One legend tells of a player in the far north who made an offering to the "Nix," inducing him to teach him his tunes. When he learned to play them, he found he couldn't stop, and his violin strings had to be cut to end his playing.

These dances are usually accompanied by the Hardanger fiddle or violin. This instrument came from Hardanger, Norway, and in appearance is like an ordinary violin, only more ornamented. It has eight strings, four upper and four lower. The lower strings give forth a drone sound similar to that of Scotland's bagpipe when the upper strings are bowed. The composer, Edvard Grieg, was much interested in this instrument and enjoyed hearing a performer play folk tunes on it. Johan Halvorsen, another composer of Norway, helped to perfect the fiddle.

Another instrument of Norway is the "langleik" (lang'lake), a harp-shaped instrument that was used by bards of old when singing their sagas or legendary stories about their Norse heroes and gods.

EDVARD GRIEG

From these fanciful but sturdy people and from this country of massive grandeur came Edvard Grieg (1843-1907), Norway's greatest composer. As a child he listened to the thrilling stories of adventure and the playing of Ole Bull, famous Norwegian violinist. Interest in this violinist influenced Grieg's earliest efforts and encouraged him to turn to music for his life work.

In the following years of study, both in Germany and at home, the

155

desire to express himself and his country in his compositions became foremost in his mind. The interest of Ole Bull and other Norwegian musicians did much to turn Grieg's attention to the music and folklore of his own country. He is considered now to be one of the greatest nationalistic composers. He once wrote: "I have sought to create a national art out of this hitherto unexploited expression of the folk-soul of Norway."

National pride found an outlet in another channel. Living at the same time as Edvard Grieg was Henrik Ibsen, Norwegian playwright and poet. His plays were performed with much success in all the large centers of northern Europe. It is not surprising that Ibsen turned to Grieg for incidental music to his greatest drama, *Peer Gynt* (Pair Ghint), written first as a poem and later as a play. Grieg wrote two suites (sweets), which he named *Peer Gynt* I and II. It is the first suite with which we are more familiar. How strange and haunting are the minor chords of "Ase's Death" (Aw'seh), and how suggestive of mountain gnomes and their haunts is "In the Hall of the Mountain King"!

Grieg wrote numerous other compositions for piano which are charming to hear as well as to play. The *March of the Dwarfs,* as the name suggests, is weird and fantastic with its jerky, characteristic rhythms. You are familiar, perhaps, with his *Norwegian Bridal Procession.* It is suggestive of the pastoral scene with the faint tune of the piper heard far away in the distance. Gradually, as the whole procession comes closer, we can hear the definite rhythm of the dance and in our mind's eye enjoy the boisterous, wholehearted gaiety of the peasants. They are with us but a moment and go on their way up the narrow mountain path, leaving only the lilting tune of the happy piper.

Grieg was usually content to write short pieces — songs and short compositions for piano or for orchestra, but his few ventures into larger forms were successful. His one Piano Concerto, written before he was thirty, remains today one of the best-loved concertos in the concert repertoire. Singers hold his songs in high regard. The best-known of all his songs, *I Love Thee,* was written for Nina Hagerup, to whom he became betrothed in 1864. They were married three years later.

His intense patriotism impelled Grieg to choose subjects from Norwegian history. His famous *Landsighting* for baritone solo and men's chorus celebrates an early king of Norway, Olaf Trygvason. Another work deals with Sigurd Jorsalfar (Sigurd The Crusader) and from it comes the often-heard *Triumphal March.*

In appreciation of his beautiful compositions and his interest in

156

the music of his own country, the Norwegian government endowed Edvard Grieg with a yearly salary which enabled him to spend the greater part of his time and energy on his composing. Being an ardent lover of nature, he built his home high on a cliff facing the sea and surrounded by rocky cliffs and tall pines. It was here that he dreamed and wrote and poured into his music the characteristics of his people, the poetic stories of the northern lands, gay village dances, queer elfin-like strains, and strong, leaping rhythms.

Like Schubert, Tschaikowsky, and Chopin, whose melodies have a widespread appeal, the music of Grieg has come to be widely known and his tunes have been frequently borrowed by the writers of popular music. A successful musical play of recent years, *Song of Norway*, derives most of its musical material from the music of Edvard Grieg.

Christian Sinding (Zind'ing) is a Norwegian composer, known especially for his *Rustle of Spring* for piano. Johan Svendsen also achieved prominence among Norwegian composers, and F. Melius Christiansen, founder of the St. Olaf College Choir at Northfield, Minnesota, is a native of Norway. From Norway also comes Kirsten Flagstad, celebrated soprano.

QUESTIONS

1. Name the Scandinavian countries.
2. Who were the Vikings?
3. Why has the home of the Scandinavian meant so much to him?
4. From what sources have the Scandinavians received their inspiration for song?
5. Write a paragraph telling some interesting facts concerning Edvard Grieg.
6. Who was Henrik Ibsen?
7. What famous drama did he write?
8. Tell something about the incidental music that Grieg wrote for his drama.
9. Have you ever played or sung any music by Grieg? Name the composition.
10. What famous light opera was produced recently which featured the life of Grieg and the folk music of Norway?

LISTENING SUGGESTIONS

Anitra's Dance — Grieg
I Love Thee (Ich liebe dich) — Grieg
In Holberg's Time — Grieg
Landsighting — Grieg
Last Spring, The — Grieg
March of the Dwarfs — Grieg

Norwegian Bridal Procession—Grieg
Norwegian Dances — Grieg
Peer Gynt Suites 1 and 2 — Grieg
Piano Concerto — Grieg
Rustle of Spring — Sinding
Solveig's Song — Grieg

157

SWEDEN

The fertile farm lands and the happy, industrious people of Sweden have instilled in her life a spirit of contentment, which in turn is reflected in the songs she sings, songs that are rarely gloomy, rarely tragic — even those in minor keys are plaintive rather than sad, and all are very beautiful.

The struggle for existence in the vast stretches of farming country is not so intense as that of Norway or Greenland. Protected from icy winds and cruel ocean storms by the towering mountain peaks of Norway, Sweden's rich soil during the summer months yields to its workers a plentiful harvest. The people of Sweden are happy and prosperous, strong and robust. They work long hours every day and in their leisure time play with equal intensity. Loyalty to their country and their families is of greatest importance to these sturdy folk and forms the theme of many of their favorite songs. Perhaps you have heard *Vermeland, Thou Lovely Vermeland,* so beloved by the Swedish people.

In the north of Sweden, we find the customs and conditions very similar to those of northern Norway. The same strange legends are told, queer haunting minor chords are used in their songs, and the people have a common enemy in the intense winter cold. The north is covered with dense forests — miles and miles of white birch — which provide wood for the large cities of the south.

Even in the large industrial centers, the factory workers and businessmen feel the call of the soil. Every home has its garden; every workingman has his plot of ground which he may rent by the season from the government for a very small amount for cultivation in his free time. The streets and parks are filled with beautiful, gay-colored flowers. Visiting foreigners say of Stockholm, the capital of Sweden, that it resembles a lovely flower garden and always looks as though it were just freshly washed.

Sweden is noted for pretty girls — girls and women who are capable as well as attractive. Their handwork is very famous and certainly mention must be made of their delicious breads and cakes and good coffee. Added to these accomplishments, many of the Swedish women have beautiful voices. In fact, Sweden long has been called the "land of singers." The musical people of all countries were delighted with the beautiful voice of Jenny Lind, a famous nineteenth-century singer who was called the "Swedish Nightingale." Three prominent singers of today were born in Sweden — Kerstin Thorborg, contralto, Jussi Bjoerling (Byair'ling), tenor, and Set Svanholm, tenor.

Sweden has had many contacts with the other countries of Europe.

158

Participation in the Thirty Years' War subjected her to many foreign influences. It is not surprising that these influences are noticeable in her songs. In fact, many of the individual Scandinavian characteristics have been lost. In Napoleon's time an alliance was made with France, and the courts of Stockholm were patterned after the French courts. During this time, some French characteristics found their way into the music of Sweden.

The dances have remained practically untouched by these outside influences. The dances of Sweden are very vigorous and are charming to watch as well as to dance. The pantomime folk dances, where the dancers enact little stories by using hands and movements of their heads, are enjoyed by the people of Sweden today. It is delightful to see a group of these peasants in their bright-colored costumes whirling and stamping out the accents in their gay dance.

August Johan Södermann (Say'der-mahn) (1832-1876) was one of the leading composers of Sweden and is probably best known for his *Swedish Wedding March*. In it one feels all the vigor and rustic charm of a peasant wedding. Emil Sjögren (Shay'gren) (1853-1918) was another of Sweden's composers, noted for his beautiful songs and small compositions. The orchestra music of Hugo Alfven (1872-   ) has also come to be known in America.

QUESTIONS

1. What is the general character of Swedish folk music? Why is this true?
2. What are some of the personal characteristics of these people?
3. Name a famous singer who was Swedish.
4. Why do many Swedish folk songs reflect the influence of other countries?
5. What interesting alliance with another country was made during Napoleon's time?
6. Tell something interesting concerning Swedish dances.
7. Name and spell correctly two well-known Swedish composers.

LISTENING SUGGESTIONS

Any Swedish folk songs or dances
Oh, Vermeland — Folk

Swedish Wedding March — Södermann

DENMARK

Jutting out into the North Sea, a close neighbor to Germany, is Denmark, smallest of the Scandinavian countries. Within her close boundary limits we find a painstaking and artistic people who have contributed many varied and useful gifts to civilization. As is char-

159

acteristic of all Scandinavians, the Danish people turn to the soil for their livelihood, and in the course of time have transformed their flat, elongated country into neat, prosperous farms. Denmark has had many contacts with the other European countries. Flags of every nation in the world are seen waving from ships anchored in her port at Copenhagen.

The music of Denmark, for the most part, reflects these outside influences. Her songs, a large percentage of which are composed, are very similar to those of Sweden. In one section of Denmark, Jutland, which was originally settled by Celts, the songs resemble those of Wales. These are said to be the most beautiful of all Danish songs. Germany has also left her impression on the music of Denmark, whereas the grace and charm of some Danish songs are due to French influences.

As for her dances, again we find a marked similarity to those of Sweden. An exception, and one of the favorite dances of the country, is the *reel*, somewhat like the famous "reel" or "jig" of Scotland and Ireland.

The foremost composer of Denmark and the "father of Scandinavian music" was Niels Gade (Gah'deh) (1817-1890). In his compositions he consciously reflected the Scandinavian folk material and ideas. It was he who influenced many of the younger composers of his time, namely Edvard Grieg, Christian Sinding, and others, to express in their writings the characteristics of their people.

In addition to her beautiful music, Denmark has given many gifts of value to the other countries of the world. Children of all lands are familiar with the famous Hans Christian Andersen *Fairy Tales*. Danish pottery is prized the world over. One of the world's greatest sculptors, Thorvaldsen, came from Denmark, and other Danish men have won fame in various fields. In our own time the operatic tenor, Lauritz Melchior, has brought fame to his native Denmark.

Her people are great enthusiasts of the drama. In fact, Copenhagen is noted for its theaters and wonderful ballets. The Danish people are promoters of all that is beautiful and bring to their art centers the finest art expressions of many lands.

QUESTIONS

1. Flags of all nations are seen waving from ships anchored in Denmark's port at Copenhagen. How does this fact affect her folk music?
2. Name a famous Danish composer who used folk music as the basis for many of his compositions, who influenced other Scandinavian composers, and was known as the "father of Scandinavian music."
3. What noted operatic tenor came from Denmark?

FINLAND

Finland brings to our minds bleak and cold marsh lands, dense forests, and thousands of silvery lakes. This country is peopled with a race that for generations has struggled for liberty. With this as her tradition, she has given to the world a wide collection of unusual and interesting folk music. We have only to read her history of six centuries of Swedish rule followed by another century of tyrannical Russian domination to feel a great admiration for this country which has so persistently preserved her language, legends, and songs.

It is strange that the Finnish people, living so close to Norway and Sweden, should be of a different stock from their Scandinavian neighbors. They are said to resemble the Magyar (Mod'yar) race of Hungary, and in some of their music one can recognize Hungarian strains. In personal appearance and temperament they show definite Asiatic tendencies.

The language of the Finnish people is very melodious and because the accented syllables fall in an irregular pattern, their speech has a curious rhythmic effect. This accounts for the unusual five and seven beat measures in their poetry and music.

Their legends are intensely interesting and have much charm. From Finland comes one of the greatest national epic poems of all countries called the *Kalevala* (Kahl-a-vahl'a). The following is a translated excerpt of this poem, referring to the cuckoo:

> *Call at morning, call at evening,*
> *And at noon-tide call thou likewise*
> *To rejoice my plains surrounding*
> *That my woods may grow more cheerful,*
> *That my coast may grow more wealthy*
> *And my region grow more fruitful.*

These verses sung to a typical folk melody show the queer chant-like qualities of Finnish folk music. They are sung in five-beat phrases - - - - - - — — with six short syllables and two long ones.

You have heard similar lines before? Compare them with the following quotation from a well-known American poem:

> *By the shores of Gitche Gumee,*
> *By the shining Big-Sea-Water,*
> *Stood the wigwam of Nokomis,*
> *Daughter of the Moon, Nokomis,*
> *Dark behind it rose the forest,*
> *Rose the black and gloomy pine trees,*
> *Rose the firs with cones upon them.*

161

It was from a translation of the *Kalevala* that Longfellow patterned his *Story of Hiawatha*.

The *Kalevala* and many other legends are still sung in Finland to the accompaniment of a very old and much-used folk stringed instrument, the "kantele" (kan-tel). In the *Kalevala* we find a description of the origin of this instrument, as though it came from the very lives and hearts of the people:

> *The Kantele of care is carved*
> *Formed of saddening sorrows only;*
> *Of hard times its arch is fashioned*
> *And its wood of evil chances,*
> *All the strings of sorrow twisted.*

Its "strings of sorrow twisted" are of copper and are five in number, *g, a, b, c,* and *d.* Many Finnish songs are based on these same five tones, just as the Scotch songs use the five tones of their folk instrument, the bag-pipe.

An ancient custom of merry-making known as "rune singing" is still enjoyed by the Finnish peasants of today. Let us picture, for a moment, a crude peasant hut on a cold winter night, dimly lighted, to which neighboring family groups have gathered for a few hours recreation. Two men seat themselves in the center of the room facing one another, hands outstretched and clasped, and begin to rock back and forth until they sway in perfect rhythm. One, the leader, sings one line and the other answers with a second phrase, slightly changed. Often the whole gathering joins the second singer. In this manner, many hours of the long winter nights are passed in song.

JEAN SIBELIUS

A native of Finland is Jean Sibelius (1865-   ), who has done much to preserve the music of his people and who has used their melodies and strange rhythms in his compositions. One of his orchestral compositions, *Finlandia,* is so descriptive of Finland and so expressive of the lives and hardships of the people that it has inspired great patriotism in his fellowmen. It is said that Russia forbade the playing of this composition because it aroused such depth of national feeling in the hearts of the Finnish people. It stirred the Finns so deeply that they took the melodious second theme and used it as their national hymn. It is often sung in this country to the words "Dear Land of Home." Composers often have used national songs in their compositions, but so far as we know, this is the only example

162

of a people who, of one accord, have taken a melody from a large composed work and made it their own. Even those who are not native to Finland can feel that this composition expresses the sorrows and struggles of the people and their longing for liberty.

The career of Jean Sibelius has, in some respects, paralleled that of Edvard Grieg. Both composers studied in Germany but returned to their native countries to devote their efforts to a national music. Both were granted incomes by their governments so that they might be free to compose. Grieg and Sibelius shared a deep love for nature and both were impassioned patriots.

There are important differences in the music of these two Scandinavian composers. Grieg was at his best in short lyric pieces. Sibelius did small things well, but large things better. His symphonies have been called great tonal landscapes or epic poems in sound. It has been said that no composer has heard Nature more surely than Sibelius, and the sights and sounds of his native land appear in the seven symphonies of Sibelius. Each of the symphonies is now regarded as important, and no two of them are alike, thus testifying to the imagination of Sibelius which, after producing nationalistic music, such as *Finlandia*, passed to music of universal appeal.

Sibelius often drew upon the *Kalevala* for inspiration, and his *Swan of Tuonela* had its source in the famous poem. Best known among the shorter pieces of Sibelius is the descriptive *Valse Triste*.

Another present day composer of Finland is Selim Palmgren (1878-   ), who has also based much of his writings on the music of his own people. He has written orchestral suites, many compositions, large and small, for the pianoforte and some fine choruses for male voices. Piano students are familiar with his *May Night* and have employed the mystic, tender impressionism that Palmgren expresses so beautifully in his music. Another Finnish composer who should be mentioned is Armas Järnefelt whose *Berceuse* (Bair'suhs) and *Praeludium* are often heard.

QUESTIONS

1. Tell something about the geography of Finland.
2. Why should we admire the Finnish people for having preserved their folk songs, their language, and their legends?
3. In what way do the Finnish people differ from their Scandinavian neighbors?
4. Tell something interesting regarding their language.
5. What famous epic poem comes from Finland?
6. Its meter resembles what well-known poem written by an American poet?

163

7. Name a composer of Finland who is among the most famous of twentieth century composers.
8. Tell some interesting facts concerning one of his compositions, *Finlandia*.
9. Trace some parallels between the careers of this Finnish composer and a famous Norwegian composer.

LISTENING SUGGESTIONS

Berceuse — Järnefelt

Finlandia — Sibelius

May Night — Palmgren

Praeludium — Järnefelt

Swan of Tuonela, The — Sibelius

Symphonies (1-7) — Sibelius

Valse Triste — Sibelius

Violin Concerto — Sibelius

⇜ 16 ⇝

CENTRAL EUROPEAN COUNTRIES

CZECHOSLOVAKIA

THE MAP of Czechoslovakia (Check'o-slo-vak'e-ah) has been likened to a gigantic lizard with its head entering Germany and its tail resting on the eastern Carpathian Mountains. Following World War I the territories which comprise Czechoslovakia — Bohemia, Slovakia, Moravia, Silesia, and sub-Carpathian Ruthenia — were united under one government. Music in Czechoslovakia has thus been subjected to various influences and the native folk music of Bohemia and Slovakia has in some degree been affected and augmented by Russian and German influences. The Czechs have many beautiful folk songs, of which *Came a-Riding* and *Morning Comes Early* are fine examples.

Because of the central position of this country, it has been subject to aggression from the south, east, north, and west. This has of necessity caused the Czech (Check) to fight in defense of his homeland. History records that as he fought he sang, and his songs carried him into victory. In the fifteenth century the "Hussite Hymn" of the one-eyed warrior Zitka was the Czechs' conquering hymn, and it is interesting to note that it was this same "Hussite Hymn" which they sang in World War I when they were victorious. The "Hussites" were followers of John Huss, who broke away from the established church in the fourteenth century. Huss gave much attention to singing in his religious services, and in 1501 his followers published the first hymnbook of which there is any record.

There is evidence that the Slavs were in these regions as far back as 500 B.C. Prague, the capital of Bohemia, is a very ancient city and had its beginning back in the early Middle Ages. In the fifth century A.D., Czech, who was the leader and ancestor of the Bohemians, entered the country with his followers. In the tenth century, "Good King Wenceslaus" (later known as Saint Wenceslaus), who as Duke of Bohemia ruled the country, laid the foundation of the famous cathedral at Prague. During his reign of nine years he wove the Czech tribes into close political unity, at the same time instilling

165

into them the Christian spirit of the West. He will be remembered as the inspiration for the famous Christmas carol, *Good King Wenceslas*.

When thinking of the music of Czechoslovakia, we turn instinctively to Bohemia, for in few countries has music been such a part of the people. The strolling street musicians and singers, the town pipers, all have had their part in keeping alive the music of the people. Before the World Wars almost everyone in Bohemia sang or played, and the violin was the best-loved instrument of the people. An important industrial effort in many towns was the making of violins, and because they were not expensive, any one who wished to play was able to purchase an instrument. The violin could be carried into the fields or the forest, and it has been said that "throughout the entire land it is difficult to escape the sound of the fiddle at some time during the day."

The music of the Czechs and Slavs affords great contrasts. It is either slow and sombre or very fast and fiery. The *polka* is one of their most popular dances, but there are others deserving of attention: the *furiant* in $\frac{3}{8}$ time (the dancer having a girl on either side of him), the *dupak,* a stamping dance, the *medved,* a bear dance, and their great national dance called *beseda* which is composed of folk songs, the songs being sung with the dancing.

With the advent of Frederick Smetana (Smay'tah-nah) (1824-1884) Bohemian music became known to the world. His music reflects the spirit of his country. He has been called the Bohemian Beethoven, for many of his finer compositions were composed after he was stone deaf. In the United States he is best known for his symphonic cycle, entitled *My Fatherland,* of which "The Moldau" is a part, and his comic opera, *The Bartered Bride.* His polkas are said to be to Bohemia what Chopin's mazurkas are to Poland.

Another composer, Antonin Dvořák (Dvawr'jok) (1843-1904), is even better known. He was a poor peasant boy, son of an innkeeper and butcher. At an early age he showed a love for music. His father wished him to become a butcher, but he preferred to follow the strolling players and loved to play the violin and to sing. When quite young and beginning his work as a composer, he became a member of Smetana's orchestra. The great master befriended him and helped to foster his love of the national spirit in music. Franz Liszt, of Hungarian fame, aided him as he did all struggling young artists, and gradually Dvořák came to take his place as one of the great composers of the world. His *Slavonic Dances* are evidence of his Bohemian background, and his *New World Symphony* shows his interest in the Negro and Indian music of our own country. It was while he was Director of the New York Conservatory of Music that he

166

became interested in our Negro music which inspired many of the themes in this symphony. During his American stay he made an extended visit to the little town of Spillville, Iowa, where he played the organ in the village church and wrote some of his compositions. To the world at large, he is probably best known for his piano composition *Humoresque* and the song, *Songs My Mother Taught Me*.

Dvořák, a poor boy, lived to enjoy success and honors. He was very popular in England, and Cambridge University made him a Doctor of Music. He was the first musician to be appointed to the Austrian Upper House. His countrymen recognized in Dvořák's music his love of country and his deep appreciation of the folk music of his own land.

Two prominent composers of our own time came to us from Czechoslovakia. Jaromir Weinberger (Vine'bair-ger), who has spent much time in America, is well known for his opera, *Schwanda, the Bagpipe-Player*. The Polka and Fugue from this opera are often heard at symphony concerts. Weinberger includes among his works a Concerto for Tympani, and he has frequently written variations on American and British folk melodies. The best-known of these is his orchestral variations on *Under the Spreading Chestnut Tree*.

The other prominent Czech composer is Bohuslav Martinu, whose works for violin and orchestra command increasing attention.

All violin students are familiar with the name of Ottokar Ševčik (Sef'chik), who was born in the section of Czechoslovakia once known as Bohemia. One of his pupils was Jan Kubelik, a world famous violinist a half-century ago. Rafael Kubelik, son of Jan, continues to add to the family reputation as a recent conductor of the Chicago Symphony Orchestra.

Bright colors seem to predominate in Czechoslovakia, and when this country is mentioned, we are likely to think of brilliant beads, colorful pottery and textiles of every kind. Her cathedrals and palaces are famous, and her mineral spas are very numerous, the best known being that of Carlsbad.

QUESTIONS

1. What small countries were united under the government of Czechoslovakia?
2. Why have the people had to engage in so many wars?
3. Who was the early leader in this region?
4. Tell something about "Good King Wenceslaus."
5. What part of Czechoslovakia is considered the center of musical interests?
6. Name several dances popular in the country.

167

7. Briefly state some interesting facts concerning Frederick Smetana.
8. Who was Antonin Dvořák and why should Americans be especially interested in him?

LISTENING SUGGESTIONS

Dances from *The Bartered Bride* — Smetana

Humoresque — Dvořák

Moldau, The — Smetana

Overture to *The Bartered Bride* — Smetana

Polka and Fugue from *Schwanda* — Weinberger

Slavonic Dances (any) — Dvořák

Songs My Mother Taught Me — Dvořák

String Quartets and Quintets (any) — Dvořák

Symphony No. 5 in E Minor (From the New World) — Dvořák

Under the Spreading Chestnut Tree — Weinberger

HUNGARY

Hungary is a country filled with musical surprises! When thinking of European shrines of music and art, people often forget Hungary This is because it is off the beaten track of the average tourist and is not visited so frequently as other countries. Now, as a Communist country, Hungary is no longer in friendly contact with us, but her musical offerings have been great and her history fascinating.

The capital, Budapest, is really two cities in one with the picturesque Danube separating the ancient city of Buda from the more modern city of Pest. Buda is very old, dating back to 150 A.D., while Pest was founded several centuries later. For many years gypsies formed a colorful part of the throngs mingling in the streets, and the orchestras and bands in nearly every inn and hotel were largely made up of these care-free people.

In view of Hungary's musical past, it is not surprising to learn that a conservatory of music existed in Budapest as early as 1839, several years before the famous conservatory at Leipzig was started. Budapest is today the musical center of the country and the home of the National Conservatory. All branches of music have flourished in Hungary, and there is a long list of famous composers, pianists, violinists and singers. There has been great interest in symphonic music, and opera has been featured with many Hungarian works performed.

It is one thousand years and more since the Magyars (Modyars), who are the real Hungarians, wandered into what is now known as the Great Plain of Hungary. There, about 895 A.D. under their leader Arpad, they decided to settle. Today we find their descendants inhabiting a small country about the size of Florida, for Hungary lost much of her land after World War I. Nearly 2,000,000 Magyars, with

168

the same folk lore and music, are now living within the present boundaries of the country.

Two distinct types of music have come to us from Hungary. The first is that type known as Hungarian-Gypsy music — music which perhaps was originally Hungarian in character, but has been changed by the playing of the Gypsies until it is difficult to tell what is Hungarian and what is Gypsy. The second type is the real or pure Hungarian music without the musical decorations of the Gypsy.

Gypsy tents were in Hungary long before the Magyars led by Arpad conquered the land. It is thought by many that in some far distant past the Magyars and Gypsies were one people, for the Magyars long ago were a wandering or nomadic group. If this is true, it is easy to understand why the Gypsies were treated better in this land than in others, and, being thus treated, lived better and more orderly lives.

When we hear music which makes us exclaim, "Oh, that is gypsy music," it is more than likely to be Hungarian-Gypsy music. The Gypsy has the habit of taking the music of the country through which he roams and embellishing it with his own twists and turns, trills and runs. He plays without notes, improvising and making up the melodies as he performs. The older players cannot read music but the younger ones are learning to read. Their music has been passed on from one generation to another, just as any folk music is, and most of the players are able to repeat a number after one or two hearings.

Among the Hungarian Gypsies there have been several noted musicians. When one noted Gypsy fiddler died, thousands of people are said to have marched in his funeral procession. He was considered the King of the Gypsies and had played for the leading rulers of Europe. A Gypsy Queen was another romantic figure, traveling through Hungary and playing on her Amati violin. It is believed by many that she brought the *Rákóczy March* (Rah-koh'tshee) to the Hungarian people. This was their National March and greatly beloved by them.

Hungarian-Gypsy music has been an inspiration to many of the greatest composers. We have only to turn to the *Gypsy Rondo* of Haydn, the *C Major Symphony* by Schubert, the *Hungarian Dances* of Brahms and the Liszt (List) *Hungarian Rhapsodies* to find evidence of this inspiration. Perhaps the Rhapsodies of Liszt should be called "Gypsy Rhapsodies." It is said that Franz Liszt often visited the Gypsy camps and roamed the fields and woods with the Gypsies in order to absorb their delightful music.

However, the modern composers of Hungary do not feel that the Hungarian-Gypsy music is representative of the real folk and composed music of the country. They remind us that the Gypsies are but a

169

small part of the population of the country, and that gypsy music is only one type of Hungarian folk music. Béla Bartók (Bay'la Bar'tuk) (1881-1945), a recent Hungarian composer who spent years in studying the folk music of his country, maintained that much Hungarian music is Oriental and Byzantine (Biz'zan-teen) in character. Bartok is said to have collected from six to seven thousand folk tunes. In his music and that of other modern composers of Hungary you will find examples of this belief and a use of these old Hungarian tunes with modern harmonizations. Béla Bartók and his wife were excellent pianists, and their duo-piano concerts, in the United States and Europe, presented much of Bartók's music based on Hungarian sources.

The violin is a very popular instrument in Hungary, but the most beloved folk instrument is the *cimbalom* (tshim'bah-lom). It resembles a small piano with the cover open. Steel wires are spread on a horizontal board like those of a grand piano and are struck with two wooden sticks, the ends of which are covered with cloth. In Hungary there are said to be more than 10,000 of these instruments in use. The people love music and will listen for hours to their folk songs played on the cimbalom. The older folk have a special liking for sad songs. This is illustrated by the story of an elderly Hungarian count, who, when some very old Hungarian themes were being played for him, suddenly burst into tears. Of course the players stopped, but his wife cried, "Go on! Go on! He is enjoying it so much!" The *tarogato* (tar-oh-gah'to), a deep-toned clarinet-like instrument, is a popular old instrument. It was used in olden times to sound a warning of impending Turkish attacks.

The favorite Hungarian dance is the *czardas* (char'das), deriving its name from the inn where it was first danced. It has two parts, a slow part called the "lassu" or "lassen" and a fast part called the "friss" or "friska." These contrasting parts are found in Liszt's *Second Hungarian Rhapsody*. You can remember the fast part by associating it with the word "frisky," for it gets faster and faster until at the end the dancers finish in a veritable whirlwind.

Perhaps the greatest surprise of this rather small country is the number of composers who have risen within its borders. The most important among these composers is Franz Liszt (1811-1886). Be certain that you know about this man, who was a splendid musician, a great pianist, and a remarkable man. Liszt used folk tunes as the themes for many of his great works. The folk tune "Herons Homeward Flying" is found in his *Rhapsody No. 1* and also as the first theme of his *Hungarian Fantasy* for piano and orchestra. As a boy Franz Liszt knew the same great estates of the Esterhazy family on which Haydn had lived, for Liszt's father was employed by the Esterhazy's, though

170

not as a musician. The young Franz displayed such musical talent that friends sent him to Paris to study. This marked the beginning of one of the most remarkable careers in the history of music. Liszt's life was, in fact, a combination of several highly successful careers, for he became the greatest pianist of his time and also achieved world-wide fame as conductor, teacher, and composer.

Audiences all over Europe were electrified by Liszt's tremendous gifts as a pianist. Wherever he played he received unprecedented acclaim. Kings and queens bestowed honors upon him, and many women fell in love with him, for he was, by the standards of his day, a handsome and romantic figure.

As a teacher, he guided many of the foremost musicians of the nineteenth century, for Americans and Europeans alike sought to study with him. As a conductor at the German Court of Weimar (Vy'mar) he befriended young composers, among them Richard Wagner, who became the husband of Liszt's daughter, Cosima.

Concert audiences know and esteem Franz Liszt as the composer of *Les Préludes* and other symphonic poems, the Hungarian Rhapsodies and two famous Piano Concertos. Everyone knows him as the composer of the much played *Liebestraum*. Late in life Liszt became deeply engrossed in religion and wrote music for the church.

Also among Hungarian composers we should mention Karl Goldmark. He was very gifted and wrote many works, among them the well-known *Rustic Wedding Symphony*. The name of Stephen Heller is familiar to nearly every person who has been a student of piano music. Perhaps you have played some of his many studies and piano pieces that are still popular and used today. Erno von Dohnányi (Do-nahn'ye) is a splendid composer as well as one of the world's greatest living pianists. He now lives in America. Zoltán Kodály (Ko-dah'yee) is a modern composer, interested in the pure Hungarian music, who brings us compositions similar to those of Bartók, though perhaps not quite so ultra-modern.

Among Hungarian violinists are world-famous names. The memory of Leopold Auer (Ow-er) is beloved by hundreds of violin pupils in Europe and America. Joseph Joachim (Yo'ahk-im), one of the great violinists and teachers, was a composer as well. Jenö Hubay (Oo'bye), who studied with Joachim, had practically all of the outstanding violinists in Hungary as his students. Mention should be made of the virtuoso, Edward Reményi (Reh'men-yee), whose tours were always greeted with wild enthusiasm. It was through him that Brahms is said to have become interested in Hungarian melodies and it was to Reményi that he dedicated his Hungarian Dances.

Hungary has truly produced an extraordinary array of artists.

171

Among them are several symphony orchestra conductors now prominent in America. George Szell (Sell), conductor of the Cleveland Orchestra, Eugene Ormandy, conductor of the Philadelphia Symphony Orchestra, and Fritz Reiner are natives of Budapest, while Antal Dorati, conductor of the Minneapolis Symphony Orchestra, is also Hungarian-born.

QUESTIONS

1. Why is Hungary often forgotten in connection with European centers of music and art?
2. Tell something about the capital, Budapest, and the musical interests there.
3. Who were the Magyars?
4. Describe the Hungarian-Gypsy music and explain the difference between it and the real Hungarian music.
5. Who was Franz Liszt?
6. What famous non-Hungarian composers have been inspired by Hungarian music?
7. Describe the popular Hungarian instrument.
8. What is the favorite Hungarian dance and how did it receive its name?
9. Name some famous Hungarian-born composers.
10. Name several Hungarian musical artists who have attained world-wide recognition.

LISTENING SUGGESTIONS

Concerto for Orchestra — Bartók
Háry János Suite — Kodály
Hungarian Dances — Brahms
Hungarian Fantasy — Liszt
Hungarian Folksongs — Bartók
Hungarian Rhapsodies — Liszt
Les Préludes — Liszt
Liebestraum No. 3 — Liszt
Mephisto Waltz — Liszt

Piano Concertos (1-3) — Bartók
Piano Concerto No. 1 in E Flat — Liszt
Psalmus Hungaricus — Kodály
Rakoczy March — Berlioz
Rustic Wedding Symphony — Goldmark
Te Deum — Kodály

POLAND

Early in the nineteenth century (1810) the composer-pianist, Frederic Chopin (Sho-pan) was born in Poland. Born of a French father and a Polish mother, Chopin's loyalties were divided between France and Poland. Most of his life was spent on French soil, but throughout his short life-span of thirty-nine years he maintained a

172

deep love for Poland, and when he was buried in Paris, in 1849, Polish soil was placed in his grave.

To listen to a dashing mazurka or a stately polonaise by Chopin is to be reminded of Poland and its national dances. Chopin was a piano "specialist" and nearly all of his compositions were written for the piano. Today every pianist plays his preludes, etudes, waltzes, ballades, and polonaises. They are of universal interest, but in many of them is the national accent of the Poland he loved so dearly.

Ignace Paderewski (Een'yahss Pahd-eh-reff'skee) (1860 1041) is another celebrated Polish pianist who became the greatest concert artist of his day. He was a composer also, though not of the prominence of Chopin. Every student pianist, however, knows Paderewski's *Minuet in G.* Like Liszt, Paderewski had more than one career, and in his later life this famous Pole became a noted statesman and was the first Premier of Poland following World War I.

Chopin and Paderewski head a long list of renowned pianists of Polish birth. Although Poland boasts of many celebrated singers, the folk music of this country seems to have felt the influence of a national love of instrumental forms. Because of this influence their songs employ a wide melodic compass, they use chromatics freely, and their rhythms are complicated and varied.

The Poles are a Slavic nation and their folk music has many points in common with that of other Slavic peoples such as the Russians. On the other hand, some of their musical characteristics are quite different. Most of the Polish people have been devout Catholics for many centuries and it is thought that this influence of the Church brought them into closer touch with western Europe and gave them a different outlook from that of Russia and other Slavic nations. The Oriental influence which manifests itself in some Russian music is seldom heard in Polish music.

The Polish people have enjoyed only occasional periods of political freedom, and it is not surprising that a melancholy note dominates many of their songs. However, they generally employ a major scale and only now and then in their music do they use a minor scale, and then usually in a modified form.

There was a long period in the history of Poland when Polish society was greatly influenced by the elegance and the stately manners of the French court. This doubtless accounts for the fact that there are to be found in Polish music a certain polish and perfection of form as well as delicacy and grace. Polish songs and dances are very romantic in character. They are often intense, passionate, and filled with fire.

The best-known national dances of Poland are the *mazurka* and

173

the *polonaise*. In dancing the mazurka, the peasants did some improvising and added new steps as they went along, and therefore there are many variations of this dance. In its original form, the mazurka was a folk dance sung in $\frac{3}{4}$ meter, the accent falling on the second beat. The dancers provided an accompaniment by singing and clapping their hands. The polonaise is written in $\frac{3}{4}$ meter but, unlike the mazurka and the well-known waltz, which also have three beats to the measure, it was used as a dignified processional or grand march. It was inspired by days of pomp and splendor and was often danced at courts and at important social functions.

The most typical peasant dance of Poland is the *obertass*. It is usually written in $\frac{3}{8}$ measure and is the most rollicking and boisterous of all their dances. Another lively Polish dance is the *cracovienne* or *krakowiak* (krak-awv'yak) named for the city of Krakow. Paderewski was very fond of this dance.

Chopin and Paderewski were not the only celebrated pianists to come from Poland. Josef Hoffman came to America from Poland as a boy and made his debut at the Metropolitan Opera House when only eleven years old. Fifty years later, in 1937, he played the same program in the same auditorium. Moritz Rosenthal and Leopold Godowsky were celebrated concert pianists early in our century, and the Polish-born Theodor Leschetizky (Lesh-eh-tits'kee) was the teacher of Paderewski, Artur Schnabel, and many other famous pianists. Artur Rubinstein, well known to present-day concert and cinema audiences, is a native of Poland, while Wanda Landowska (Lahn-doff'ska), distinguished harpsichord player, is also Polish-born.

Frederic Chopin is the most illustrious name which Poland has given to creative music, but there have been other Polish-born composers who have achieved more than local recognition. The violin compositions of Henri Wieniawski (Vee-nee-ahff'skee) (1835-1880) have enjoyed favor. In our own time Alexandre Tansman (1897-   ) has won a reputation as a composer, particularly for the orchestra. Like Chopin, he has spent much time in Paris, and he has also lived in America.

QUESTIONS

1. What two great pianists and composers were born in Poland?
2. In what way does Polish folk music show instrumental influence?
3. How does the music of Poland differ from that of Russia?
4. What are the chief characteristics of Polish folk dances and folk songs?
5. Name two national Polish dances and tell something about each of them.
6. Name a famous Polish pianist and a noted Polish-born harpsichordist.

174

LISTENING SUGGESTIONS

Berceuse — Chopin
Concertos 1 and 2 for Piano — Chopin
Concerto for Violin (any) — Wieniawski
Etudes (any) — Chopin
Funeral March — Chopin

Minuet in G — Paderewski
Nocturnes (any) — Chopin
Polonaise in A — Chopin
Polonaise in A-flat — Chopin
Preludes (any) — Chopin
Waltzes (any) — Chopin

♉ 17 ♊

MUSIC IN OTHER COUNTRIES

The Netherlands

WHEN CONSIDERING The Netherlands, we usually think of both Holland and Belgium. Each has its own government at the present time, but there have been periods in history when they were under one rule. *Netherlands* means "low lands" and because much of this country is below sea level, this part of Europe is usually referred to as the "low countries."

HOLLAND

Holland means "hollow land" and it is easy to understand why this remarkable country was so named. With no point of land more than one hundred and twenty miles from the sea, it presents an interesting picture of lakes, rivers, dunes and dikes with a network of canals connecting with the North Sea. The *Zuyder Zee*, so famous in folk song and story, was once an ancient lake. With "water, water, everywhere" it is easy to understand why these people have a fondness for sailor songs and songs of the sea, and why the "hornpipe" is one of their favorite dances.

Holland's proximity to both England and Germany accounts for the fact that her folk music was greatly influenced by that of these countries. When the Protestant religion first flourished in Holland, the hymns which were sung were similar to the German Chorales, and even today many of these old Psalms and hymn tunes are heard in the Dutch Reformed Church. One of these fine old songs, the *Prayer of Thanksgiving*, we hear each year at Thanksgiving time.

Much of the music of both Holland and Belgium shows the influence of the thirteenth, fourteenth, and fifteenth centuries, when these countries led the world in developing a great contrapuntal school of writing. "Contrapuntal" is a type of music in which each voice sings an independent melody. This highly intellectual type of expression left its imprint on Netherlands folk music and because of this influence

176

many of the songs and dances are quite formal in type. This does not mean, however, that the Dutch did not enjoy many lively songs and dances. Any people as wholesome and as happy as they would find some way to express their feelings.

Most of us, even though we have had no first-hand opportunity to become acquainted with the Dutch, have vivid impressions of their characteristics and mode of living. These impressions have come to us from song and story and from their great artists, such as Rembrandt and Vermeer, who have given us remarkable portrayals of their people both at work and at play. We are all familiar with the paintings of Dutch girls dressed in colorful costumes, red and blue predominating, wearing white aprons, caps set demurely on their heads, and their feet clad in wooden shoes ready to tap out the rhythm of a dance. We also know the pictures of sturdy, rosy-cheeked Dutch boys, who, in some paintings, are pictured with the girls, ready to join in a game or dance, and in others, skating on the frozen canals wearing warm coats, long pantaloons and colorful scarfs and mittens. The Dutch now dress as we do, but it is quite certain that their former, quaint attire can still be seen in some rural sections of their country and that they doubtless use these costumes for festivals of dance and song held in Holland and in parts of Belgium where the population is predominantly Dutch.

QUESTIONS

1. How has the geographical location of Holland affected its folk music?
2. Why is much of the folk music of Holland more formal in type than that of other countries?

BELGIUM

The history of Belgium has been one of struggle for independence and not until 1830 did Belgium as we know it come into existence. During World War I this country suffered tragic experiences and rose bravely from the bondage of that time, rebuilding her towns and cities only to experience the terrors of World War II.

The area of Belgium is equal to that of our State of Maryland, but has five times its population, with a score of thriving cities and more than one hundred small towns and villages. Much of her countryside looks like that of Holland. The people of Belgium have had to build dikes to protect their country from the ravages of the sea, and they have been able to irrigate the sandy stretches by running streams and sluggish canals.

During the fourteenth and fifteenth centuries, western Belgium

177

was known as Flanders and today the people of this section are largely of Flemish ancestry. Their customs, costumes and language are closely akin to that of the Dutch. Some of the loveliest folk music of this region is found in its Christmas carols.

The people in southern Belgium are of French ancestry. They are known as "Walloons" and speak a dialect of the French language. The folk songs and dances of this section are particularly charming. Some of the oldest were introduced into the country by the trouvéres of France. A famous dance of the Walloons who lived in this section of Belgium was the *cramignon* (cra-meen'yon), a dance not unlike the French *farandole*. The farandole was a dance very popular in France, parts of Italy, and in Spain. The music is written in $\frac{6}{8}$ time and the participants form a procession and dance through the village streets. They imitate the leader and the tempo increases in speed until it comes to a rollicking climax.

Belgium, like Holland, shows English and German characteristics in her folk music and, like Holland, was influenced by the highly developed school of contrapuntal writing in the fourteenth, fifteenth, and sixteenth centuries.

On every side in Belgium one sees church towers and spires. Some of these churches are as beautiful in architecture as any to be found in Europe. For many centuries, when Belgium was divided into many small kingdoms, the important towns demanded the right to build belfries from which curfew could be rung each night. The church bell was also used to sound an alarm when the town was threatened by fire or by an invading army.

Perhaps this early interest in bells had something to do with the fact that today Belgium leads the world as the home of the carillon. A "carillon" is a chime of bells. Originally there were but four of these bells in a chime, but today some of the more elaborate chimes have as many as sixty or seventy bells tuned to different pitches. These can be played by means of a keyboard or console arranged like the manuals and pedals of an organ or can be mechanically operated by a clock-work mechanism. In Belgium and Holland there are as many as one hundred and thirty carillons of importance. In the past these chimes have sometimes been played hourly. The carillonneur plays programs which include songs and tunes of both national and local interest. The people of the Netherlands know their folk music better than others and this is in great measure due to the fact that for many years they have heard these melodies played hourly. The carillon is the most democratic of all instruments since a whole city constitutes its audience.

The city of Bruges has been famous for its carillon music, im-

178

mortalized in a well-known poem by our American poet, Longfellow. In Holland, also, there are great carillons, twenty of importance, and one hundred in all. We now have many carillons in this country, on college campuses and in church and other towers. Perhaps the most famous is in the Bok Tower at Lake Wales, Florida.

The saxophone was invented in Belgium by Adolphe Sax, who worked in Brussels. It was invented there about 1840. Its importance in present-day American popular music is known to all.

The eighteenth century opera composers of Belgium were important. Andre Grétry wrote over fifty operas and François Joseph Gossec became identified with musical life in Paris during and after the French Revolutionary period. Another famous Belgian musician was François Gevaert (Ghay'vahrt) (1828-1908). He was a distinguished teacher and author and collected and arranged many folk songs.

The violinists, Henri Vieuxtemps (Vee-oo-tahn') and Eugène Ysaye (Y-sah'ay) were the greatest of the nineteenth century Belgian violinists. They were both born near the city of Liege.

The most famous composer of Belgium was Cèsar Franck, who was born at Liege and studied at the Conservatory there. He became so definitely identified with French music that we often forget that he was born in Belgium. His musical contributions are discussed in the chapter on France.

The great importance of the Netherlands, musically speaking, was due to the wonderful school of counterpoint or part writing which flourished there from the fifteenth to the seventeenth centuries. We use the term "school" here to refer to a group of composers. The importance of this school of Holland and Belgium was not confined to those two countries, because, for many years, it set the pattern for musical composition throughout Europe. Many compositions of this period are still sung today, such as the *Ave Maria* of Arcadelt, *Born Today* composed by the greatest of all Dutch organists, Sweelinck, and *Matona, Lovely Maiden,* and the *Echo Song* by the most famous composer of this school, Orlando di Lasso.

QUESTIONS

1. What part of Belgium was once known as Flanders?
2. What name was given to the people of southern Belgium?
3. What countries influenced the folk music of Belgium?
4. (a) Name a folk dance which is popular in southern Belgium.
   (b) What French dance does it closely resemble?
5. What is a carillon?
6. Do you know where carillons are located in America?
7. Name a famous Belgian composer.

179

LISTENING SUGGESTIONS

Ave Maria — Arcadelt   *Echo Song* — di Lasso
Choral music — di Lasso   *Prayer of Thanksgiving* — Folk
Choral or organ music — Sweelinck

BULGARIA, YUGO-SLAVIA AND RUMANIA

There is distinctive music in the smaller countries of Europe, although it is not as well known to us as the music of Great Britain, Germany, France, and Spain. We have had less opportunity to know the music of such countries as Yugo-Slavia and Rumania, but enough has come to us to show that in the area in Southeastern Europe once known as the Balkan States, there are interesting types of folk music.

The music of Bulgaria, Yugo-Slavia, and Rumania, as we might expect, represents a blend of Eastern and Western influences. The history of these countries is one of many changes. The Greeks, Romans, Tartars, Turks, and Russians all have ruled this area at various times, and the culture and customs reflect a blend of European and Oriental influences.

All of these people are fond of dancing, and their folk culture includes many dances. They are group dances in which the men and women join hands and promenade gaily or leap and bound, depending upon the spirit of the music. They do not dance in couples as we are accustomed to do. Sometimes the dances are slow and the music is melancholy. In others there is lively movement, as in the Yugo-Slavian *kolo*.

The folk songs of Bulgaria, Yugo-Slavia, and Rumania are usually short and often very simply constructed. They are accompanied by rather primitive instruments, such as the *tamburitza*, somewhat like a mandolin, and the *gusla*, an instrument resembling a violin, although smaller and with less tone. Often they show the characteristics of gypsy music, for these nomadic people have been an important element in these countries, just as they have been in Hungary and Spain. The violin is a favorite instrument, and one of the best known examples of present day music from this part of Europe is the often-played violin number, *Hora Staccato*, by the Rumanian composer, Dinicu, a piece frequently included in the concert programs of Jascha Heifetz and other violinists.

The popular Rumanian Rhapsodies of Georges Enesco (1881-   ), played by symphony and school orchestras, give us an idea of Rumanian folk music, since their themes are either folk tunes or modeled after folk tunes. Enesco has attained international recognition as a violinist, teacher, conductor, and composer. He has appeared in this country as guest-conductor of several of our leading symphony orchestras. As a teacher, he helped to train such noted artists as Yehudi Menuhin.

GREECE

History tells us that music was held in high esteem by the early Greeks, who had achieved a remarkable development in many of the arts hundreds of years before the Christian era. Enough remains of their beautiful temples and works of art to show that Greece produced remarkable artists and architects. Their plays and books of philosophy have survived to support their reputation for literature, but unfortunately their music did not survive. We know from their art work and their writings that they had instruments resembling the flute, harp, and bagpipe, but we know little of the type of music they played. It is said, however, that there are Greek folk songs which maintain the character of the ancient Greek music.

America has reason to be grateful to the country of Greece for producing at least one great interpreter of music. Dmitri Mitropolous (Mee-trop'o-los), the celebrated conductor, was born in Athens and came to this country in 1937.

PORTUGAL

Although neighboring countries, Portugal and Spain and their types of music present marked differences. Both countries were influenced by the Moorish invasion, but the Portuguese are a less excitable people than the Spaniards, and their melodies are less elaborate and usually more serious than the tunes of Spain.

Now and then a Portuguese melody has found its way to this country. Usually it has been a sailor song, for the Portuguese have followed the sea, and sometimes it has been a Christmas carol, for Portugal, like many another country, has its interesting folk customs and songs connected with the Christmas season. When we sing *Adeste Fideles* (O Come, All Ye Faithful), we may be singing a Portuguese tune, for it is said to have come from Portugal to England. Some authorities, however, believe it to be of English origin.

SWITZERLAND

Because Switzerland is surrounded by Germany on the north, Italy on the south, and France on the west, her folk music has been greatly influenced by that of her neighbors. It seems likely, in fact, that the only really distinctive Swiss folk music is the Ranz des Vaches

181

(Rahn′day-Väsh), a dance song based on the calls of the cowherds and shepherds, and the yodel calls heard in all mountainous countries. Rossini gives us an example of the Ranz des Vaches in Part III of the Overture to *William Tell.* In this overture the composer strove to describe life in the Swiss Alps and the third section, known as "The Calm," relates the shepherd's thanksgiving after the storm, and the pastoral melody of the Ranz des Vaches is played by the flute and English horn.

Several distinguished musicians have come from Switzerland, but their music does not often bear any distinctive characteristics associated with their native land as in the case of many American, German, or Russian composers. Ernest Bloch, born in Geneva but long a resident of America, is deeply interested in Hebrew music, and many of his compositions have been influenced by Hebraic musical traditions. Bloch has paid tribute to the country of his birth in a composition entitled *Helvetia* (the old name for Switzerland) and to his adopted land of America in a symphony entitled *America,* in which he makes use of American folk tunes.

Arthur Honegger, also born in Geneva, has lived for many years in Paris and is considered a "modernist" composer. He is known for his descriptive piece for orchestra, *Pacific 231,* and his oratorio, *King David.* Rudolph Ganz, a native of Zurich, has spent most of his life in the United States, where he has won distinction as pianist, conductor, composer, and teacher. Switzerland also produced the noted teacher, Emile Jaques-Dalcroze (Zhahk-Dahl-kroz) (1865-1950), who developed the system of musical training through physical movement known as Eurythmics.

ISRAEL

The Jewish people probably have the world's oldest musical traditions. The Old Testament is full of references to music, both vocal and instrumental. A thousand years before the Christian era, King David established the use of music in the services in the Temple at Jerusalem. The chanting of the Psalms and other parts of the Scriptures have been featured in Jewish religious observances for several thousand years.

After the fall of Jerusalem in 70 A.D. and the dispersal of the Jews to many lands, the Jewish musical traditions were kept alive through the traditional chants in the synagogues. These chants were handed down from one generation of cantors to another and for hundreds of years were not even written down. In the nineteenth century an organized effort to preserve the ritual music of the Hebrews was

182

made, largely through the work of Solomon Sulzer, Louis Lewandowski, and Samuel Naumburg.

As this music became better known outside of the synagogues, it began to have an effect on composers, particularly those of Jewish origin. The twentieth century composer, Ernest Bloch, has probably provided the best expression in contemporary music of the Jewish musical tradition. Many of his works, such as the *Sacred Service*, the *Israel Symphony*, the *Three Jewish Poems*, and *Schelomo* (Solomon) were directly inspired by the ancient chants and by Jewish folk song, even though the themes are nearly always original with Bloch, rather than being based on actual folk melodies.

Other composers of our own time, including Joseph Achron, Leonard Bernstein, Aaron Copland, and Frederick Jacobi have found inspiration for some of their compositions in traditional Hebrew music. The recreated nation of Israel gives much attention to music, and a new generation of composers is developing there.

With their long tradition of instrumental music it is not surprising that as our modern instruments became perfected some of our foremost musical interpreters are of Jewish origin. Among the great pianists of Jewish blood may be noted Anton Rubinstein, Moritz Rosenthal, Leopold Godowsky, Myra Hess, Artur Schnabel, Artur Rubinstein, and Vladimir Horowitz. Noted violinists of Jewish origin include such virtuosi as Leopold Auer, Mischa Elman, Jascha Heifetz, Nathan Milstein, and Yehudi Menuhin. Some of our great conductors have also inherited the Jewish musical tradition — among them being Alfred Hertz, Bruno Walter, and Serge Koussevitzky.

QUESTIONS

1. Why does the music of Bulgaria, Yugo-Slavia, and Rumania represent a blend of Eastern and Western cultures?
2. What great interpreter of music was born in Greece?
3. Name three prominent musicians who were born in Switzerland.
4. What noted present-day composer has based much of his work on traditional Hebrew music?

LISTENING SUGGESTIONS

Concerto Grosso — Bloch
Hora Staccato — Dinicu
Rumanian Rhapsody No. 1—Enesco

Rumanian Rhapsody No. 2—Enesco
Sacred Service — Bloch
Schelomo — Bloch

Maestro Toscanini

184

⫷ 18 ⫸

THE SYMPHONY ORCHESTRA

A LMOST EVERYONE today has access to a radio or a phonograph and is thus able to hear, through broadcast or recording, the music of the world's splendid symphony orchestras. Before the development of these reproducing devices, only the favored few who lived in large cities were able to attend symphony concerts. Now it is possible for all of us to have this privilege.

To be sure, we cannot enter into this pleasure as completely as those in actual attendance in concert halls, but with the aid of television it may soon become possible for those outside of cities to see, as well as hear, our great orchestras. Moreover, the symphony orchestra is no longer confined to the large city. Many of our smaller cities have community orchestras, and so many of our colleges, universities, and larger high schools have their own orchestras that opportunities for hearing orchestra music have greatly increased.

It is an exciting experience not only to hear, but to see, a symphony orchestra in action. It is impressive to see the bows of each string section moving together, each individual player giving his best. It is interesting to watch a good conductor leading his players, often without a score, and it calls forth our admiration and profound respect.

The word "symphony" comes to us from the Greek "symphonia," which meant a concord or agreement of sounds. The Greeks also applied the word to musical instruments. In the seventeenth century musicians began to use the word "symphony" to designate instrumental introductions or interludes in operas or other vocal compositions.

THE STRING CHOIR

The largest section (or choir) of the orchestra is the string choir. Frequently the seating arrangement places the first violinists to the left of the conductor and the second violinists to his right. Directly in front of the conductor is the principal cellist (chellist) and parallel to the first violinists are the remaining cellists. The viola players are in the same relative position to the second violinists. Back of the violins and cellos are the double bass players.

Conductors do not always follow this arrangement, however, and some other groupings have been found in certain concert halls to give better resonance and blend.

A large symphony orchestra will include sixteen to eighteen first violins, fourteen to sixteen second violins, ten to twelve violas, the same number of cellos, and ten double basses. Like the seating arrangements, these numbers will vary in different orchestras.

The instruments of the string choir may be compared to the voices in a vocal quartet. The first violin is the soprano, the second violin the alto, the viola the tenor, and the cello the baritone. The double bass is like a low bass voice. For many years the cello played the bass part of the string music and the double bass played the same part an octave lower. Composers finally realized that the cello had great expressive possibilities for singing melodies and began to assign important melodies to it. When you listen to the cello theme in the Andante of Beethoven's *Fifth Symphony* or the equally lovely theme in the second movement of Schubert's *Unfinished Symphony*, you realize how much the earlier composers missed by not using the cello for such melodies. And composers since the time of Beethoven and Schubert have frequently called upon the cello to play some of their best melodic ideas.

It was probably Claudio Monteverdi (Mont-eh-vair'dee) who first appreciated the musical possibilities of the string choir. This is not strange, since he was born in the little town of Cremona, Italy, at a time when the Amati family was developing the violin into the splendid instrument we now know. The viol, as the ancestor of the violin was known, was a common instrument in the fourteenth and fifteenth centuries. King Henry VIII of England was fond of the viols and wrote music for them. During the sixteenth and seventeenth centuries the viol was improved to become the instrument so familiar to us now. This improvement took place largely in two small towns in the north of Italy — Brescia (Bres'chee-a) and Cremona. The instrument-makers to whom we owe the violin were Gasparo di Salo, who worked in Brescia, and three famous families of violin-makers, the Amati, Stradivari (Strahd-ee-vahr'ee) and Guarneri (Gwahr-nay'ree), all of whom lived in Cremona. Jacobus Stainer, who lived in the Tyrol, was the most celebrated German violin-maker. These artisans worked with the greatest attention to details, and since they knew secrets as to the fitting and seasoning of woods and the preparation of varnish, their instruments have never been surpassed. Violinists have paid many thousands of dollars for their instruments, and many of these famous violins are in use today.

The "Strad" is still the aristocrat among violins. Antonio Stradivari

186

lived to the age of ninety-three and continued to fashion his lovely instruments even in the final years of his life. His creations are often designated by the Latinized form of his name, Stradivarius, and similarly a Guarneri violin is known as a Guarnerius.

Monteverdi, who is known to us also as one of the first opera composers, had access to these wonderful instruments and began to realize their expressive powers in the orchestra. It was he who suggested the use of the tremolo, a string effect resulting from rapid up-and-down movements of the bow. The tremolo is used to add power to the tone and is sometimes employed as a descriptive device. Mendelssohn, in his Overture to *A Midsummer Night's Dream*, uses it to suggest the dancing of the fairies, and sometimes the tremolo creates effects of weirdness or excitement.

Monteverdi was one of the first to use the *pizzicato* (pit-se-ka'to) in which the strings are plucked with the fingers instead of bowed. This effect is often heard in orchestral music, and Tschaikowsky wrote an entire symphonic movement (the second movement of his Fourth Symphony) in which the string players do not use their bows, all notes being played pizzicato.

By the late seventeenth century such composers as Alessandro Scarlatti in Italy and Henry Purcell (Pur'sell) in England had adopted the five-part violin choir which is standard today. For many years each of the five instruments played a single part, but more recent composers frequently divide the first and second violins, and even the violas and cellos, into two or more parts.

Each group of players in the string choir has a leader, or "principal." The leader of the first violins is called the "concertmaster." Sometimes he is referred to by the German term "concertmeister" (con'cert-my' ster). It is his duty to mark all bowings and fingerings, and, since he is near the conductor, the entire section follows him as to attack, release, tempo, and style of bowing. The man beside him is known as the assistant concertmaster and is always ready to assist or replace the "first chair man."

The second violins, violas, cellos, and basses all have similar leaders, whose duties parallel those of the concertmaster in the first violin section. You will find, in fact, that each choir of the orchestra has its leader who is responsible for the phrasing, breathing, and fingering of the music that is being played.

The Violin. This instrument evolved from the rather clumsy old viol (vee'ol) and was first called "the little French fiddle." The word "fiddle" is still an informal name for the violin, and we often hear the term "fiddler's tunes." The violin is perhaps the most important

The violin   *Courtesy of the NBC Symphony Orchestra*

188

The viola

instrument in the orchestra and expert violinists can play passages of many notes with amazing rapidity and accuracy, or they can draw from the instrument, in voice-like tones, lovely sustained melodies.

Look at a violin closely, and you will be interested in its delicate structure, which comprises seventy-five to eighty parts. Notice the strings, the bridge, fingerboard, and the sounding post. The four strings are tuned to G, D, A, and E, and when violinists tune up at the beginning of a concert they tune to A above middle C which has a pitch of 440 vibrations per second.

All instruments of the violin family are played with bows which vary slightly in size and shape. A good bow is almost as important as the violin itself and the art of bow-making has long been important. The standard violin bow has changed very little since about 1775 when it was established by Francois Tourte (Toort), a Frenchman, regarded as the greatest of violin bow-makers. Bows are made from choice woods and are strung with horsehair.

The Viola. An instrument that looks like an oversized violin, the viola (vee-o'la) is held and played in the same manner as the violin. Each string is tuned five notes lower than the corresponding string of a violin. The viola tone is deeper than that of the violin and suggests a beautiful contralto voice, although it is the third, or tenor, part in the string choir. A trained ear is required to distinguish between the low notes of a violin and the high notes of a viola. Likewise, the lower notes of the viola resemble the higher notes of the cello.

The viola was developed before the violin, particularly by Gasparo di Salo, about 1540. Viola players read from the so-called "alto" or "C" clef on which Middle C is found on the third line. Good violinists can play the viola without special preparation after they have mastered the C clef.

The Violoncello. The full name of the 'cello is "violoncello" (vee-o-lon-chel'lo), not "violincello," but custom has made it known simply as the "cello." It is shaped like a violin, but is much larger, and when played it stands on the floor in front of the player. It developed from the "knee fiddle" of the seventeenth century. It is one of the most-beloved instruments in the orchestra, because of its rich, sonorous tone and its capacity for expressing deep emotion. Someone has referred to the cello as "the sighing lover" of the orchestra.

The Double Bass (Contrabass). The double bass, like the violoncello, stands on the floor, but the player instead of being seated on a chair, as is the cellist, must stand or sit on a high stool because

190

The violoncello

The double bass

192

the instrument is so tall. Its tones sound an octave lower than the music is written, and it gets its name from the fact that, until the time of Beethoven, it was always used to double, or duplicate, the part of the violoncello an octave lower. When, in his *Fifth Symphony,* Beethoven gave interesting passages to the double basses, Berlioz, the famous master of orchestration, said the music reminded him of the gambols of an elephant.

Stringed Instruments as Solo Instruments. The violin, viola, and violoncello are all used frequently as solo instruments, and many celebrated virtuosi (skilled players) have been developed. Some of the great violinists of our time are Nathan Milstein, Jascha Heifetz (Hi'fetz), Zino Francescatti (Frahn-ces-kaht'tee), Mischa Elman, and Fritz Kreisler. William Primrose is famed as a viola player, and Pablo Casals (Ka-sahls') and Gregor Piatigorsky (Pee-at-i-gor'skee) are celebrated cellists. Even the double bass has had a few noted soloists, especially the late Serge Koussevitzky, long conductor of the Boston Symphony Orchestra.

THE WOOD WINDS

When we arrive a little early at an orchestra concert, we see the players entering singly or in small groups. Those who seat themselves in the center of the stage are the wood-wind group, whose instruments are possibly the most romantic of the entire orchestra. By listening to the "pre-concert" bits of music from their instruments, we get an idea of the kind of music this section of the orchestra will give us. The wood-wind players have to "warm up" their instruments, not for practice, but because the instruments must be warmed by the breath of the players to put them in tune.

What fascinating bits of melody we hear from them! Light, airy runs and trills, grunts and rumblings, and odd, oriental-sounding scales. Now it will be plaintive pastoral music, and again it may be bird calls or fairy music. Or, if the bassoons are heard, it may be grotesque or humorous passages.

The Flute. The flute is one of the oldest instruments and one consistently used in the earlier orchestras. Except for the piccolo, it is the highest in pitch among the wood-wind voices. At first one or two flutes were used, but since the time of Haydn it has been customary to use three flutes. The tone of the flute is produced by blowing across the hole in the side of the instrument. All other wood winds produce their tones through the vibration of reeds, double or single.

193

The flute

194

195

The bassoon

The clarinet

The light silvery tones of the flute are most attractive and are often employed in the orchestra. Brilliant passages are easily played on the flute and its little brother, the piccolo, which plays brilliant, sometimes shrill, notes an octave higher than the flute. Although included in the wood-wind family, the flute and piccolo are nearly always made of metal rather than wood.

The Oboe. Someone has termed the oboe "an ill wind that nobody blows good." It is, in truth, not an easy instrument, but in the hands of a skilled player it adds a flavor to the orchestra that cannot be had from any other source. Its nasal, penetrating quality may be easily heard in the pre-concert "warming up." The other players listen carefully to it, for since it deviates from pitch less than any of the other instruments, its "A" is accepted as the standard for tuning the orchestra.

The oboe is certainly one of the oldest of the instruments, for it descended from the shawm, an oboe-like instrument which has been found in Egyptian tombs dating back to 3700 B.C. The oboe has a conical bore and its tone comes from the vibration of a pair of reeds in the mouthpiece. The reeds are blades of very thin cane. The pitch of the tone is controlled by finger-holes and keys, and unusual breath control is demanded, since the air pressure on the reeds must be very light.

The oboe was a member of the earliest orchestras. Bach and Handel were very fond of it, and a pair of oboes has been standard in all symphony orchestras since their time. Composers call on the oboe for sad, plaintive, or mysterious music and sometimes for a saucy or whimsical tune.

The English Horn. Sometimes musical terms are not so exact as we might expect, and this is true of the English horn, which is neither English nor a horn. It is, instead, an alto oboe, pitched five notes lower than the oboe and with a richer, darker quality, although still nasal. It originated in Italy and succeeded an earlier double-reed instrument of similar range (the oboe da caccia (cach'ee-ah) often used in early orchestras. Rossini, who used the English horn in his opera, *William Tell*, was among the first to establish it in the orchestra.

The Clarinet. This is a versatile and important member of the orchestra which may play brilliantly, like the flute, or expressively, like the oboe. It can also increase or lessen its tone with great ease. Its lower tones are resonant and beautiful. This part of its range is often called the "chalumeau" register, a term which comes from the chalu-

198

meau, the instrument from which the clarinet is descended. The word "register" refers to a part of the compass of an instrument or voice, which is said to have lower, middle, and upper registers.

The lower middle notes of the clarinet are not always true, but the upper middle register is of great beauty. The very highest clarinet tones are likely to be shrill.

Mozart introduced the clarinet into the symphony orchestra, although Haydn and Gluck had employed it in opera scores. Since Beethoven's time the clarinet has been established in the orchestra, and composers normally employ two or three clarinets, often adding the bass clarinet, which sounds an octave lower than the clarinet.

Many clarinetists in symphony orchestras use two clarinets — one pitched in A for sharp keys and one in B flat for flat keys.* In school orchestras and bands the B-flat clarinet is universally used. All clarinets are single-reed instruments. The player blows into the mouthpiece and the reed vibrates, setting in motion the air within the instrument and producing the tone, which is regulated as to pitch by finger-holes and keys.

The Bassoon. This instrument is the bass voice of the wood-wind section, and what a bass! It is one of the most versatile instruments in the orchestra, and its tones may be rich, somber, sad, or playful. It can grunt or cackle, and its great variety of sound effects has caused it to be termed the "clown of the orchestra." Composers, since the seventeenth century, have been fond of the bassoon and have used it consistently in the orchestra. Beethoven, Mendelssohn, and others have exploited its humorous effects. It often adds a serious note of beauty however. The bassoon is a tube, nine feet long but doubled back on itself. The Italians gave it the name of *fagotto* (fa-got'to), meaning a bundle of sticks. It is a double-reed instrument.

The Contrabassoon. An even lower bass voice is available to the wood-wind section in the contrabassoon. It plays the bassoon notes an octave lower in the same fashion that a double bass plays an octave below the violoncello. A wit once observed that

> A contrabassoon may be had
> Just twice as long and twice as sad.**

---

* When the A clarinet is used, the player reads a minor third higher than the instrument sounds. Thus when he reads C-D-E the instruments plays A-B-C sharp. With the B-flat clarinet the player reads a tone higher than the sound. Thus, he reads C-D-E and the sounds are B flat-C-D.

**From *People of Note*, by Lawrence McKinney. Used by permission of E. P. Dutton & Co., Inc.

Listen to a recording of the *Polovetzian Dances* by Borodin or *The Sorcerer's Apprentice* by Dukas and you will hear the very low bass notes of the contrabassoon.

THE BRASS CHOIR

The brilliant, shining array of instruments usually seen in the right center of the orchestral group is the "brass choir." Who does not thrill to the brilliant notes of the trumpet, the soft beauty of the French horn, or the majestic tone of the trombone? In orchestral music many of the great climaxes result from the full rich voices of the brass section. The modern orchestra customarily calls for three trumpets, four horns, three trombones, and tuba.

The Trumpet. We know the trumpet is a very old instrument, for the Old Testament contains many references to it. The Psalmist, in Psalm 150, exhorts us to "Praise the Lord with the sound of the trumpet," and a favorite Bible story relates that the walls of Jericho were leveled to the ground by a great blast from trumpets of rams' horns, blown by Joshua's priests. Through the ages the trumpet has been widely used by man to sing songs of triumph, to call soldiers to battle, and to add brilliance to religious or patriotic festivals. The trumpet we know today is made of brass, is normally pitched in B flat and through a series of valves can play in any key. An Irishman, Charles Claggett, invented the valve trumpet about one hundred fifty years ago, and it was gradually improved into the instrument we have today. Before the valve trumpet, players changed keys by changing the "crook," which was an accessory piece of tubing which would lengthen or shorten the instrument and thus lower or raise the pitch. There were "crooks" for various keys and a trumpet player had to keep several at hand to allow for the changes of key during a program.

Bach and Handel were fond of the instrument and often used three trumpets in order to play chords. Their instruments were pitched higher than those of today and added a remarkable brilliance to their music. These two composers were among the first to use the trumpet as a solo instrument. Perhaps you have heard the trumpet obbligato in "The Trumpet Shall Sound" in Handel's *Messiah* or the solo trumpet in Bach's *Second Brandenburg Concerto*. The latter, played by a trumpet in F, is an excellent example of the old high-pitched trumpet.

Much of Bach and Handel's music is majestic, and the trumpets add grandeur. It is interesting to recall that Mozart, whose music is more elegant and delicate, disliked the trumpet and even rewrote

200

some Bach and Handel trumpet parts for clarinet. Wagner, who demanded a large orchestra for his grand impressive works, made great use of all the brass instruments and practically all composers since his time have given much attention to the brass choir.

The French Horn. Placed near the wood winds in the orchestra will be noted the French horns, usually four in number. A French horn is really a long tube (about 18 feet) coiled around and around and ending in a large flaring bell. The French horn we know descended from the hunting horn, which was also coiled in a circle and could be slipped over the head of the mounted hunter. The hunting horn had no valves or crooks and was largely limited to one key. Our modern French horn has valves, and can play in any key. For many years, however, horn players had to use horns of different pitches or resort to crooks, as in the case of trumpets, for changes of key. The valve-horn was invented as long ago as 1827, but many composers preferred the older horns, and even Brahms only seventy or eighty years ago specified horns in various keys for some of his symphonies. Today, however, only the French horn in F is used in orchestras. Since the fundamental note is F the player reads a perfect fifth higher than the instrument sounds. Thus to play middle C and the D and E above, the player reads G-A-B.

Lully is said to have introduced the French horn into the orchestra in 1664. Bach frequently used two horns and Handel even more often, as you can hear in the *Water Music* or the *Royal Fireworks Music*. Haydn and Mozart called for two horns in many of their symphonies, but it remained for Beethoven to add the third and finally the fourth horn. Wagner, with his usual lavishness, sometimes called for as many as eight.

The horn brings mellowness to the orchestral tone and adds a great richness to the body of tone. It has a most expressive sound and is frequently called upon by composers as a solo instrument. You may often hear it playing lovely melodies, such as the first theme of the slow movement of Tschaikowsky's *Fifth Symphony* or the opening of the Overture of *Mignon* (Meen'yohn) by Thomas (To-mäh'). Or you may hear it, alone or in harmony, sounding horn calls which suggest military or hunting scenes. Beethoven's *Eroica Symphony* provides excellent examples of such passages for three horns.

Perhaps you have wondered why a horn player sometimes inserts his hand into the bell of the instrument. He may be "muting" the horn to give the effect of sound from a distance or a muffled, veiled effect. He may also be "stopping" the horn, which raises the pitch a half or full tone, depending upon the degree of "stopping."

The trumpet   *Courtesy of the Chicago Symphony Orchestra*

The French horn

The tuba

204

The trombone

The horn is the most difficult to play of the brass instruments. The player's lips serve as a reed and set in motion the column of air within the tube. This requires a special and not easily achieved embouchure (ahm'boo-shure'), which means a particular position of the lips and tongue. A slight variation of this position or of the control of the breath will easily bring about a wrong note, as even experienced players have found, to their discomfiture.

The Trombone. Back of the trumpets and French horns and a little to the right are the trombones. At first glance they look like long trumpets, but observation shows that the players are pulling or pushing a long slide. This slide varies the length of the trombone tube and thus raises or lowers the pitch. The trombone player therefore does not use valves or keys. This makes it necessary for him to think his tone before he plays it, and to be sure he moves the slide to just the right place.

The trombone provides the right tone for solemn and majestic passages in music, and it may, on occasion, be martial or sad, or even humorous, as it sometimes is in a dance orchestra. In the latter case the calisthenics of the player add to the amusing musical antics of the instrument. In the symphony orchestra, composers have made splendid use of the trombone's impressive tonal capacities, commonly using three trombones with a tuba to form a quartet of lower-voiced brass instruments. In a band or orchestra the trombones correspond to the tenors and basses in a mixed chorus.

An instrument called the *sackbut* (meaning *drawpipe*) was the ancestor of the trombone in fifteenth century Italy. Trombones were used in the early operas, and Mozart made excellent use of them in *Don Giovanni* (Gee-o-vahn'ee). For some reason, however, no composers took them into the orchestral family until Beethoven, never afraid of a new idea, brought them into the last movement of his *Fifth Symphony*. Mendelssohn, it is said, regarded them as "too sacred" for frequent use. Wagner knew how to make the best use of this noble instrument. You will feel their power in the Overture to *Tannhäuser* and many other Wagnerian passages.

The Tuba. The deepest voice in the brass choir is that of the tuba, the large bulky brass instrument with a large, upright bell, placed next to the trombones. It is played with valves and provides a deep, full-sounding bass for the brass harmonies. Sometimes it is used with other instruments to bring out an important melody. Wagner uses the tuba in this fashion in the Overture to *Die Meistersinger*.

206

THE PERCUSSION SECTION

The percussion section of the orchestra carries much responsibility. When a percussion player is busy, he is very busy, having sometimes the responsibility for half a dozen instruments. When he is not busy, he still must be thoroughly alert in order to perform his part at exactly the right time. One boom or cymbal crash on the wrong beat will ruin a performance.

In the percussion section you will see the timpani (tim'pa-nee), looking much like copper kettles, and often called kettledrums. These are flanked by the bass and snare drums, the cymbals, triangle and other instruments played by striking with sticks or hammers. These instruments help in adding color and accent to orchestral music. They are the rhythmic foundation of the orchestra, and they are especially valuable in achieving great climaxes in the music.

The Timpani. Timpani (singular is timpano) are the only percussion instruments which must be tuned to definite pitches. Bach, Handel, Haydn, and Mozart used two timpani and tuned them to the tonic and dominant of the piece. Since the tonic and dominant (first and fifth of the scale) are important notes which appear in many chords, this tuning enables the timpani to give a bass support to much of the music.* Timpani played with trumpets formed a sort of team in military music for hundreds of years. Beethoven, again the innovator, experimented with new tunings and freed them from the trumpets. Weber in 1807 added a third kettledrum. The timpani rest on metal tripods and are usually made of copper.

Stretched across the top of the timpano is a parchment head, kept in place by an iron hoop and tightened by a set of screws. In the older type of timpani the performer loosens or tightens these screws to change the pitch. The newer instruments are tuned by means of a foot-pedal. When you see a player turning screws and keeping his ear close to the instrument, you will know that he is changing the tuning. Beethoven and Wagner and more recent composers have sometimes used the timpani to announce a short theme or note pattern, and all composers have called on these instruments for loud and dramatic passages.

The Bass Drum. The sight and sound of a bass drum is familiar to all who have seen and heard a band. Most small boys have had an ambition to play it. Made of wood, its hollow barrel is covered at

---

* The tonic is the keynote or number one of the scale, while the dominant is number five. Thus, in the scale of A the tonic is A and the dominant is E.

207

The kettledrums   *Courtesy of the Chicago Symphony Orchestra*

The cymbals

Courtesy of the Chicago Symphony Orchestra

211

both ends with taut parchment. It is beaten with a stick which ends in a felt-covered knob. Its greatest service is to mark the rhythm with steady strokes, although a drum roll can be performed with two sticks, and a muffled effect is sometimes achieved by loosening the heads. Muffled drums are often used in funeral marches. While the bass drum is more prominent in the band, it has had a part in the symphony orchestra for nearly two hundred years, or since the time of Gluck and Mozart.

The Snare Drum. The snare drum, or side drum as the English call it, has a cylindrical body of wood or metal with tightly stretched heads over both ends. The upper head of the snare drum is called the "batter-head," the lower, the "snare-head." Under the snare-head are the snares, which are tightly stretched strings of catgut or metal. When the player, using wooden sticks, strikes the "batter-head," the snares vibrate against the "snare-head" and produce the rattling sound with which we are all familiar. Rapid alternation of the two sticks produces the familiar drum-roll. The tone can be muffled by inserting cloth between the snares and the "snare-head."

The Cymbals. These are large brass plates usually twelve or more inches in diameter. They are sounded by striking their edges together with a sliding movement. For certain effects the percussion-player may strike them with the wooden or felt-covered drumsticks, and it is possible to produce a roll effect, somewhat in the fashion of a drum-roll. Cymbals are used in marches and other strongly rhythmic music and are called upon in other music to accentuate a climax or a sudden change of mood. The cymbal is a very ancient instrument, and we read in the Bible, "Praise Him upon the high sounding cymbals."

The Triangle. This is a steel bar, bent into triangular shape with the ends left a short distance apart. It is struck with a steel rod and gives forth a ringing, penetrating tone which helps to mark the accent of the music. It is frequently heard in ballet music.

The Xylophone and Marimba. Xylophones (Zí-lo-phones) and marimbas are familiar instruments found in most dance orchestras, but only occasionally in the symphony orchestra. Each instrument consists of a series of wooden plates tuned to form a chromatic scale, of three octaves in the xylophone, and four octaves in the marimba. Under the plates are tube-like resonators. The tone is produced by striking with hard or soft mallets. The marimba, which is said to have

212

originated in Guatemala, has a softer and more mellow tone than the xylophone and is often used in Latin-American music. A notable example of the use of the xylophone in the symphony orchestra is in *Danse Macabre* (ma-cahb′) by Saint-Säens, where it depicts the dancing of the skeletons.

Orchestra Bells and Cathedral Chimes. The orchestra bells, often called "glockenspiel" (glock′en-shpeel), comprise a series of steel plates, tuned to the chromatic scale, and played with mallets. The tones are clear and bell-like and are used to give point to high-pitched melodies.

The cathedral chimes are a series of long metal tubes mounted on a rack. The tones are produced by striking the tubes near the upper end with a wooden mallet. They are used to represent church bells or other chime effects.

The Celesta. A celesta consists of a series of steel plates, under each of which is a wooden resonator. The instrument is played by means of a piano-like keyboard. It produces a charming, bell-like tone, and because of its delicacy is used in light orchestral passages in connection with the upper strings or flutes. You can hear the celesta used to excellent effect in the "Dance of the Sugarplum Fairy" in Tschaikowsky's *Nutcracker Suite.*

The Gong. The gong comes to us from the Orient, where it is often featured in the music of China and Japan. It provides awe-inspiring or sinister effects, usually in compositions of an Oriental character.

The Castanets. These instruments are associated with Spanish music, especially dance music. They resemble the halves of a chestnut (meat) and are clicked together in the player's hands or clicked at the end of a stick. Traditionally the larger pair is played by the left hand to mark the basic rhythm and the smaller pair is played by the right hand to mark additional rhythms.

The Tambourine. A member of the drum family, this is a very old and rather primitive instrument which is played by shaking, as well as striking. It is a small wooden hoop with parchment stretched on one side. Small metal disks are inserted at intervals in the hoop, and they produce the jingling sound when the instrument is shaken or rapped. The tambourine is often used in Spanish or gypsy music. Percy Scholes points out that the tambourine of today appears to be exactly the same instrument as pictured on ancient monuments.

213

QUESTIONS ON THE ORCHESTRA

Strings

1. Describe how the violins, violas, and cellos of the orchestra are generally placed.
2. How many of these instruments are usually found in large symphony orchestras?
3. Tell something about famous makers of the violin.
4. What is meant by the term "pizzicato"? What effects are gained by the use of the tremolo?
5. What are the duties of the leaders of each section?
6. Describe the viola and compare it to the violin.
7. Why is the cello such an important instrument in the string section?
8. How did the double bass get its name?
9. Name a great violin virtuoso, a famous viola player, an outstanding cellist, and a former symphony conductor who was an accomplished bass player.
10. Can chords be played on a violin?
11. Find out from a violinist or cellist what is meant by "the positions."
12. What famous violinist have you heard on recordings or on the air and what did he play?

Wood Winds

1. Which of the wood winds has the highest pitch?
2. How is the tone produced on a flute?
3. Suggest an orchestral composition in which the flute is prominent.
4. Tell something of the history of the oboe.
5. How are its tones produced?
6. How does the English horn differ from the oboe? Is it a horn?
7. What is the most numerous wood-wind instrument in a band?
8. How would you describe the tone of an oboe? Of a clarinet? Of a bassoon?
9. What are some of the musical effects that are characteristic of the bassoon?
10. How is the bassoon constructed?

Brass

1. Tell something of the earliest uses of the trumpet.
2. How did the ancient instrument differ from the modern one?
3. What effects are gained by the use of the trumpet and what type of music is best suited to its use?
4. What composers used the trumpet to great advantage in their orchestra works and also were the first to use the trumpet as a solo instrument?
5. Describe the construction of the French horn.
6. From what instrument did it descend?

7. What famous composer was the first to write compositions which called for the use of four horns instead of two?
8. What composer sometimes scored his works for as many as eight horns?
9. Describe a trombone and tell how the slide is used.
10. List the possible effects to be gained by the use of this instrument.
11. Who was the first composer to employ trombones in his orchestral family?
12. What is the deepest voice in the brass choir?
13. What music have you heard in concert or on the air which featured (a) trumpets; (b) trombones; (c) horns?
14. Suggest two different combinations of instruments which might form a satisfactory brass choir.

Percussion

1. What are the most important instruments of the percussion section?
2. Which ones are tuned to definite pitches? How is this accomplished?
3. Describe the construction of the timpani.
4. Tell something about the snare drum and how it is made.
5. Describe the cymbals and tell how they are made.
6. What composition did Tchaikowsky write where the celesta is used to advantage?
7. Tell how the celesta is constructed and describe the character of its tone.
8. Castanets are generally associated with the music of what country?

LISTENING SUGGESTIONS

All Instruments
Columbia Album Set X250.
The Young Person's Guide to the Orchestra — Britten

Violin
Brandenburg Concerto No. 4 — Bach
Any Concerto or Sonata for Violin
Any Concerto Grosso by Handel or Vivaldi

Viola
"In the Village" from *The Caucasian Sketches* — Ippolitov-Ivanov
Symphony No. 6 (opening of 1st movement) — Tschaikowsky

Violoncello
Any Concerto or Sonata for Violoncello

Symphony No. 3 (3rd movement) — Brahms
Symphony No. 6 (2nd movement) — Tschaikowsky

Double Bass
Symphony No. 5 (3rd movement) — Beethoven
Symphony No. 8 (*Unfinished*) (1st movement) — Schubert
Symphony No. 2 (introduction, 2nd movement) — Sibelius

Flute
Italian Symphony (4th movement) — Mendelssohn
Prelude to the Afternoon of a Faun — Debussy
Suite No. 2 in B Minor — Bach

Piccolo
"Procession of the Sardar" from *The Caucasian Sketches* — Ippolitov-Ivanov

215

Oboe
> *Symphony No. 2* (3rd movement) — Brahms
> *Symphony No. 4* (2nd movement) — Tschaikowsky

English Horn
> *Symphony in D Minor* (2nd movement) — Franck

Clarinet
> "In the Garden" from *Rustic Wedding Symphony* — Goldmark
> *Symphony No. 1* (3rd movement) — Brahms

Bassoon
> *In the Hall of the Mountain King* — Grieg
> *The Sorcerer's Apprentice* — Dukas
> *Symphony No. 6* (introduction to 1st movement) — Tschaikowsky

Contrabassoon
> *Polovetzian Dances* — Borodin

Trumpet
> *Leonore Overture No. 3* — Beethoven
> Overture to *Rienzi* — Wagner

French Horn
> *Symphony No. 7* (introduction to 1st movement) — Schubert
> *Symphony No. 5* (2nd movement) — Tschaikowsky

Trombone
> *Ride of the Valkyries* — Wagner
> *Russian Easter Overture* — Rimsky-Korsakoff

Tuba
> Overture to *Die Meistersinger* — Wagner

Timpani
> *Symphony No. 1* (3rd movement) — Sibelius

216

THE PIANO AND THE HARP

THE PIANO

W E CALL IT the "piano," although its full name is the "pianoforte." And if we were to translate it into English, we might say, "I am now going to play upon the soft-loud," for *piano* means soft and *forte* means loud. These are Italian words, and it is entirely appropriate that they be used to designate the instrument we know so well, for the pianoforte was invented by an Italian, almost 250 years ago.

Any history of artistic developments seems inevitably to have a connection at some time with the city of Florence, Italy, and it is not surprising to find that the first pianos were built in Florence by Bartolomeo Cristofori (Chreest-o-foh′ree). Christofori was a harpsichord maker and among his patrons was Prince Ferdinand de Medici (Med′eh-chee), a member of the family prominent in the cultural and political history of Florence for several hundred years.

The idea of the keyboard was not new, since organs, harpsichords, clavichords, and virginals, all played by keyboards, had been in common use for a couple of centuries. The clavichord, said to have been a favorite instrument with Bach, resembled a small rectangular piano except that it often had no legs, and was placed upon a table. The harpsichord, with a larger tone than the clavichord, looks much like a small grand piano, although it frequently has two keyboards, rather than the one keyboard which the modern piano possesses. The harpsichord-player, like the present-day harpist, has to devote much time to tuning the instrument before playing. Harpsichords are still made in this country and in Europe and several artists play them in concert and for recordings. Wanda Landowska (Lahn-doff′ska) is perhaps the best-known performer on the harpsichord in our own time.

Cristofori's contribution to the piano was the development of the hammer action (which may not have been an entirely new idea) whereby the strings of the piano were struck by hammers instead of being plucked by quills, as in the harpsichord, or pressed by metal bars, as in the clavichord. There was no way of sustaining or varying the tone of the harpsichord, and while the tone of the clavichord could be to some extent sustained, it was so small as to be almost inaudible in a large room. Musicians, therefore, were in search of an instrument that would be more flexible and more brilliant and Cristofori found the answer.

Cristofori's earliest pianos were shaped a great deal like our present-day "grand" pianos. They were considerably smaller, however, and their keyboard range was smaller, usually extending from four to four and a half octaves in comparison with the standard 88-note keyboard, or seven and a third octaves, on pianos of our time. One of Cristofori's first pianos, made in 1720, may be seen today in the Metropolitan Museum of Art in New York City.

While Cristofori evolved the hammer action and thus gave the piano a much greater volume of sound than the harpsichord could produce, it remained for others to perfect the pedals and thus bring about the great variety of expressive musical effects which the modern piano can produce. The *damper* pedal, often wrongly called "loud" pedal, is said to have been invented by John Broadwood of England. The damper is a piece of felt which stops the tone after the strings have been struck by the hammer in the piano action. When the damper pedal is depressed, the dampers are raised, allowing full vibration of the strings. Properly used, the damper pedal enables tones to be prolonged, but when used too much, a jumble of tones results.

The development of the so-called "soft" or *una corda* (one string) pedal is attributed to Andreas Stein of Vienna. This pedal shifts the action so that the hammers strike but one string, instead of the usual two or three, for each key, thus producing a softer tone.

About 1862 the middle pedal on grand pianos, known as the *sostenuto* pedal, was invented by a French piano-maker, Montal. Its use, when the damper pedal is not down, prolongs tones without confusion with others played after them.

At first pianos were made by hand in small shops in contrast to the large factories in which they are made today. For some years many musicians preferred the harpsichord and clavichord. It is related that Silbermann, the first German piano maker, persuaded Johann Sebastian Bach to try some of his instruments. Bach indicated that he liked his clavichord much better. Later, however, as the instruments improved, Bach's opinion of them improved, and while the great composer is said never to have owned a piano, at least two of his sons were prominent in winning public favor for the new instrument. Carl Philipp Emanuel Bach, court musician for Frederick the Great of Prussia, liked the piano and induced the king to purchase several of Silbermann's pianos. John Christian Bach, another of the

218

composer's sons, went to London in 1759 and is said to have given the first piano recital in England.

The early pianos had a larger tone than the harpsichord, but they were still best adapted to music which had lightness, clarity, and brilliance, the sort of music we associate with Haydn, Mozart, and Scarlatti. As the piano was improved and its tone grew in power and expressiveness, piano music became more dramatic and more poetic. Composers who were also pianists, such as Beethoven, Schumann, and Liszt, developed the dramatic and exciting qualities of piano music, while others, such as Chopin and Debussy, explored its poetic possibilities.

Eventually the piano could do so many interesting things with sound, that its ancestors, the harpsichord and clavichord, were largely forgotten and concert-goers took to the piano with enthusiasm. It became a household instrument and great firms developed to supply the demand for pianos. Such piano makers as Broadwood in England, Stein in Austria, Bechstein in Germany, and Erard and Pleyel in France grew rich and famous.

In our country the first piano is said to have been built in 1775 by John Behrent of Philadelphia. John Hawkins, also of Philadelphia, made an important contribution by building the first piano to have a full iron frame. Other manufacturers started in New York and Boston, among them the Chickering firm, founded in Boston in 1823 and the Steinway Company, founded in New York in 1853 by a German family which had made pianos in Hamburg.

The first music published especially for the piano was a set of three sonatas composed and published in 1773 by Muzio Clementi, an Italian who lived in London. Much music written for the harpsichord is, of course, now played upon the piano, and any person who learns to play the piano has available to him a vast treasure house of music. Mozart, Beethoven, Schubert, Schumann, Chopin, and many other composers have enriched the literature of piano music, and the person who can play the piano has at his fingertips much of the musical riches of the world.

QUESTIONS

1. What is the full name for the piano and what does the word mean?
2. Explain the difference between the harpsichord and the piano.
3. By whom were the first pianos built? Describe their appearance.
4. In what way did Johann Sebastian Bach's sons win favor for the piano?
5. What composers developed the dramatic qualities of piano music and which composers explored the poetic possibilities of the instrument?
6. Who were several famous American makers of pianos?
7. Name different styles of pianos that are in use today.

LISTENING SUGGESTIONS

Concerto for Piano — Grieg
Any Concerto for Piano by Mozart,
  Beethoven, or Brahms
Concerto for Piano — Schumann
Jeux d'eau — Ravel

Moments Musical — Schubert
Preludes — Debussy
Any Sonata for Piano by Beethoven
Any Waltzes, Impromptus, Ballades,
  Etudes by Chopin

THE HARP

One of the oldest of musical instruments, the harp is at the same time one of the most beautiful. It is often mentioned in the Old Testament, and pictures of harps appear in Egyptian art dating back to 1300 B.C. For more than a thousand years the harp was a favorite instrument with the musicians of Ireland, Scotland, and Wales, and the harp is still popular in these countries. The Irish and Welsh harps, however, are smaller and simpler in design than the modern harp we know.

For many hundreds of years the harp could be played in but the one key in which it happened to be tuned. The player could not change the pitch of the strings by shortening them as is now possible. Early in the eighteenth century a German invented a harp with foot-pedals which could change the length of the strings. This development was perfected by the Frenchman, Sebastien Erard, who in 1810 made his first double-action harp. The harps of today differ but little from Erard's model. Erard also built the first piano made in France and for many years his firm manufactured harps and pianos in France and England. In America the manufacture of harps was introduced and is continued today by the firm of Lyon & Healy in Chicago, Illinois.

The harp of today is a graceful and impressive instrument always seen in the large symphony orchestras and frequently used as a solo instrument or as one of a small group of instruments. When you examine it you will note that the harp has forty-seven strings and eight pedals. One of the pedals near the center of the base of the harp affects the loudness or softness of the tone, but the other seven pedals are for transposing purposes. The harpist can play in any key by setting the pedals to produce the particular scale he needs.

Although its tone is not powerful, the harp can contribute brilliant effects to the orchestral performance, and you may have seen a harpist sweep her fingers across the entire expanse of strings, sounding them all in a wave of sound. This is known as a *glissando* and the same effect can be produced from a piano by drawing one finger rapidly across the white keys.

The harpist can play melodies and chords, or a melody with one hand and accompanying chords with the other. Harp music makes much use of *arpeggios* (ar-ped'jos). "Arpeggio" is an Italian term, derived from the word "arpa" (a harp), and it means a chord played one note after the other, in the style of the harp.

Listen to a recording of the "Waltz of the Flowers" from Tschaikowsky's *Nutcracker Suite* and you will hear the harp give a good account of itself. You will hear it often in the music of Debussy and other French composers. Wagner employed the harp frequently, but the older composers, such as Bach, Handel, and Haydn gave little attention to it, perhaps because in their time its possibilities were somewhat restricted.

QUESTIONS

1. Find some Bible references to the harp.
2. What well-known compositions can you name where the harp adds much to the beauty of this music?
3. Many years ago the harp was a favorite instrument of what countries?
4. Is it still popular with these same people?
5. How did these harps of earlier days differ from those of today?
6. Tell something about the use of the pedals on the harp.

LISTENING SUGGESTIONS

Danses Sacrée et Profane — Debussy
Introduction and Allegro — Ravel
Symphony in D Minor, second move-
ment — Franck
Waltz of the Flowers, Introduction
— Tschaikowsky

221

⇘ 20 ⇙

THE BAND

Iᴺ ᴏᴜʀ ᴛɪᴍᴇ the term "band" is used to describe a group of wind and percussion instruments playing together. In concert bands, string basses are frequently found, and the harp is sometimes used. The band is an important part of our school life because it figures not only in the musical life of the school but also has an important part in many outdoor school activities, especially athletic events.

The band is important in another way in American life because many towns and cities maintain municipal bands supported by tax funds. The weekly band concert on summer nights is still a custom in many American communities, and some cities provide nightly concerts in parks through the summer months.

The military band has also been a factor in the musical activities of this and other countries. Band music, therefore, reaches and has reached practically every American at one time or another. Almost every boy or girl thrills to the music of the band, and now for some years many of our American boys and girls have enjoyed the privilege of playing in bands.

As was stated in the chapter on The Symphony Orchestra and Its Instruments, the trumpets and drums have been associated almost since the dawn of history with military affairs. For hundreds of years military instructions have been given by means of trumpet and bugle signals, just as today a soldier's day starts with the call of "Reveille" and ends with "Taps." The music of trumpets and drums has long been used to quicken the step of soldiers and to bolster their spirits in battle.

Kings and princes throughout hundreds of years of the world's history have maintained bands, as an inspiration to their soldiers and as a source of music on state occasions. Five hundred years ago trumpets and kettledrums were reserved for the use of rulers, and their use was denied to the minstrels and troubadours who were the popular musicians of the day. Henry VIII of England, and Queen Elizabeth, his daughter, maintained bands of trumpets and trombones. Elizabeth's group in 1587 is said to have comprised ten trumpets, six trombones, and a few other instruments. Louis XIV

222

of France commissioned his court composer, Lully (Lüh'lee), to organize regimental bands in the French army, and a little later Frederick the Great of Prussia took great interest in his bands. Napoleon Bonaparte likewise gave considerable attention to the bands in his armies. With the patronage of rulers and generals the band has long been solidly recognized as part of military and government establishments. Such bands as The Coldstream Guards and the Grenadier Guards in England, and the Garde Republique in France have become famous. In our own country we have the United States Marine Band, founded in 1798 as a fife and drum corps and changed to a brass band in 1802. We also have the United States Army Band, the United States Navy Band, and the Air Force Band, thus representing all branches of our defense forces.

The "town band" has been taken for granted by several generations of Americans, and perhaps some of them have thought of it as an American institution. It is really quite an old tradition — older, in fact, than America itself. Some European cities have had "town musicians" for five or six hundred years. Johann Sebastian Bach's father was a member of his town's music staff, and his duties were to help provide music for public affairs.

The employment of musicians by towns and cities grew out of the musicians' efforts to improve their position. In the Middle Ages musicians, except in the church, went from town to town, like gypsies, and lived from hand to mouth. They were really "wandering minstrels," to quote Nanki-Pooh in *The Mikado*. Some of the more enterprising found that "it pays to organize," and the groups they formed led to the Guilds (described in the chapter on Germany) and also to the employment by towns and cities of groups of musicians to perform official duties. The first of these groups was The Brotherhood of St. Nicolas, founded in Vienna, Austria, in 1288.

Today in many countries it is possible for people to spend an hour or two on pleasant summer evenings listening to the music of a band. Many cities provide a series of band concerts in parks. The Goldman Band, conducted by Edwin Franko Goldman, has given summer concerts in Central Park in New York since 1918 and Mr. Goldman's best known march is named *On the Mall*, commemorating these concerts.

In towns and small cities it is now quite common for the high school band director to have charge of the summer municipal band, and such bands often include many high school players. In such communities the bands are highly useful in providing music for outdoor festivals and patriotic observances.

The orchestra as a school music activity is considerably older than the band, and there are records showing that orchestras were organized

223

as far back as 1878 when one was established in the high school at Aurora, Illinois. From 1896 on, high schools began to organize orchestras, but for some years they rehearsed after school hours and were maintained by the efforts of the students themselves, assisted by an interested teacher.

One of the first school bands was organized in Connersville, Indiana, and soon afterward school administrators and boards of education began to see the value of instrumental music in the public schools and to give it tangible support. Many school bands were formed, and the movement really hit its stride immediately after World War I. During this war America became band-conscious, and the armed services maintained three divisional directors in Europe, each of whom had some sixty bands under his supervision. Following the war, schools were able, as a result of this activity, to secure as teachers many young men who had been trained as band leaders during their military service.

For many years bands played light, often trivial, music — and some of them still do — but the quality of music and performance has been vastly improved through the influence of our college and university bands.

It is still common to hear a band referred to as a "brass band." This is now a misnomer, for all bands, military, school, or municipal, are a blend of brass, wood-wind and percussion instruments. There was a time when small bands were sometimes made up entirely of brass instruments, or entirely of wood winds. In eighteenth century France a band might be all oboes and in England all trumpets and trombones, but as the orchestra gradually adopted various instruments into its family, the band made similar changes. The German bandmaster, Wilhelm Wieprecht, more than a hundred years ago had bands which included flutes, oboes, E-flat and B-flat clarinets, bassoons, cornets, trumpets, trombones, tubas, and French horns. French bands of about 1860 were similar except for the addition of saxophones.

The instrumentation of our school bands of today is much the same. Some years ago the National School Band Association suggested the following instrumentation for symphonic band for Class A schools:

     5 flutes (one or two interchangeable with piccolo)
     2 E-flat clarinets (2 E-flat clarinets may be replaced by 2 additional C or E-flat flutes, or 1 E-flat clarinet and 1 or more C or E-flat flutes)
   24 or more B-flat clarinets
     2 alto clarinets
     2 bass clarinets

224

2 or more oboes (one doubling English horn when called for in
  score)
2 or more bassoons
5 saxophones (soprano, alto — or two altos — tenor, baritone,
  and bass. Large bands may double this number).
4 or more B-flat cornets
2 or more B-flat trumpets
2 Fluegelhorns
4 to 8 French horns
4 to 6 trombones
2 to 4 baritones
2 E-flat tubas
4 BB-flat tubas
2 string basses
1 harp (if available and called for in score)
1 set of timpani
3 other percussion

Total 75 or more players

This combination of instruments is pretty generally followed except
for the Fluegelhorns, for which additional trumpets or cornets are
substituted, and E-flat flutes which are quite uncommon. Bands in
smaller schools have fewer clarinets, horns, and cornets, and they
usually substitute at least some E-flat altos or mellophones for part
of the French horn section, but the general balance of instruments
is quite similar.

Most of the instruments used in the band have already been described in the chapter on the orchestra, but there are a few instruments
used in the band, but not in the orchestra, which should be mentioned here:

The Alto and Bass Clarinets. The alto clarinet is an E-flat instrument,
larger and lower in pitch than the B-flat clarinet. The bass clarinet
is one octave lower than the B-flat clarinet. It is more widely used
in bands than in orchestras.

The Baritone Horn. With its upright bell, the baritone horn seems to
be a small edition of the tuba. It is pitched in B-flat and sounds an
octave lower than the cornet or trumpet. It is esteemed as a solo
instrument with the band and has rich quality and great power.

The Cornet. One of the important solo instruments of the band is the
cornet. It closely resembles the trumpet, but is somewhat shorter
with a larger bore (trumpets and cornets are long cylindrical tubes

225

and the bore refers to the size of the tube). The cornet has a cup-shaped mouthpiece like that of the trumpet but somewhat deeper. The cornet is somewhat more flexible and easier to play than the trumpet.

The E-flat Clarinet. Smaller and higher-pitched than the B-flat clarinet, the E-flat clarinet adds brilliance to the upper ranges of the band. Inclined to be shrill, it is now sometimes replaced by another flute.

The Euphonium. Like the baritone, the euphonium is really a small tuba. It may, however, have as many as five valves instead of the three found on the baritone horn. A euphonium has the large upright bell of the tuba and sometimes a smaller one also, giving it the appearance of a horn with two openings, or bells.

The Fluegelhorn. This instrument looks like a large cornet which, in fact, it is. It has a larger bore, broader tone, and somewhat lower range than the cornet. It is found in some large bands but is not in common use.

The Mellophone. Resembling a French horn, the mellophone is often used as a substitute for it. It is easier to play but lacks some of the richness of the French horn tone. It is often called an E-flat alto because its fundamental tone is E-flat rather than F, as in the French horn.

The Saxophone. This is a hybrid instrument, since it is made of brass but is played by means of a single reed mouthpiece, like a clarinet. It also employs metal keys which regulate the pitch, as in a clarinet. Invented in 1840 by the Belgian, Adolphe Sax, the saxophone is widely used in bands and is occasionally required in symphonic orchestra music. It is, of course, a mainstay of the dance orchestra. School bands use the E-flat alto, the B-flat tenor, and the B-flat baritone saxophones. There are also soprano and bass saxophones and a C-melody saxophone which is used in dance orchestras.

The Sousaphone. The largest instrument in the band, the Sousaphone was named for John Philip Sousa, for whom it was developed. It is a large tuba, and its shape was designed so that it might be more easily carried when bands were marching.

Some of the instruments play much the same part in the band as in the orchestra. Thus the tuba and trombone provide the bass

226

support for the music and the French horn gives richness and fullness to the inner harmonies, likewise serving frequently as a pleasing solo instrument. The cornets and trumpets add brilliance to the band ensemble as well as the orchestra, but in the band the cornet is often a solo instrument, while it is never so used in an orchestra. The trumpet, frequently heard as a solo instrument in the orchestra, is more likely to appear as a supporting instrument in the band.

In both the band and the orchestra the flute is used for high lyrical passages and for reinforcing the principal melody. The oboe is likely to be used for solo spots in either the band or the orchestra groups. The clarinet, however, has an altogether different function in the band as compared with its orchestral use. In the orchestra it is a member of the wood-wind choir and an occasional soloist, but in the band the clarinet has much more responsibility. It becomes the mainstay of the band, just as the violin is the mainstay of the orchestra, playing many important melodies and supplying much harmonic background. The B-flat clarinet section of a modern band is divided into three, and sometimes four parts, thus functioning much like the first violin, second violin, and viola sections of an orchestra.

The term, "symphonic band," is now often used, especially in schools, and it means a band designed to play concert music. Bands do not often play complete symphonies as do orchestras, but they frequently play movements from symphonies and often play standard overtures, such as *William Tell, Rienzi, Oberon,* and others which once were available only to orchestras. Much orchestra music has been transcribed for band and an increasing amount of original music is being written for it. Students of music, unless they are studying a wind instrument, do not usually appreciate the extent to which composers have been interested in writing music for wind instruments. Handel was fond of the wind instruments and wrote his *Royal Fireworks Music* for a "wind-band." Mozart liked the wood winds and wrote concertos for them and serenades and other pieces for groups of wood winds. Beethoven wrote numerous works for groups of wind instruments. So did Haydn and Schubert. Berlioz wrote a symphony for band and used four small bands of brass instruments in his colossal *Requiem.*

In our own time some of the foremost composers have produced works written especially for band. Holst, Vaughan Williams, Milhaud, Respighi, and Stravinsky have all written works for band, and in our own country such men as Paul Creston, Roy Harris, William Schuman, and Percy Grainger have added to the band repertoire.

In one form of music, the march, the band is supreme. No orchestra, however skillful, can quite match a good band in playing a march. And while the band is no longer limited to military associations, marches are still important in its repertoire. An American, John Philip Sousa, had such a gift for writing stirring marches that he became known as the "March King," just as Johann Strauss was called the "Waltz King." Appropriately enough, John Philip Sousa, whose music has thrilled Americans on so many patriotic occasions, was born in Washington, D.C., in 1854. His father's name was Antonio So, to which, according to the story, he added the letters U.S.A., and the family name became known as Sousa. John Philip was for twelve years conductor of the U. S. Marine Band, a post which he gave up to organize his own band. For forty years his band gave concerts, toured Europe several times, and became the best-known of all professional bands.

No one has ever seemed to capture the spirit of the military march quite as well as Sousa, and his marches are played by bands everywhere. *El Capitan, The Thunderer, Washington Post, King Cotton,* and especially the *Stars and Stripes Forever* are a part of our American tradition, for they seem to typify the young, vigorous America which Sousa knew as a young man. Musicians generally regard the *Stars and Stripes Forever* as without a peer in military marches. John Philip Sousa died in 1932, after a long and distinguished career.

Band

1. Name some of the different types of bands to be heard in our country.
2. Name some famous European rulers who gave much attention to bands.
3. What instruments were particularly popular with Henry VIII of England and with his daughter, Queen Elizabeth I?
4. Tell something of interest concerning the musicians during the middle ages.
5. Name the wood winds and brass that generally make up the instrumentation of a good concert band.
6. Describe the baritone horn and the Sousaphone.
7. Tell something of interest concerning John Philip Sousa.
8. Name two of his famous marches.

LISTENING SUGGESTIONS

An Outdoor Overture — Copland
Circus Polka — Stravinsky
El Capitan — Sousa
First Suite for Band — Holst
King Cotton — Sousa
National Emblem March — Bagley
On the Mall — Goldman
Second Suite for Band — Holst

Semper Fidelis — Sousa
Stars and Stripes Forever — Sousa
Suite Française — Milhaud
The Thunderer — Sousa
Toccata Marziale — Vaughn Williams
U. S. Field Artillery March — Sousa
Washington Post — Sousa

228

❧ 21 ❧

CHORAL MUSIC

WHEN WE SING in a choir or glee club, we are following one of the oldest musical traditions. Singing together has been a musical custom observed for many hundreds of years in many lands. The ancient Greeks held contests in singing and dancing, and wealthy Greeks twenty-five hundred years ago devoted considerable time and money to the training and costuming of choruses which took part in contests, not unlike our school contests of today.

The early Christian Church, according to historians, made extensive use of groups of singers. These early choruses sang in unison, not in parts as we do today. Harmony as we know it, had not then been developed. Some of the unison singing of the early church, known as *plain song* or *plain chant,* is widely used today in the Roman Catholic and Episcopal services. The ancient Greeks sang in unison also, and although their melodies have not come down to us, we have some idea of their character because we know the scales from which they were constructed. These are known to students of music as the "Greek modes."

When musicians discovered that they could make harmony by singing two melodies at the same time, the art of part singing began to develop. At first only the trained choirs in the cathedrals and large churches were able to undertake singing in parts. The people who went to church were good listeners, however, and eventually the harmonic or part-song style was adapted to secular music. Some of the peoples of the world seem to have an instinctive feeling for harmony. The Russians, Germans, and Scandinavians have long been accustomed to singing in parts, and the Welsh people, according to historians, sang in harmony a thousand years before our time. The Negroes likewise developed their own style of part singing in their spirituals.

The church supported music and trained its singers from an early day, and eventually the secular rulers did likewise. If you sing in an *a cappella* choir, you may be acquainted with the delightful *Echo Song*

229

by Orlando di Lasso in which one group of singers echoes the phrases of another. This is one of several hundred choral compositions written by di Lasso, who was director of choral music in the sixteenth century for Duke Albert of Munich. The Duke engaged di Lasso and brought him from Flanders (Belgium) to Munich, where he maintained a staff of sixty singers and thirty instrumentalists. It was di Lasso's duty to train these singers and compose music for them. Concerts were given after dinner on weekday nights, and on Sundays the musicians provided the music for the chapel services. Di Lasso spent thirty-seven years in the service of the Duke.

Other princes and wealthy men provided the money and opportunity for musical development. The Italian rulers of the Renaissance period, such as the famous families of the Medici, Este, and Sforza, supported music as well as the other arts and encouraged the development of choral singing. Their activities helped to originate the singing of madrigals and the establishment of such important musical forms as the opera and the oratorio.

In England in the seventeenth century one of the highest honors a boy could attain was membership in the Chapel Royal. These boys lived in the King's palace and accompanied him on journeys away from the court. They sang at the royal chapel services and on state and less formal occasions. They received the best education and musical training which the time afforded and when a boy's voice changed the King sent him to Oxford or Cambridge. Some of England's most distinguished musicians came from the boys of the Chapel Royal. Often they returned from the universities and became "Gentlemen of the Chapel Royal."

In the England of the first Queen Elizabeth's reign, which was about the time the Pilgrims sailed to America in the Mayflower, choral singing was so highly regarded among educated people that if one went to a dinner party and failed to follow his part in the madrigal singing which followed, eyebrows were raised as to his social fitness. And in those days, printing was so expensive that four or five singers gathered around a small table had to use one book. Today a group of high school madrigal singers often follows this tradition in sitting about a table, although each singer can have his own copy of music instead of reading only his own part on a portion of one page.

A little later in England one of the chief amusements at the court of Charles II was the singing of rounds and catches. (A catch is something like a round.) The children of today, and sometimes the older folks, still sing rounds, and have a good time with such time-honored favorites as *Three Blind Mice* and *Row, Row, Row Your Boat*. The rounds and catches were followed in the eighteenth century by

230

the glee, from which we get the term "glee club." The glee was a part-song in which the voices had considerable independence, but it was less complex than the madrigal.

When we sing *a cappella* (without accompaniment) we are following an ancient tradition, for *a cappella* means "as in the chapel" and derives from the custom long employed in Rome and elsewhere of singing without instrumental accompaniment. That is why the music of Palestrina, Vittoria, di Lasso, and others who wrote in the sixteenth and seventeenth centuries is always sung unaccompanied. It also explains the practice of singing Russian church music "*a cappella*," for the Russian Church, in pre-Soviet days, was a part of the Greek Orthodox Church which did not permit instruments in the church.

Singing to the accompaniment of instruments is very old, however, for the Bible tells of singing with the harp, psaltery and other instruments. And in the eleventh century the famous choir in the Monastery of St. Gall in Switzerland had, for festival occasions, an orchestra accompaniment of harp, flutes, organ, cymbals, triangle, bells, and the seven-stringed psaltery. In England and Germany much of the choral music written after 1700 was accompanied. This became true in other countries also and was due to the advances in the development of the organ, piano, and the instruments of the orchestra.

Today a mixed chorus is made up of four types of voices — the sopranos, the higher voices of women or girls; the altos, the lower voices of women or girls; and the tenors and basses, which are, respectively, the higher and lower voices of men. For hundreds of years, however, the church choirs and many singing groups outside the churches were made up entirely of men and boys. Boys sang the soprano and alto parts, as they still do in some churches. Even as late as 1846 when Mendelssohn's *Elijah* was performed for the first time, the sixty altos in the festival chorus at Birmingham, England, were all young men or boys. His "bearded altos," Mendelssohn called them. This was an exception, however, for by the time of the American and French Revolutions, women had been admitted to amateur choral societies, and many such were founded in America, England, and Germany. One of the oldest — the Stoughton Musical Society — was founded in 1786 in Stoughton, Massachusetts. The Handel and Haydn Society of Boston, founded in 1815, was the first American choral society to present the great works of Handel, Bach, Haydn and Mendelssohn, and it still presents, each year, performances of the *Messiah* and other masterworks. Cincinnati had a choral society as early as 1816, although the present well-known Cincinnati Festival Chorus did not come into existence until 1873. The Apollo Club of

Chicago was established in 1872, first as a male chorus, but it became a mixed group in 1876.

Singing as a public school activity in the United States is well over a hundred years old, thanks to the activities of Lowell Mason, who established the teaching of vocal music in the public schools of Boston. The name of Lowell Mason is well known to church choirs and congregations because of the many hymn tunes which he composed and arranged. Many of them are still widely sung. Singing groups in colleges and universities are of considerably older origin, and it is recorded that the great Johann Sebastian Bach conducted a university chorus in Leipzig, Germany, more than two hundred years ago. The study of various branches of music in universities is still older, for Cambridge University in England was granting degrees in music as long ago as 1463.

Many high school singers take part each year in festivals which bring together hundreds of choristers, often with orchestra or band accompaniment. Sometimes choruses from several schools participate in such an event, and it often becomes a thrilling musical experience for the singers. The idea of musical contests and festivals dates back to early history. The Greeks, before the Christian era, held competitions in singing, instrumental music, poetry, and dancing. Centuries later the Minnesingers and Troubadours in Europe held their festivals of song. Two of Richard Wagner's music-dramas, *Tannhäuser* and *Die Meistersinger,* tell us of these contests. The musicians of Wales maintain today, as they have for hundreds of years, their "Eisted-fodds" (Eye-steth'vods) a sort of combination music contest and festival. The festival idea which brings together large numbers of singers in massed singing has long been popular in America, Great Britain, and the Scandinavian countries. One of the first of these annual festivals, which continues to this day, is the Three Choirs Festival, established in 1724 and combining singers from Gloucester, Worcester, and Hereford in England.

The spread of choral singing was greatly aided when music began to be published on a large scale so that copies could be purchased at a moderate cost. For hundreds of years choirs had to sing from manuscripts which had been laboriously copied. Printed music was known as long ago as the time of Christopher Columbus, but it was scarce and expensive, and it was not until George Washington's time that printed music became generally available. Pioneers in the publication of choral music were Breitkopf and Härtel in Germany, Vincent Novello in England, and Oliver Ditson in the United States.

It is quite common for high school and college choirs to sing music that was written three to four hundred years ago. The period of

1500-1700, in fact, is known as the "Golden Age of Choral Music." Many great composers, such as Palestrina, Vittoria, di Lasso, Byrd, Morley, Gibbons, and a host of lesser composers were actively at work during these two centuries. The piano was unheard of at that time, and its ancestors, the virginals and the harpsichord, were considered solo instruments and were not used for accompaniment. Some of the instruments of the band and orchestra did not exist before 1800, and all of them excepting the violin family have been greatly improved since that date. Instrumental music is thus of more recent development than choral music, and it was not until the time of Bach and Handel that the custom of singing to the accompaniment of instruments became really well established. Much instrumental music and less choral music was produced from 1750 to 1900, although choral music was not entirely neglected. Schumann, Mendelssohn and Brahms all composed extensively for choruses, and their compositions included works for choruses of men and choruses of women as well as for the conventional mixed voices. Since 1900 many composers have interested themselves in choral writing and they have produced a great variety of original compositions and arrangements of folk songs in choral settings.

Today in America and in numerous other countries almost every boy and girl has a chance to sing. A considerable part of the world is thus realizing the hope expressed more than three hundred years ago by William Byrd, a great English composer, who wrote, "Since singing is so good a thing, I wish all men would learn to sing."

QUESTIONS

1. What famous musician during the reign of Queen Elizabeth felt that it would be a good thing if all men "learned to sing"?
2. How did the choruses of the early days differ from those of today?
3. Tell something of interest concerning di Lasso, composer and director of choral music who lived in the sixteenth century.
4. What privileges were accorded boys who were able to attain membership in the Choir of the Chapel Royal?
5. Tell something of interest concerning the singing of madrigals in Queen Elizabeth's time.
6. What is meant by "a cappella" singing?
7. When were women first admitted to choral organizations?
8. Who first established the teaching of vocal music in the public schools in Boston?
9. Tell something about the history and development of choral festivals.
10. How long ago was printed music to be had?
11. When did it become available at a price that the public could afford to buy it?

12. Name two composers who made a great contribution to choral music in the period of 1500-1700?
13. Singing to accompaniment became really well established during the time of two famous composers. Who were they?
14. Name some other famous composers who later wrote great music for choruses.

LISTENING SUGGESTIONS

Alto Rhapsody — Brahms

Cantatas (Any one) — Bach

Ceremony of Carols — Britten

Choral compositions by Holst, Vaughn Williams, Parry, Kodály, Randall Thompson

Concert or radio programs by high school, college, or professional choirs

Elijah — Mendelssohn

A German Requiem — Brahms

Madrigals (any) by Morley, Gibbons, Wilbye, Weelkes, Palestrina, or other sixteenth and seventeenth century composers

The *Messiah* — Handel

Motets (any one) — Bach

Mount of Olives — Beethoven

Negro spirituals (any)

Passion according to St. John — Bach

❧ 22 ❦

RELIGIOUS MUSIC

IF YOU WANT TO READ an interesting chapter in the story of music, make a study of the hymnbook used in your church. You will find that the tunes came from many sources, particularly if it is a Protestant hymnbook. There will likely be tunes from plain song (the original music of the Christian church), together with Lutheran chorales, folk songs from many lands, melodies from Beethoven, Schumann, and other masters, and tunes by present-day musicians. There have always been differences of opinion as to what should properly be considered sacred music, but in general the people have selected the tunes they wanted for their hymnbooks. They have followed the lead of Rev. Rowland Hill, an early minister, who is credited with having said that he saw no reason why the devil should have all the good tunes, and although the early Methodists frowned on dancing, more than one dance tune found its way into their hymnal. Of course it assumed greater dignity in its hymn form, just as did the famous chorale, *O Sacred Head,* which Bach used so much. He liked this tune and did not hesitate to transform it into a hymn tune, even though it had been originally used for a love song. Through experience the people and their composers have found that a good tune can often serve more than one purpose.

In the early Christian church music was accorded a prominent position, and since it had so much to do with education, it is not surprising to find that one of the early heads of the Roman Catholic Church, Pope Sylvester, decreed that singing schools should be established in the churches. A little later Bishop Ambrose assembled and improved the words and tunes of the hymns then in use. Still later, in the seventh century, the famous Pope Gregory established the scales, or modes, which still greatly influence the music of the Roman Catholic Church and have indirectly influenced the music of practically all Christian churches. The early music of the Roman Catholic Church is often referred to as Gregorian.

During the period known as the Dark Ages, after the downfall of

the Roman Empire, the great mass of mankind had little or no learning and the only centers of art and culture were the churches and
monasteries. These were the only sources of trained singers, and church
music thus became a function of priests and musicians who were
specially educated for it. The people could only listen. That they did
listen and sometimes remembered what they heard is indicated by the
melodies of folk songs which often bear a resemblance to the early
music of the church.

When harmony was discovered, church music almost immediately
became complex. Although the unison Gregorian and Ambrosian
tunes were still used in certain parts of the service, these and other
tunes were made the very basis of a very elaborate music which could
be performed only by highly trained directors and singers. An English
composer once wrote a piece of music which called for forty separate
parts, ten times as many voice parts as we now normally use in a
church choir made up of sopranos, altos, tenors, and basses.

All this emphasis on elaborate musical structure detracted from
the worshipful character of the music, so that church music became
a sort of musical mathematics and had little to do with genuine
religious feeling. Sometimes composers even used street songs as
the main themes of Masses and motets, and one group of singers
would be singing these non-religious words while others at the same
time were singing the sacred texts of the service, just as though a
present-day composer were to take the words and tune of a Hit Parade
song and mix it up with the text and music of a Psalm or hymn. This
condition eventually became a scandal and is said to have given the
distinguished composer, Palestrina, his first great opportunity.

Palestrina worked in Rome, as did the Spanish-born Tomas de
Vittoria, whose *O Magnum Mysterium* is frequently heard on present-
day programs. At about the same time there were fine musicians
working in Flanders (now Belgium), in Germany, and in England.
Orlando di Lasso, who spent many years in Germany, helped to
improve church music, as did William Byrd, Orlando Gibbons, and
others in England.

Other changes affected church music. Shortly before Palestrina's
time, Martin Luther had broken away from the Church of Rome and
founded the church which today bears his name. Luther and his
followers believed that the members of the church congregation
should have a greater part in the musical portions of the service instead of always listening to the choirs of trained singers. He and
his followers translated Greek and Latin hymns into the German
language and fitted them to various tunes. Some Luther wrote himself, such as the celebrated *Ein Feste Burg ist Unser Gott* (A Mighty

236

Fortress Is Our God). At first the melodies were always given to the tenor, with supporting parts for the bass and treble voices. This custom was widely followed in Europe and America and still persists among some American groups, such as the Sacred Harp Singers in our southern states.

Luther and his followers called these hymns "Chorales," and the first book of them was published in 1524, which happens to be the year of Palestrina's birth. In a later edition of Luther's *Chorales*, published in 1586, the tunes were given to the sopranos and this manner of singing chorales and hymns has generally prevailed until the present time, although some churches, especially in England, prefer to sing their hymns in unison.

About the same time that Martin Luther established his church, King Henry VIII of England was having his historic quarrel with the Church of Rome. This led to the establishment of the Church of England and, later to that branch of the church known in the United States as the Protestant Episcopal. King Henry's disagreement with Rome did not have to do with music, but the founding of the English church resulted in changes which helped to shape the church music we know today in many American Protestant churches, not the Episcopal alone, but the Methodist, Baptist, Presbyterian, and many others. After the time of Henry VIII, music was sung in English, rather than in Latin, and there came into use the type of sacred composition which we know as the "anthem." The anthem occupies much the same place in the English and American services that the "motet" does in the Roman Catholic service. The *Adoramus Te* is called a motet, while *Praise Ye the Father*, by Gounod, is known as an anthem.

Anthems are sung by the choir, in contrast to the hymns sung by the congregation, and are today a feature of most Protestant church services. Sometimes an anthem is written for voices alone, but often it is composed for voices with organ accompaniment. When intended for special or festival occasions, anthems may have an accompaniment for orchestra. Handel wrote numerous anthems to be performed with orchestra. The anthem may or may not have solo sections for individual voices. Henry Purcell, England's great seventeenth century composer, wrote many anthems with important solo parts and brilliant accompaniments to please the taste of his royal patron, Charles II, and the soloist was prominent in much church music written during the eighteenth and nineteenth centuries, Catholic and Protestant alike. In more recent times the display of solo voices has been discouraged and composers have written generally for chorus alone, or for chorus with minor solo parts. Often when we attend church today we hear choruses from an oratorio or a Mass sung in place of an anthem. A great many churches, for example, include the "Hallelujah Chorus," from Handel's *Messiah,* in their Christmas services, or we may hear "The Heavens Are Telling," from Haydn's *Creation,* or the "Sanctus" from Gounod's *St. Cecilia Mass.*

The "oratorio" developed from the church custom in medieval times of teaching the people the stories of the Bible through the enactment of pageants. These were known as mystery or miracle plays and were often used to tell the Christmas and Easter stories to the people who, in those days, usually could neither read nor write. These plays gradually led to a type of musical play on a sacred subject. This was given in the *oratory,* the chapel for prayer, and came to be called an "oratorio." St. Philip Neri (Nay'ree) (1515-1595), for whom churches and schools are sometimes named, was a pioneer in developing these sacred musical plays in Rome. His ideas were taken up by others and the first work which might be considered an oratorio was composed by Emilio di Cavalieri and presented in Florence in 1600. The first oratorio was thus presented in the same city and at about the same time as the first opera.

In time much of the pageantry and the dramatic features of the oratorio disappeared, and it assumed the form which we know today in such works as the *Messiah, The Creation,* and *Elijah.* The eighteenth century was the great period of oratorio when Handel wrote many such works and Haydn and Bach also produced great choral works. Those of Bach were usually settings of the Passion story — that is, the last days of Christ on earth and his resurrection. *The Passion according to St. Matthew* is regarded as one of Bach's greatest works. Mendelssohn continued with the oratorio in the nineteenth century, giving us such great works as *Elijah* and *St. Paul* and still later some English composers produced oratorios, notably Sir Edward Elgar, with *The Apostles* and *The Dream of Gerontius.* The American composer, Horatio Parker, is perhaps best known for his oratorio, *Hora Novissima,* and a few present-day musicians have worked in this form. William Walton of England has achieved fame for his *Belshazzar's Feast,* and Arthur Honegger's *King David* and *Joan of Arc* are other contemporary examples.

When Johann Sebastian Bach presided over the music of Leipzig's churches, he could not, as do present-day choirmasters, enter a music store and have his choice of thousands of published compositions. There was some published music, but even at this period, a little over two hundred years ago, much of the music had to be copied by hand and·sung from manuscript. Often it was not possible to find just the right piece for a particular church ceremony, and so Bach used to write his own. His particular form of service called for considerable music, and his Sunday service, which included solos, organ interludes and preludes, chorales, and longer choruses, is known as a "cantata." Bach wrote several hundred of them, providing for every season and occasion of the Lutheran Church year. His *Christmas Oratorio* is not a true oratorio, but is a compilation of six short cantatas which cover the Advent, Christmas, and Epiphany seasons. A great many cantatas have been written since Bach's time, and a cantata is often the featured musical work in the Christmas and Easter services in our Protestant churches in America.

The oldest musical tradition in religious music is that of the Jewish faith. The Old Testament tells how David played and danced before the Ark of the Covenant and how the Levites conducted the music in the Temple of Solomon. After the fall of Jerusalem in 70 A.D. the Jews abstained from instrumental music and their religious music for many centuries was limited to the chanting of the Psalms and other Scriptural passages by the cantors who were especially trained for the service. The technical name for this type of chanting is "cantillation" and the chants were passed, by oral tradition, from one generation of cantors to another. The music of the cantors is very elaborate, but the basic melodies had a considerable influence upon the music of the early Christian church.

It was not until the eighteenth century that instrumental music again became a part of the synagogue service, and the introduction of the organ was associated with a change in the Jewish services known as the Reform Movement. Choral singing had been employed in some synagogues in Italy in the seventeenth century but did not come into wide usage until after 1800 when the Reform Movement had become well established. Today the Reform synagogues (usually known as "Temples") have organs and choirs of mixed voices which present not only Hebrew music but many hymns and anthems from other sources which are sung in the language of the country in which the temples are located. The Orthodox synagogues, however, cling to the old traditions of the cantor and the unaccompanied solo chants.

Like secular music, church music has often been influenced by the conditions under which it is presented. Thus music for the Russian Orthodox Church of pre-Soviet times was always written without accompaniment, because instruments were prohibited in the Russian and Greek churches. In contrast, the Germans, who contributed greatly to the development of the organ, have always employed it extensively in their church music. In sixteenth-century Venice, music was written for two choirs singing antiphonally (answering one another). It happened that St. Mark's Church in Venice was built with two organs and two choir lofts, and composers therefore adjusted their music to these conditions.

Fifty years ago American churches nearly always maintained a quartet of paid or volunteer singers instead of a chorus choir. The anthems used were intended for quartets of solo voices. Today these quartets have largely been replaced by chorus choirs of from twenty to fifty voices — sometimes even more — and the more recent church music is planned for such choirs.

Many churches have two or more choirs — some as many as five or six — thus providing choirs for children and young people of various age groups. Many anthems and a few larger works have been written for these multiple choir groups. This development of large choirs in the churches is largely a result of the past twenty-five years of choral activity in the schools of the United States where thousands of young people have acquired a taste for singing good choral music. Fortunately many churches are providing opportunity for our young people to continue or to increase, while still in school, their participation in choral singing.

THE ORGAN

This chapter on church music would not be complete without some reference to the organ, that great instrument which is so important in most church observances. The modern pipe organ with its hundreds of pipes which produce such a mighty and varied volume of tone is a far cry from the organ mentioned in the Bible and in ancient Greek writing. The organ began as a series of pipes bound together through which air was forced, at first from the lungs and later by hydraulic or pneumatic pressure. That the organ early became a powerful instrument is indicated by writers who mention an organ in Jerusalem, in 420 A.D., which could be heard a mile away. Another interesting reference to an early organ concerns an instrument which was presented in 822 to the Emperor Charlemagne by Haroun Al Raschid, of Arabian Nights fame. Somewhat later, in the tenth century, English writers described an organ which required the services of three musicians to play, while seventy men worked the bellows to supply the wind.

The first organ to be played from a keyboard is said to have been built at Magdeburg, Germany, about the end of the eleventh century. It had but sixteen keys and it was not until the fourteenth century that the organ was equipped with the chromatic scale keyboard which we know in the organ and piano of today. Some of these early organs had keys that were as much as five inches wide, and the keys had to be struck by the fist rather than depressed by the finger. The pipe organ of today, with its three to five manuals (keyboards) controlling hundreds of pipes and its pedal keyboard played by the feet, is the most elaborate musical instrument we have.

For many years hand power or water power was employed for the wind pressure. In some cases gasoline engines were used, but after electricity was discovered and developed, organ builders found a way to use electric power, and when you examine the mechanism of a present-day organ you find that it includes a maze of electric wires and connections. The use of electricity has also given rise to the electronic organ, a small compact instrument which dispenses with pipes. Such organs are frequently found in small churches and in restaurants and homes, for they are often used for secular, as well as church music.

Today, in most church services, the first and last music you hear will be that of the organ prelude and postlude, and the instrument is played throughout the service in responses and offertories and for accompanying the choir and congregation in hymns and anthems. For three hundred years the organ has been a source of inspiration to composers, and such musicians as Bach, Handel, Mendelssohn, Franck, and a host of others have produced some of their finest compositions for this great instrument.

QUESTIONS

1. Tell something about the part played by music in the early days of the Christian Church.
2. Who established the scales or modes which still greatly influence the music of the Roman Catholic Church?
3. Why did congregational participation change during the Dark Ages?
4. What happened to church music soon after harmony was discovered?
5. What bad effect resulted from the very elaborate music that was used?
6. Tell something of interest concerning Palestrina.
7. What changes in church music took place in Martin Luther's time?
8. What effect was had by the founding of the Protestant Episcopal Church in England?
9. How did the oratorio have its start?
10. Name two famous oratorios.
11. Why did Bach write the music that was sung and played in the church where he was organist?
12. Describe the characteristics of traditional Hebrew music.
13. Distinguish between Jewish religious music as presented in Orthodox and Reform synagogues.
14. State some interesting facts concerning the organ and its evolution.

241

LISTENING SUGGESTIONS

Anthems by Clokey, Noble, Geoffrey Shaw, Thiman, Titcomb, Willan and other twentieth century composers.

Cantatas (any) — Bach

Cherubim Song — by any Russian composer

Chorales (any) — Bach

Gregorian Chants (any)

Hymns — from any hymnbook

Masses (any one) — Palestrina

Motets by Palestrina, di Lasso, Victoria, Byrd, Morley, Gibbons, and other sixteenth and seventeenth century composers

Sacred Service — Bloch

⇒ 23 ⇐

MUSIC PRINTING AND PUBLISHING

O NE OF THE most important events in the history of civilization
was the invention of printing. The application of printing to
music was likewise of tremendous importance. As long as music had
to be copied laboriously by hand there could be only a limited supply
and only a small number of persons could read and perform it.

Just as the Bible was the first book to be put into print, the earliest
examples of printed music are for the Church. The first book of music
to be printed was produced in Rome in 1476 by Ulrich Hahn. It
presented the melodies of the early music of the church, which we
know as plain song. The staff was printed in red and the notes in
black. This required a double printing and for some time music was
printed in this way, with diamond-shaped, rather than round, notes.

For many years music was printed from hand-set type, although it
was a cumbersome process which involved the use of many small
pieces of type. In 1501 an Italian, Ottaviano dei Petrucci (Peh-
troo'chee), printed the first collection of part music, consisting of
ninety-six madrigals and motets, mainly by composers from France
and The Netherlands. Music printing was quickly taken up by England, France, and Germany. In England Queen Elizabeth gave to
such distinguished composers as Thomas Tallis, William Byrd, and
Thomas Morley special patents for printing music.

Experiments were made with printing from wood blocks and metal
cuts, but the next important step was the application of engraving.
The music was engraved on plates of copper and then printed from
the plates. One of the earliest examples of such printing was an
English collection of music for the virginal (an early keyboard instrument). It was called "Parthenia" and was issued in 1611. Some of
the first music engraved in America was done by Paul Revere, the
famous American patriot.

Toward the end of the seventeenth century the process of engraving was improved by a method of "punching" the notes, rests, and
other symbols. The engravers worked with a series of punches, each
having a different type of notehead or rest at its end. These were

243

stamped into the plate and the notes could thus be made uniform. The engravers also substituted pewter or zinc for the more expensive copper.

Another important advance occurred about 1800 with the discovery of the process of lithography. This made it possible to transfer an impression from the engraved plate to a lithographic stone and then reproduce the music by lithography. This enabled the printers to retain the engraved plates with but little wear and to print several thousand copies by the lithographic process.

Today much music is still stamped on metal plates and then printed from other offset plates made by photographing transfers from the original plates. Some music is reproduced by photographing a carefully prepared manuscript copy on offset plates and printing from these plates. In this process the engraving step is omitted and the resulting economy makes it a process often used in reproducing large scores for band or orchestra.

For about two hundred years music printing was confined entirely to books of music. No one seemed to see the possibility of printing a single song or instrumental piece as a separate number. Finally this idea occurred to an English publisher, Thomas Cross, who began to issue single numbers about 1700 and who may thus be considered the originator of the idea of sheet music.

Music printing had been well established for some time before the business of music publishing developed. The first music printers apparently did little to advertise or sell the music, and this responsibility was left to the composers or to the patrons who ordered the printing of the music. Perhaps the first man who thought of music publishing as a special and separate business through printing and offering for sale the works of various composers was the English bookseller, John Playford, who established a music publishing business in London about three hundred years ago. His collection, *The English Dancing-Master,* published in 1651, is still famous as a source of English folk dances. He and his successor published a considerable quantity of music and maintained a store where it was sold.

Early in the eighteenth century, John Walsh became the leading music publisher in England and was the first to be granted the title of "Music Seller to the King." He and his son were long prominent in music publishing and brought out many of the works of Handel.

These early publishers in England were followed by others who founded firms which are operating today. Vincent Novello, an organist and teacher, founded Novello and Company in 1811. His son, Joseph Alfred Novello, should be honored by all who sing in choirs and choral societies, since he was the first publisher to see the advantage of making available at moderate prices editions of anthems, oratorios, and part songs. It was he who started the publishing of choral music in octavo size now universally used in schools and churches. Chappell and Company, founded in 1812, is still prominent in Great Britain and America as publishers of musical works for the stage. It was this firm which first published the operettas of Gilbert and Sullivan.

The firm of Boosey and Company was founded in 1816 and is today, under the name of Boosey and Hawkes, a prominent publisher in Great Britain and America. The Oxford University Press, also well known in Britain and America, did not begin its musical activities until 1923.

In Germany Breitkopf and Härtel, established in 1719 as a publisher of Bibles, has been prominent for two hundred years as a publisher of music. In 1790 Nikolaus Simrock of Bonn, and later, Berlin, who had been a horn-player in Beethoven's orchestra, founded a publishing house which issued many of Beethoven's works and later became the publisher for Brahms and Dvořák. Another famous house was established in 1814 in Leipzig by Carl Friedrich Peters, who published the first complete editions of Bach and Haydn.

Much of the music of French composers which we know was first published by Durand and Company, founded in Paris in 1847. In Italy the most prominent music publishing firm is G. Ricordi and Company, established in 1808 by Giovanni Ricordi.

In our own country the first music publishing firm to reach a position of importance was the Oliver Ditson Company, founded in Boston, Massachusetts, in 1835. In 1931 the Ditson Company was purchased by the Theodore Presser Company of Philadelphia, Pennsylvania, which maintains publications under the Ditson imprint as well as others under the Presser name. Theodore Presser was a teacher of piano who established the publishing company and also the magazine, *The Etude*, about 1880.

G. Schirmer, Inc., was founded in New York City in 1861 by Gustave Schirmer, who had come to this country from Germany in 1837. Also from Germany came Carl Fischer, who began the publication of music in New York in 1872 and built the firm of Carl Fischer, Inc. The firm of J. Fischer and Brother of New York was established in 1864 and was first located in Dayton, Ohio.

Also in New York is located the Music Publishers Holding Corporation, comprising the catalogs of Witmark, Remick, and Harms, and including much of the music of Victor Herbert, Sigmund Romberg, George Gershwin, and the other composers in the entertainment field.

245

Other New York publishers such as Mills, Chappell, and The Big Three, long prominent in popular music, have now become well known in the educational field.

Several music publishers claim Boston as their home. C. C. Birchard & Company was founded in 1901 by Clarence C. Birchard, who specialized in music for schools and music by American composers. The Arthur P. Schmidt Music Company was started in 1876 and featured American composers, especially the works of Edward MacDowell.

Composers and publishers of music alike have been benefitted by the legal protection known as "copyright." This confers upon a composer, author, or publisher the exclusive right to copy, publish, and sell, for a stated period of years, books or musical compositions which are his property. Those who copy or reproduce copyrighted music without permission of the owner of the copyright are violating the copyright law.

The idea of copyright as applied to music dates back to 1491 in Venice, but in this case the right was given to Petrucci, the printer, rather than to the composers. Protection to the composer and author was first afforded in England. In America there has been at least some copyright protection since the Continental Congress in 1783. The Copyright Act has been amended several times. At present the life of an American copyright is twenty-eight years, plus an optional renewal of twenty-eight years. In other countries the copyright period varies from fifteen years to the lifetime of the composer or author plus fifty years following his death, as in England.

Copyright protection includes not only publication rights but the rights to use the music in public performances for profit and the rights to reproduce it through phonograph recordings, radio and television performances. In 1914 the American Society of Composers, Authors and Publishers (ASCAP) was founded by Victor Herbert and others to help protect American creative musicians from illegal public performance of copyrighted music. In practically all of the European countries there exist similar societies for the protection of creative musicians and their publishers.

This book has tried to show music as a part of life, in different forms, in different countries, and in various presentations. It is our hope that through listening, studying, and active participation you, too, may have a part in "music throughout the world."

246

FOLK SONGS TO SING

OTHER SONGS WITH ILLUSTRATIONS

Accompaniments to the songs listed above will be found in *Sing!* and in the accompaniment books for *The Twice 55 Brown Book, The Twice 55 Green Book,* and *Singing America,* all published by C. C. Birchard & Company. The source for each accompaniment is shown immediately below the title.

The Erie Canal

(Sing!, Page 80)

Traditional

American Folk Song

1. I've got a mule, her name is Sal,
2. We'd bet-ter get a-long our way,
Fif-teen miles on the

E-rie Ca-nal. ___ She's a good old work-er and a
'Cause you bet your life I'd nev-er

good old pal,
part with Sal,
Fif-teen miles on the E-rie Ca-nal. ___ We've
Get

hauled some barg-es in our day, Filled with lum-ber,
up there, mule, here comes a lock, We'll make Rome 'bout

coal and hay, And we know ev-'ry inch of the way From
six o'-clock, ___ One more trip and back we'll ___ go, ___

CHORUS

Al-ba-ny ___ to ___ Buf-fa-lo. ___
Right back home ___ to ___ Buf-fa-lo. ___
Low bridge,

ev-'ry-bod-y down! Low bridge, for we're go-ing thro' a town;

And you'll al-ways know your neigh-bor, You'll al-ways know your pal,

If you've ev-er nav-i-gat-ed on the E-rie Ca-nal. ___

249

Jeanie with the Light Brown Hair
(*Twice 55 Brown Book*, № 131)

S.C.F.

STEPHEN COLLINS FOSTER

Tranquillo

1. I dream of Jean-ie with the light brown hair, Borne like a va-por
2. I long for Jean-ie with the day-dawn smile, Ra-diant with glad-ness,

on the gold-en air. I see her trip-ping where the bright streams play,
warm with win-ning guile; I hear her mel-o-dies at-tuned to___ love.

Gay-as the dai-sies a-long her way. Man-y are the fond notes her
Warm as the sun light-ing heav'n a-bove.

mer-ry voice would pour, Ech-oed by the birds in the grove, o'er and o'er.

Ah!_____ I dream of Jean-ie with the light brown hair,

A-float__ like__ va-por on the soft sum-mer air.

The Old Chisholm Trail
(*Twice 55 Brown Book*, № 144)

Anonymous

Cowboy Song

With spirit

1. — Come a-long, boys,__ and__ lis-ten to my tale, I'll__ tell you
2. — Woke up one morn-ing on the old__ Chis-holm trail, With a rope__
3. It's ba-con and beans most ev-'ry__ day, I__ would-n't

REFRAIN

all my trou-bles on the old Chis-holm trail.
in my hand__ and a cow by the tail. Com-a ti yi youp-y,
mind a change if it was prai-rie__ hay.

1 and 2   3

youp-y ya, youp-y ya, Com-a ti yi youp-y, youp-y ya.   ya.

250

Home on the Range
(*Sing!*, Page 120)

Anonymous

Cowboy Song

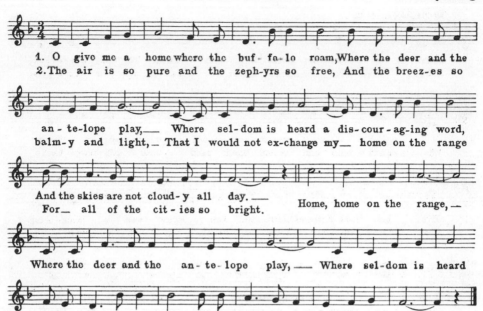

1. O give me a home where the buf - fa - lo roam, Where the deer and the
2. The air is so pure and the zeph-yrs so free, And the breez-es so

an - te-lope play,___ Where sel-dom is heard a dis-cour-ag-ing word,
balm-y and light,__ That I would not ex-change my__ home on the range

And the skies are not cloud-y all day.___
For__ all of the cit - ies so bright.   Home, home on the range, __

Where the deer and the an - te - lope play, ___ Where sel-dom is heard

a dis-cour-ag-ing word, And the skies are not cloud-y all day. __

She'll Be Comin' 'Round the Mountain
(*Sing!*, Page 91)

Southern Song

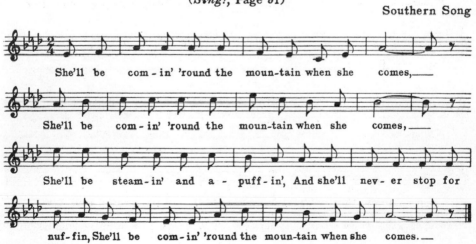

She'll be com - in' 'round the moun-tain when she comes,___

She'll be com - in' 'round the moun-tain when she comes,___

She'll be steam-in' and a - puff-in', And she'll nev - er stop for

nuf-fin, She'll be com - in' 'round the moun-tain when she comes. __

Dogie Song*
(*Twice 55 Brown Book,* No 143)

Anonymous   Cowboy Song

1. As I was a-walk-ing one morn-ing for pleas-ure,
2. It's ear-ly in spring that we round up the do-gies,

I spied a cow-punch-er all rid-ing a-long;
We mark them and brand them and bob off their tails;

His hat was throwed back and his spurs was a-jing-ling,
We round up our hors-es, load up the chuck wag-on,

And as he ap-proached he was sing-ing this song.
And then throw the do-gies out on-to the trail.

Whoop-ee ti yi yo,— Git a-long, lit-tle do-gies,

It's your mis-for-tune and none of my own;

Whoop-ee ti yi yo,— Git a-long, lit-tle do-gies.

You know that Wy-o-ming will be your new home.

* From *Songs of the Open Range,* by Ina Sires. C. C. Birchard & Company, Publishers.

Steal Away

(*Twice 55 Brown Book,* № 49)

Traditional   Negro Spiritual

Steal a - way, steal a - way, Steal a - way to Je - sus.

Fine

Steal a - way, steal a - way home. I ain't got long to stay here.

1. My Lord __ calls me, He calls me by the thun- der; The
2. Green trees __ bend- ing, Poor sin - ner stands a - trem-bling; The
3. My Lord __ calls me, He calls me by the light-ning; The

D.C. al Fine

trum- pet sounds with- in- a my soul! I ain't got long to stay here.
trum- pet sounds with- in a my soul! I ain't got long to stay here.
trum- pet sounds with- in- a my soul! I ain't got long to stay here.

Swing Low, Sweet Chariot

(*Twice 55 Brown Book,* № 48)

Traditional   Negro Spiritual

Swing low, sweet char - i - ot, __ Com- in' for to car - ry me home!

Fine

Swing low, sweet char - i - ot, __ Com- in' for to car - ry me home.

1. I looked o - ver Jor - dan an' what did I see, __
2. If you get there be - - fore __ I do, __

Com- in' for to car - ry me home! A band __ of an - gels
Com- in' for to car - ry me home! Jes' tell __ my frien's that

rall.   *D.C. al Fine*

com- in' aft - er me, __ Com- in' for to car - ry me home!
I'm a - com - in' too, __ Com- in' for to car - ry me home!

253

Go Down, Moses

(*Twice 55 Green Book*, № 69)

Traditional

Negro Spiritual

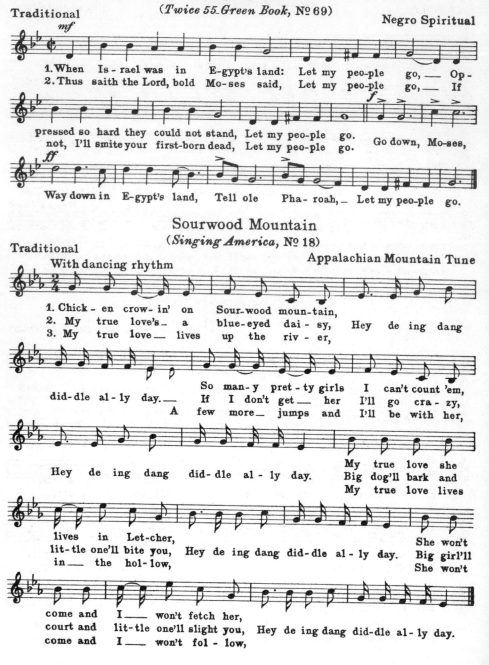

1. When Is-rael was in E-gypt's land: Let my peo-ple go, — Op-
2. Thus saith the Lord, bold Mo-ses said, Let my peo-ple go, — If

pressed so hard they could not stand, Let my peo-ple go.
not, I'll smite your first-born dead, Let my peo-ple go. Go down, Mo-ses,

Way down in E-gypt's land, Tell ole Pha-roah, — Let my peo-ple go.

Sourwood Mountain

(*Singing America*, № 18)

Traditional

Appalachian Mountain Tune

With dancing rhythm

1. Chick - en crow- in' on Sour-wood moun-tain,
2. My true love's_ a blue-eyed dai - sy, Hey de ing dang
3. My true love_ lives up the riv - er,

did-dle al - ly day. _ So man- y pret- ty girls I can't count 'em,
If I don't get_ her I'll go cra- zy,
A few more_ jumps and I'll be with her,

Hey de ing dang did- dle al - ly day. My true love she
Big dog'll bark and
My true love lives

lives in Let-cher, She won't
lit-tle one'll bite you, Hey de ing dang did- dle al - ly day. Big girl'll
in_ the hol- low, She won't

come and I _ won't fetch her,
court and lit-tle one'll slight you, Hey de ing dang did- dle al - ly day.
come and I _ won't fol - low,

Flowing River
(*Singing America*, № 47)

English by H.W.L.

Chilean Folk Tune

The Song We Sang

(*Sing!*, Page 12)

DAVID STEVENS

Viennese Melody

With expression

1. Be - side the   Dan - ube blue one moon - lit   night, I   sat a -
2. Her hair was   gold - en, then, her eyes were   blue, Her voice was

lone be - neath the gold - en   light Of days long passed a - way, when youth was
ten - der, then, her heart was true; To - geth - er,   day by day, in rain or

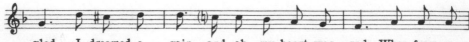

glad,   I   dreamed a - gain, and oh, my heart was   sad; When from a -
shine,   I   was her   on - ly love and she was   mine. And then a

cross the riv - er's si - lent   flow   A   song came drift - ing, ten - der, soft and
shad - ow fell, I   know not   how, 'Twas long a - go, and half for - got - ten

low,   A   song of   love whose haunt - ing, soft re - frain Turned back the
now,   But when I   heard that haunt - ing, sweet re - frain, I   lived those

CHORUS

years and made me young a - gain.   It was the   song we sang, my love and
hap - py mo - ments once a - gain.

I,   When all   the   world   was fair, and blue the   sky; Fond mem - 'ries

came that sum - mer night to   me, Re - called at   last by that sweet mel - o - dy. —

256

John Peel
(*Twice 55 Brown Book*, № 116)

English Hunting Song

With spirit

1. D' ye ken John Peel with his coat so gay? D' ye ken John
2. D' ye ken John Peel with his coat so gay, Who at Trout-beck

Peel at the break of day? D' ye ken John Peel when he's
lived in a by-gone day? D' ye ken John Peel? He is

far, far a-way, With his hounds and his horn in the morn-ing?
gone far a-way, We shall ne'er hear his voice in the morn-ing.

'Twas the sound of his horn called me from my bed, And the

cry of his hounds which he oft-times led, For Peel's view hal-loo

would wak-en the dead, Or a fox from his lair in the morn-ing.

Drink to Me Only with Thine Eyes
(*Twice 55 Brown Book*, № 35)

BEN JOHNSON (1573-1637)

English Air

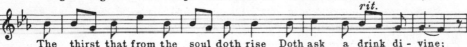

1. Drink to me on-ly with thine eyes, And I will pledge with mine;
2. I sent thee late a ros-y wreath, Not so much hon-'ring thee

Or leave a kiss with-in the cup And I'll not ask for wine.
As giv-ing it a hope that there It could not with-ered be;

rit.

The thirst that from the soul doth rise Doth ask a drink di-vine;
But thou there-on did'st on-ly breathe, And send'st it back to me;

a tempo

rit.

But might I of Jove's nec-tar sup, I would not change for thine.
Since when it grows, and smells, I swear, Not of it-self but thee!

257

Loch Lomond
(*Twice 55 Brown Book*, №102)

Unknown

Scottish Song

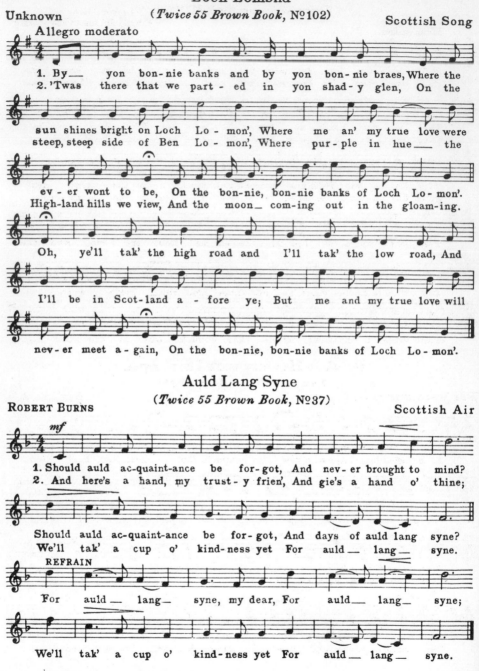

Allegro moderato

1. By— yon bon-nie banks and by yon bon-nie braes, Where the
2. 'Twas there that we part-ed in yon shad-y glen, On the

sun shines bright on Loch Lo-mon', Where me an' my true love were
steep, steep side of Ben Lo-mon', Where pur-ple in hue— the

ev-er wont to be, On the bon-nie, bon-nie banks of Loch Lo-mon'.
High-land hills we view, And the moon— com-ing out in the gloam-ing.

Oh, ye'll tak' the high road and I'll tak' the low road, And

I'll be in Scot-land a-fore ye; But me and my true love will

nev-er meet a-gain, On the bon-nie, bon-nie banks of Loch Lo-mon'.

Auld Lang Syne
(*Twice 55 Brown Book*, №37)

ROBERT BURNS

Scottish Air

mf

1. Should auld ac-quaint-ance be for-got, And nev-er brought to mind?
2. And here's a hand, my trust-y frien', And gie's a hand o' thine;

Should auld ac-quaint-ance be for-got, And days of auld lang syne?
We'll tak' a cup o' kind-ness yet For auld— lang— syne.

REFRAIN

For auld— lang— syne, my dear, For auld— lang— syne;

We'll tak' a cup o' kind-ness yet For auld— lang— syne.

258

Comin' Thro' The Rye

If   a bod-y   meet   a bod-y,   Com-in' thro' the rye,
If   a bod-y   meet   a bod-y,   Com-in' frae the town,

If   a bod-y   kiss a bod-y,   Need a bod-y   cry?
If   a bod-y   greet a bod-y,   Need a bod-y   frown?

Ev-'ry las-sie has her lad-die, Nane they say ha'e I;

Yet   a' the lads they smile on me,

When   com-in' thro' the rye.

Believe Me, If All Those Endearing Young Charms
(*Twice 55 Brown Book,* № 28)

THOMAS MOORE

Irish Air: *My Lodging Is in the Cold Ground*

Andantino

1. Be - lieve me, if all those en - dear - ing young charms, Which I
2. It— is not while beau - ty and youth are thine own, And thy

gaze on so fond - ly to - day, — Were to change by to - mor - row, and
cheeks un - pro - faned by a tear, — That the fer - vor and faith of a

fleet in my arms, Like— fair - y gifts, fad - ing a - way, —
soul can be known, To which time will but make thee more dear! —

Thou would'st still be a - dored, — as this mo - ment thou art, Let thy
No, the heart that has tru - ly loved— nev - er for - gets, But as

love - li - ness fade as it will, — And a - round the dear ru - in each
tru - ly loves on to the close; — As the sun - flow - er turns on her

wish of my heart Would en - twine it - self ver - dant - ly still.
god when he sets The same look which she turned when he rose. —

Watchman, Tell Us of the Night
(Aberystwyth)
(*Twice 55 Green Book,* № 83)

JOHN BOWRING

JOSEPH PARRY

Moderato

Watch - man, tell— us of the night, What its signs of prom - ise are,

Trav - 'ler, o'er yon moun - tain's height, See that— glo - ry - beam - ing star.

Watch - man, does its beau - teous ray Aught of hope or joy fore - tell?

Trav - 'ler, yes, it brings the day, Prom - ised— day— of Is - ra - el.

All Through the Night
(*Twice 55 Brown Book*, № 24)

Old Welsh

DAVID OWEN

Quietly
mp

1. Sleep, my child, and peace at-tend thee All through the night;
2. While the moon her watch is keep-ing All through the night;

Guard-ian an-gels God will send thee, All through the night.
While the wea-ry world is sleep-ing All through the night.

Soft the drow-sy hours are creep-ing, Hill and vale in slum-ber
O'er thy spir-it gen-tly steal-ing, Vi-sions of de-light re-

steep-ing, I my lov-ing vig-il keep-ing, All through the night.
veal-ing, Breathes a pure and ho-ly feel-ing, All through the night.

Deck the Hall
(*Twice 55 Brown Book*, № 78)

Traditional

Old Welsh Air

1. Deck the hall with boughs of hol-ly, Fa la la la la la la la la.
   'Tis the sea-son to be jol-ly, Fa la la la la la la la la.
2. See the blaz-ing Yule be-fore us, Fa la la la la la la la la.
   Strike the harp and join the cho-rus, Fa la la la la la la la la.
3. Fast a-way the old year pass-es, Fa la la la la la la la la.
   Hail the new, ye lads and lass-es, Fa la la la la la la la la.

Don we now our gay ap-par-el, Fa la la la la la la.
Fol-low me in mer-ry meas-ure, Fa la la la la la la.
Sing we joy-ous all to-geth-er, Fa la la la la la la.

Troll the an-cient Yule-tide car-ol, Fa la la la la la la la la.
While I tell of Yule-tide treas-ure, Fa la la la la la la la la.
Heed-less of the wind and weath-er, Fa la la la la la la la la.

261

A Merry Life

(*Twice 55 Brown Book*, №64)

From the Italian

DENZA

SOLO

1. Some think— the world is made for fun and frol-ic,— And so do
2. Ah, me,— 'tis strange that some should take to sigh-ing,— And like it

CHORUS   SOLO

I!— And so do I!— Some think— it well to be all mel-an-
well!— And like it well!— For me,— I have not tho't it worth the

CHORUS   SOLO

chol-ic,— To pine and sigh;— To pine and sigh;— But I,
try-ing,— So can-not tell!— So can-not tell!— With laugh—

— I love to spend my time in sing-ing— Some joy-ous song,—
— and dance and song the day soon pass-es,— Full soon is gone,—

CHORUS   SOLO

Some joy-ous song;—— To set— the air with mu-sic brave-ly
Full soon is gone;—— For mirth— was made for joy-ous lads and

CHORUS

ring-ing— Is far from wrong!— Is far from wrong!—
lass-es— To call their own!— To call their own!—

f 1st time SOLO

Hark-en! Hark-en! Mu-sic sounds a-far!— Hark-en!

p

Hark-en! Mu-sic sounds a-far! Tra-la-la-la, tra-la-la-la-la, tra-la-la-

mf < *f* >

la, tra-la-la-la-la! Joy is ev-'ry-where, Tra-la-la-la, tra-la-la-la-la!

Santa Lucia
(*Twice 55 Brown Book*, № 46)

Andantino   Neapolitan Boat Song

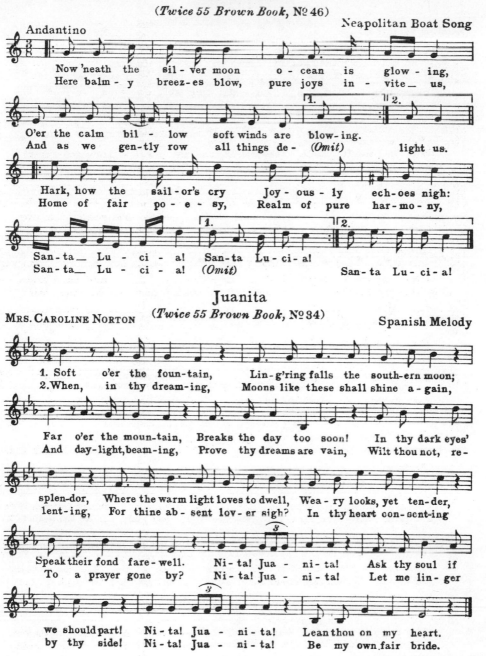

Now 'neath the sil - ver moon o - cean is glow - ing,
Here balm - y breez - es blow, pure joys in - vite_ us,

O'er the calm bil - low soft winds are blow - ing.
And as we gen - tly row all things de - (*Omit*) light us.

Hark, how the sail - or's cry Joy - ous - ly ech - oes nigh:
Home of fair po - e - sy, Realm of pure har - mo - ny,

San - ta_ Lu - ci - a! San - ta Lu - ci - a!
San - ta_ Lu - ci - a! (*Omit*) San - ta Lu - ci - a!

Juanita
(*Twice 55 Brown Book*, № 34)

MRS. CAROLINE NORTON   Spanish Melody

1. Soft o'er the foun - tain, Lin - g'ring falls the south - ern moon;
2. When, in thy dream - ing, Moons like these shall shine a - gain,

Far o'er the moun - tain, Breaks the day too soon! In thy dark eyes'
And day - light, beam - ing, Prove thy dreams are vain, Wilt thou not, re -

splen - dor, Where the warm light loves to dwell, Wea - ry looks, yet ten - der,
lent - ing, For thine ab - sent lov - er sigh? In thy heart con - sent - ing

Speak their fond fare - well. Ni - ta! Jua - ni - ta! Ask thy soul if
To a prayer gone by? Ni - ta! Jua - ni - ta! Let me lin - ger

we should part! Ni - ta! Jua - ni - ta! Lean thou on my heart.
by thy side! Ni - ta! Jua - ni - ta! Be my own fair bride.

263

The Pedlar
(*Singing America*, №80)

English by A. D. Z.

Russian Folk Tune

In brisk walking time

1. "Down the road the whole day long With my pack of goods for
2. "Ma-dame, you see be - fore you now What pret - ty things I

dame or maid: Oh, the weight on my ach - ing shoul - ders!
have to sell!" "Ah, good ped - lar, they steal my heart, In -

But to live a man must trade! Oh, the weight on my
deed I like them far too well! Ah, good ped - lar, they

ach - ing shoul - ders! But to live a man must trade!"
steal my heart, In - deed I like them far too well!"

Hai - da, hai - da, hai - da, hai - da, hai - da, hai - da, hai - da da!

poco rit.

Hai - da, hai - da, hai - da, hai - da, hai - da, hai - da, hai - da da!

Au Clair de la Lune
(*Sing!*, Page 23)

M. Louise Baum

French Folk Tune

Andante

1. With the moon's pale shim-mer, Lit-tle friend Pier - rot, Shines thy can-dle's
2. See my lan - tern flick- er, Now the light is out, Now the snow falls

glim - mer On the fall - en snow. Lend a pen I pray thee,
thick - er, Round and round a - bout. Gusts go hel - ter - skel - ter,

But a word to write, One fare-well to say thee Ere I go to - night.
Lo, the night is old, Ope and give me shel - ter Ere I die of cold.

264

Brown Eyes
(*Sing!*, Page 9)

DAVID STEVENS   Russian Gipsy Tune

Slow waltz time

1. There are eyes of blue That may shine as true
2. There are ha - zel eyes Where - in can - dor lies,

As the star - ry light On a sum - mer night; There are
And they may be true Like the eyes of blue. But my

eyes of gray Like an au - tumn day, That are cool and calm,
quest is o'er, I shall seek no more, Find - ing Beau - ty's crown

1.
With a dis - tant charm. __

2.
In her eyes of brown. __

Patapan
(*Singing America*, № 109)

English version by A.D.Z.   Burgundian Carol

As for a merry walk

p 1. Wil - lie, bring your lit - tle drum, Rob - in, take your
mf 2. When the folk of oth - er days To the King of
f 3. God and man to - day are one Like the sound - ing

flute and come: We'll be mer - ry as you play,
kings gave praise, On the flute and drum they'd play,
flute and drum, We'll be mer - ry as you play,

We'll be
Tu - re - lu - re - lu, pat - a - pat - a - pan, On the
We'll be

mer - ry as you play, For a Christ-mas should be gay!
flute and drum they'd play, And their hearts were ver - y gay!
mer - ry as you play, For a Christ-mas should be gay!

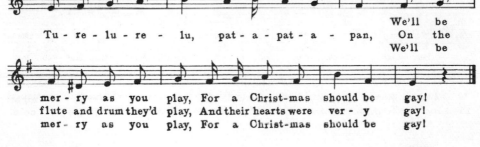

In Vossevangen

(*Singing America,* No. 75)

English by Neva Boyd
(*used by permission*)

Norwegian Folk Tune

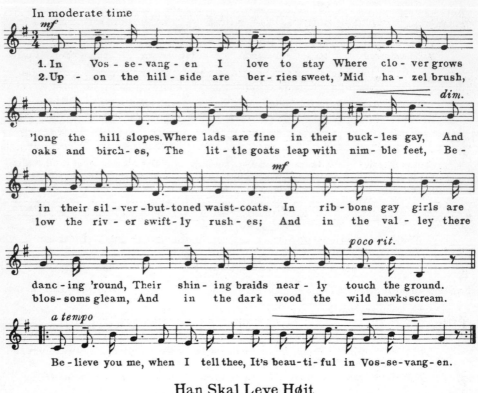

In moderate time

1. In Vos - se - vang - en I love to stay Where clo - ver grows
2. Up - on the hill - side are ber - ries sweet, 'Mid ha - zel brush,

'long the hill slopes. Where lads are fine in their buck - les gay, And
oaks and birch - es, The lit - tle goats leap with nim - ble feet, Be -

in their sil - ver - but - toned waist - coats. In rib - bons gay girls are
low the riv - er swift - ly rush - es; And in the val - ley there

danc - ing 'round, Their shin - ing braids near - ly touch the ground.
blos - soms gleam, And in the dark wood the wild hawks scream.

Be - lieve you me, when I tell thee, It's beau - ti - ful in Vos - se - vang - en.

Han Skal Leve Højt

(*Singing America,* No. 73)

Danish Honor Song

Heartily

* Han skal le - ve, Han skal le - ve, Han skal le - ve højt, hur - rah!

Faster

Hur - rah, hur - rah, hur - rah, hur - rah, hur - rah, Hur - rah, hur - rah, hur -

* Pronounced *Hahn skal lay veh hoyt*
** The small notes with their grand rise are for the last singing of this first section of the song. Its four measures are sung only once after the "bravissimo."

266

rah, hur-rah, hur-rah, Han skal le - ve, Han skal le - ve, Han skal

poco rit.   Faster

le - ve højt, hur-rah!   Bra - vo,   bra - vo,   bra - vo, bra - vis - si - mo!

Bra - vo,   bra - vo,   bra - vis - si - mo!   Bra - vo, bra - vis - si - mo,

poco rit.   *D.C. al Fine*

Bra - vo, bra - vis - si - mo,   Bra - vo,   bra - vo,   bra - vis - si - mo!

Spring
(*Singing America,* №71)

English version by A.D.Z.   Swedish Folk Tune

Soft   breez - es   blow - ing,   new   green   a - glow - ing,

Sun   warm-ly   shin-ing,   melt - ing   the snow,   Brook-lets   a - hur - ry,

on - ward they scur - ry,   Down   to   the   o - cean gleam-ing be-low.

REFRAIN *slower*

Wake,   O   my heart,   and   join   in   the   song,

New   life   is   stir - ring,   earth   is   re-born!   Horn   notes are swell-ing,

gay   car - ols tell - ing,   Sor - row   and   cold   must   go.

267

Over the Meadows
(*Singing America*, № 53)

English by A.D.Z.

Czech Folk Tune

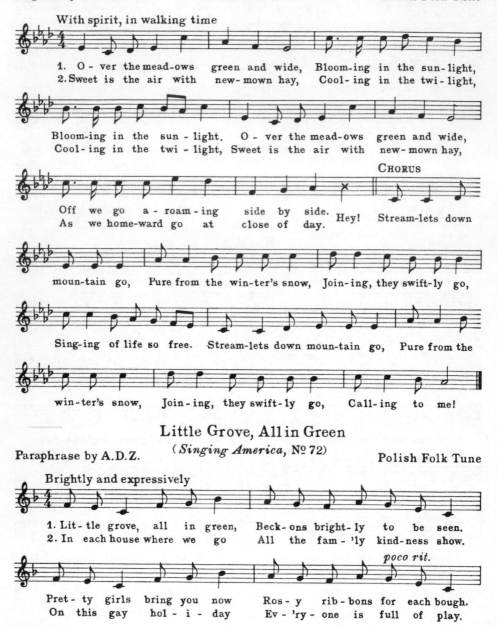

With spirit, in walking time

1. O - ver the mead-ows green and wide, Bloom-ing in the sun-light,
2. Sweet is the air with new-mown hay, Cool-ing in the twi-light,

Bloom-ing in the sun-light. O - ver the mead-ows green and wide,
Cool-ing in the twi-light, Sweet is the air with new-mown hay,

CHORUS

Off we go a - roam-ing side by side. Hey! Stream-lets down
As we home-ward go at close of day.

moun-tain go, Pure from the win-ter's snow, Join-ing, they swift-ly go,

Sing-ing of life so free. Stream-lets down moun-tain go, Pure from the

win-ter's snow, Join-ing, they swift-ly go, Call-ing to me!

Little Grove, All in Green
(*Singing America*, № 72)

Paraphrase by A.D.Z.

Polish Folk Tune

Brightly and expressively

1. Lit - tle grove, all in green, Beck-ons bright-ly to be seen.
2. In each house where we go All the fam - 'ly kind-ness show.

poco rit.

Pret - ty girls bring you now Ros - y rib-bons for each bough.
On this gay hol - i - day Ev - 'ry - one is full of play.

268

Take, each_ one, a spray of lin-den-wood, And to each house bring
Laugh-ter and sing-ing bring we ev-'ry-where, And go-ing home-ward

joy and wish-es good. Take, each_ one, a spray of
man-y gifts we bear. Laugh-ter and sing-ing bring we

lin-den-wood, And to each house bring joy and wish-es good.
ev-'ry-where, And go-ing home-ward man-y gifts we bear.

Came A-Riding
(*Singing America,* No 58)

English by
Martha C. Ramsay*

Czech Folk Tune

As for a gay, vigorous waltz

1. Came a-rid-ing by one day,
2. Pen he car-ried and a chart, Zhum ta di ya di ya.
3. "Were you al-ways kind and true,"

Suit-or jaun-ty, bold and gay,
"Write your name, give me your heart," Zhum ta di ya di ya Hey!**
"I might give my heart to you,"

Faster

Zhum ta di ya di ya Zhum ta di ya da Zhum ta

di ya di ya Zhum ta di ya da. Zhum ta di ya

di ya Zhum ta di ya da Zhum ta di ya di ya!

4. "But your pride has you misled,   5. She with green wreath on her brow,
   Not to you will I be wed!"   Gave her true love the wedding vow.

* Used by her kind permission, and some verses added.
** A merry shout.

Swiss Yodel Song

Swiss Folk Song
Arranged by Rudolph Ganz

The authors are indebted to Mr. Rudolph Ganz for this Swiss Folk Tune which was **arranged** especially for this book.

Prayer of Thanksgiving
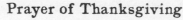
(*Sing!* Page 126)

Anonymous   Netherlands Air

1. We gath-er to-geth-er to ask the Lord's bless-ing; He
2. Be-side us to guide us, our God with us join-ing, Or-
3. We all do ex-tol Thee, Thou lead-er in bat-tle, And

chas-tens and has-tens His voice to make known; The wick-ed op-
dain-ing, main-tain-ing His King-dom di-vine. So from the be-
pray that Thou still our De-fend-er will be. Let Thy con-gre-

press-ing cease them from dis-tress-ing. Sing prais-es to His name,
gin-ning the fight we were win-ning, Thou, Lord, wast at our side,
ga-tion es-cape trib-u-la-tion, Thy name be ev-er praised

He for-gets not His own.
let the glo-ry be Thine.
and Thy peo-ple made free. Might-y and free.

Walking Song
(*Singing America,* №55)

Swiss Folk Tune

A gay, swinging walk

1. From Lu-cerne to Weg-gis fair,
2. When we row a-cross the bay, Hol di ri di a, hol di ri a,
3. Weg-gis leads to a moun-tain high,

Shoes and stock-ings we need not wear,
There we see pret-ty maid ens gay, Hol di ri di a, hol di ri a.
Gai-ly sing as we go by,

CHORUS

Hol di ri di a, Hol di ri di a, hol di ri a,

Hol di ri di a, Hol di ri di a, hol di a.

* Pronounced: Hol dee ree dee ah.

271

O Come, O Come, Emmanuel
(*Twice 55 Green Book*, №158)

Translated by
John Mason Neale

Gregorian Tune
Eighth Century

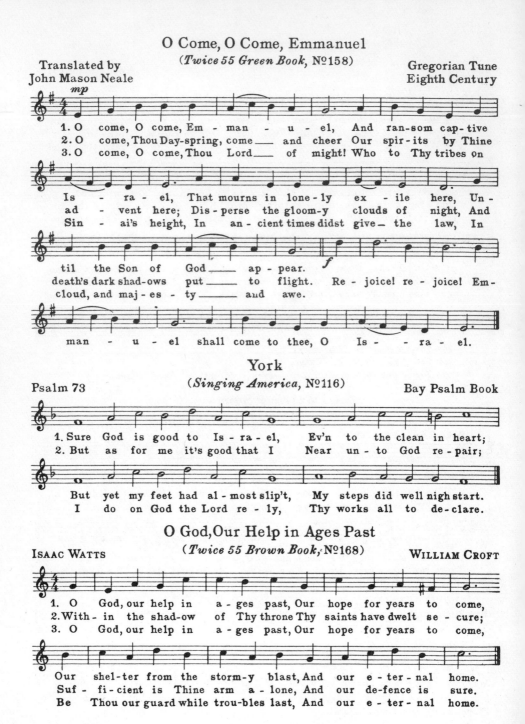

1. O come, O come, Em - man - u - el, And ran-som cap-tive
2. O come, Thou Day-spring, come and cheer Our spir-its by Thine
3. O come, O come, Thou Lord of might! Who to Thy tribes on

Is - ra - el, That mourns in lone - ly ex - ile here, Un-
ad - vent here; Dis - perse the gloom-y clouds of night, And
Sin - ai's height, In an - cient times didst give the law, In

til the Son of God ap - pear. Re - joice! re - joice! Em-
death's dark shad-ows put to flight.
cloud, and maj-es - ty and awe.

man - u - el shall come to thee, O Is - ra - el.

York
(*Singing America*, №116)

Psalm 73

Bay Psalm Book

1. Sure God is good to Is - ra - el, Ev'n to the clean in heart;
2. But as for me it's good that I Near un - to God re - pair;

But yet my feet had al - most slip't, My steps did well nigh start.
I do on God the Lord re - ly, Thy works all to de - clare.

O God, Our Help in Ages Past
(*Twice 55 Brown Book*, №168)

ISAAC WATTS

WILLIAM CROFT

1. O God, our help in a - ges past, Our hope for years to come,
2. With - in the shad-ow of Thy throne Thy saints have dwelt se - cure;
3. O God, our help in a - ges past, Our hope for years to come,

Our shel-ter from the storm-y blast, And our e - ter - nal home.
Suf - fi - cient is Thine arm a - lone, And our de-fence is sure.
Be Thou our guard while trou-bles last, And our e - ter - nal home.

272

Angels We Have Heard on High
(*Twice 55 Green Book*, № 157)

Old French Carol

An-gels we have heard on high, Sweet-ly sing-ing

o'er our plains, And the moun-tains in re-ply, Ech-o-ing their

joy-ous strains Glo - - - - -

- ri - a In ex-cel-sis De - - o. _____

Good King Wenceslas
(*Twice 55 Green Book*, № 89)

JOHN M. NEALE

Traditional

Allegro moderato

Good King Wen-ces-las looked out On the feast of Ste-phen,

When the snow lay round a-bout, Deep and crisp and e - ven.

Bright-ly shone the moon that night, Though the frost was cru-el,

When a poor man came in sight, Gath-'ring win-ter fu - - el.

273

INDEX

274

281

289

291